Primitive Elements of Grammatical Theory

This book is a compilation of manuscripts and publications from 2001 to 2010 by Jean-Roger Vergnaud, in collaboration with colleagues and students. This work is guided by the scientific belief that broader mathematical principles should guide linguistic inquiry, as they guide classical biology and physics. From this, Vergnaud's hypotheses take the representation of the computational component of language to a more abstract level: one that *derives* constituent structure. He treats linguistic features as primitives and argues that a 2 × *n* matrix allows for multiple discrete dimensions to represent symmetries in linguistic features and to derive the fabric of syntax (and perhaps of phonology as well).

Three primary research questions guide the core of these papers. (A) Methodologically, how can broadly defined mathematical/cognitive principles guide linguistic investigation? (B) To what extent do general mathematical principles apply *across* linguistic domains? What principles guide computation at different levels of linguistic structure (phonology, metrical structure, syntax)? (C) How is the computational domain defined?

In these manuscripts, Vergnaud's goal is not to radically depart from the Minimalist Program within generative grammar but rather to take the underlying goal of the generative program and bring it to an even more general scientific level. The themes of *symmetry* and *periodicity* in this book reflect his goal of scientific progress in linguistics, and he has opened the doors to new exploration of old empirical problems in linguistics that may, someday, have deeper biological and physical explanations through the theory presented in this publication.

Katherine McKinney-Bock recently completed her PhD in Department of Linguistics at the University of Southern California, USA and is joining Reed College for the academic year 2013–14 as a visiting assistant professor of linguistics.

Maria Luisa Zubizarreta is professor of linguistics at the University of Southern California, USA.

Routledge Leading Linguists

Edited by Carlos P. Otero, University of California, Los Angeles, USA

Primitive Elements of Grammatical Theory

Papers by
Jean-Roger Vergnaud and
His Collaborators

Edited by
Katherine McKinney-Bock and
Maria Luisa Zubizarreta

Routledge
Taylor & Francis Group

NEW YORK AND LONDON

First published 2014
by Routledge
711 Third Avenue, New York, NY 10017

and by Routledge
2 Park Square, Milton Park, Abingdon, Oxon OX14 4RN

*Routledge is an imprint of the Taylor & Francis Group,
an informa business*

© 2014 Taylor & Francis

Library of Congress Cataloging-in-Publication Data

Primitive elements of grammatical theory : papers by Jean-Roger
  Vergnaud and his collaborators / Jean-Roger Vergnaud ; Edited by
  Katherine McKinney-Bock and Maria Luisa Zubizarreta.
    pages cm. — (Routledge Leading Linguists ; 20)
  Includes bibliographical references and index.
  1. Grammar, Comparative and general.   2. Linguistics—
Methodology.   3. Grammaticality (Linguistics)   I. Vergnaud,
Jean-Roger.   II. McKinney-Bock, Katherine editor of
compilation.   III. Zubizarreta, Maria Luisa, editor of compilation.
  P151P745 2013
  415—dc23
  2013012620

ISBN: 978-0-415-70539-4 (hbk)
ISBN: 978-1-315-88982-5 (ebk)

Typeset in Sabon
by Apex CoVantage, LLC

Printed and bound in the United States of America by Publishers Graphics, LLC on sustainably sourced paper.

**Dedicated to the memory of
Jean-Roger Vergnaud**

Contents

Preface

This volume presents, explicates, and illustrates the core themes of Jean-Roger Vergnaud's life work in linguistics. Although the papers, in collaboration with colleagues and students, are temporally anchored in the last decade of his life, the overarching theoretical theme that preoccupied Jean-Roger is present from his earliest linguistic work. It was his deepest scientific belief that at the appropriate level of abstraction, the core building blocks of syntax shared much with those of prosodic (and possibly segmental) phonology. A basic recurring notion across his work in syntax and phonology has been that of "asymmetric headedness" across domains and the notion of occurrence of an item (or segment) as contextually defined. This preoccupation informed his early work (in collaboration with M. Halle) on vowel harmony much of which remained unpublished, but see A Formal Theory of Vowel Harmony (in *Issues in Vowel Harmony*, ed. R.M. Vago, 1980), Harmony Processes (with M. Halle in *Crossing the Boundaries in Linguistics: Studies presented to Manfred Bierwisch*, eds. W. Klein, J.M. Levelt, 1981), and On the framework of autosegmental phonology (with M. Halle in *The Structure of Phonological Representations*, Vol.I, eds. H. van der Hulst and N. Smith, 1992). For his early work on rhythmic relations in the stress systems of the world (part of which was published in *An Essay on Stress*, MIT Press, 1987), as well as his work on syllabic structure, see *The internal structure of phonological representations: a theory of Charm and Government* (with J. Kaye, J. Lowenstamm, *Phonology Yearbook* 2:305-328, 1985), and *Constituent structure and government in phonology* (with J. Kaye, J. Lowenstamm, *Phonology Yearbook* 7.2:193-231, 1990), on Case Theory, and on head raising in relative clauses (published in *Dependances et niveaux de representation en syntaxe*, J. Benjamins, 1985).

In the last decade, his main focus was to develop a graph-theoretic formalism that adequately represents overlapping grammatical relations locally and categorical symmetry, which derives noun and verb phrases from the same primitive formatives with parallel hierarchical order. He had been long convinced that phrase structure as generally conceived was inadequate to achieve this task. Jean-Roger was perhaps one of the generative linguists who took most deeply to heart the task of finding the right computational formalism to characterize natural language grammars. His thoughts were abstract, deep, and elegant, with a knack for uncovering new connections or parallelisms among divergent linguistic phenomena and subfields.

We present Jean-Roger's unfinished work in this volume with the hope that it will inspire others to pursue and explore the theoretical and empirical ramifications of the ideas contained therein. This endeavor would not have been possible without the contributions of his students Tommi Leung, Wei-wen Roger Liao, and Katy McKinney-Bock and the support of his lifetime colleagues Robert Freidin, Alain Rouveret, and Henk van Riemsdijk. Very special thanks go to Katy—without her leadership and vision, this project would have never seen the light—and to the editor of the series, Carlos Otero, for encouragement and support. We also thank Elsevier/Lingua for permission to reprint chapter 2 and de Gruyter for permission to reprint chapter 3.

—Maria Luisa Zubizarreta

1 Introduction

Katherine McKinney-Bock and
Maria Luisa Zubizarreta

This book is a compilation of manuscripts (chapters 4–7) and publications (chapters 2 and 3)[1] from 2001–2010 by Jean-Roger Vergnaud, in collaboration with colleagues and students.[2] This work is guided by the scientific belief that broader mathematical principles should guide linguistic inquiry as they have guided biology and physics, under the 'Galilean style' of science, or the "search for mathematical patterns in nature" (see chapter 2).

From this, Vergnaud's hypotheses take the representation of the computational component of language to a more abstract level: one that *derives* constituent structure. He treats linguistic features as primitives, and argues that a $2 \times n$ matrix allows for multiple discrete dimensions to represent symmetries in linguistic features and to derive the fabric of syntax (and perhaps of phonology as well).

Three primary research questions guide the core of these papers. (A) Methodologically, how can broadly defined mathematical/cognitive principles guide linguistic investigation? (B) To what extent do general mathematical principles apply *across* linguistic domains? What principles guide computation at different levels of linguistic structure (phonology, metrical structure, syntax)? (C) How is the computational domain defined?

Looking to (A), this book approaches methods used in the relatively young field of generative grammar as guided by thought in theoretical physics and biology, particular that of the Galilean style:

> A significant feature of the Generative Revolution in linguistics has been the development of a Galilean style in that field. And, to a great extent, the recent developments within MP [the Minimalist Program] must be viewed in this light-specifically, as Dirac's mathematical procedure (method) at work within linguistics. Dirac has identified two main methods within the mathematical procedure itself: one is to remove inconsistencies, the other, to unite theories that were previously disjoint (see Dirac, 1968). In linguistics, the inconsistencies primarily concern overlapping grammatical conditions, as discussed earlier, which conflict with the basic assumption that C_{HL} has an optimal design. Note further that this assumption itself

relates directly to the quest for mathematical beauty, which informs the Galilean style. (chapter 2 of this volume, p. 37)

Coming from this philosophy, an overarching theme of this book that emerges is the general principle of *symmetry* (chapters 2, 5, and 7) and how it may guide syntactic thought. Empirically, Vergnaud explores the parallels between nominal and verbal domains, *deriving* them from his grammatical architecture. To cross linguistic domains, (B), Vergnaud uses a formal notion of periodicity (chapter 3) to derive stress patterns in metrical structure and *wh*-chains in syntactic structure *in the same formal way*. Then, looking to (C), Vergnaud explores notions of *long-distance dependency* and clausal domains and what it means to be non-local. The book gravitates toward a theory that derives all grammatical relationships as inherently *local,* and the appearance of displacement (or cyclicity; see chapter 3) is a product of how the formal computational system spells out. Dealing with higher-level operations, such as coordination and *wh*-quantification, leads to an extension of copy theory that has copying and deletion *at the level of phases,* triggering phase reduplication that allows for the appearance of displacement/ movement.

The empirical applications of this book are broad, and in some sense, these manuscripts barely scratch the surface of the empirical consequences of these foundational proposals. Empirically, this book addresses relativization, the problem of split-antecedent relative clauses (chapter 6; cf. Perlmutter and Ross 1970), simple *wh*-questions and focus (chapter 5), classifier constructions in Chinese and *few/little* in English (chapter 7), as well as empirical parallels between the nominal and verbal domains (chapter 5; though see Megerdoomian 2002, 2008 for further empirical exploration as well). The book's purpose is not to resolve unresolved empirical problems (though it has some positive consequences in this direction; see chapters 6 and 7), but rather to clarify *what scientific principles can be used to guide linguistic thought*: a methodological, as strongly as a theoretical, proposal is put forth in these pages. The lines of inquiry proposed by Vergnaud in the final 10–15 years of his life open doors to further empirical research, and this book (almost by necessity) remains empirically incomplete. It is up to linguists to take the architecture proposed in this book and explore further empirical consequences.

Apparent throughout Vergnaud writings is the belief, in line with Chomskyan inquiry, that linguistic methods should have foundations in scientific methods. Using, for example "the heuristic of eliminating overlapping conditions" (chapter 2), the move from Government and Binding (GB) to the Minimalist Program (MP) allowed for the elimination of the Case Filter and government to the more general principle of Full Interpretation. Here, this work lays the foundation for an extension of the Minimalist Program, collapsing conditions such as the EPP, checking, and the Mirror Principle into a single formal mechanism (see chapter 5) based on a guiding principle of symmetry. For example, the feature/category D *is* T, but found in a general nominal context rather than a verbal context.

In the pages of this detailed introduction, we begin to introduce the key ideas and key illustrations that Vergnaud provides in the pages of these manuscripts, as well as introducing the extensions to his theory in chapters 6 and 7. The ideas and innovations remain Vergnaud's and his coauthors', and any errors in argumentation, representation and interpretation are ours to bear.

PART I: GUIDING IDEAS IN LINGUISTIC SCIENCE

Chapter 2 in this volume is a reprint/republication of Freidin and Vergnaud (F&V) 2001. Here, the roots of Vergnaud's thought leading to the final 10 years of his work is represented, on a broader scale, setting the tone for the line of inquiry pursued in chapters 3–7 in this volume. F&V explore how general mathematical principles guide linguistic theory, and how methods used in the physical sciences should be used in linguistic thought as well.

Chapter 2 compares the general use of economy principles guiding computation across scientific disciplines to those used in linguistics, appealing to notions of conceptual naturalness like simplicity or economy which have been developed in other scientific disciplines. This appeal "is not unique to generative grammar. It has been employed fruitfully in the more developed natural sciences—in particular, theoretical physics. The discussion of physics that follows [in chapter 2] attempts to elucidate this notion in a way that, ultimately, should illuminate its role in contemporary theoretical linguistics" (p. 35).

Akin to the principle of *least time* used in physics to explore light travel (Fermat c. 1650), F&V suggest that the principle of economy of derivation used in the Minimalist Program (MP), the shortest derivation or restriction to unidirectional movement, is as valid to linguistic inquiry as *least time* is to physical inquiry. But even more importantly, chapter 2 illustrates that contributions by physicists go beyond just *physical* principles—they tell us something about the general nature of *computation* rather than just facts about the physical world. This gives us a "link between physics and linguistics"—at least "metaphorically"—which allows for principles such as the one mentioned above to guide linguistic thought.

Chapter 2 pushes the idea of economy further, and proposes that a general principle of *symmetry* may govern linguistics, as it does other fields of science, such that symmetries "enhance the economy of computations" (p. 42).[3] They provide a preliminary empirical illustration of how working under a general symmetry principle derives Principle C, demonstrating that general principles can govern our linguistic research, with the right empirical consequences.

Looking to Dirac (1968), chapter 2 also explores the diversity of methods used in science; namely, Dirac's distinction between "experimental" and "mathematical" procedures. A key example of both procedures at work in physics would be the Heisenberg/Schrödinger discovery of quantum mechanics. Heisenberg used spectroscopy, experimental methods, to arrive at a similar conclusion as Schrödinger's theoretical work regarding spectral frequencies. Then, linking back to linguistics, F&V defend the "mathematical" procedure, contra an article by Lappin, Levine and Johnson 2000, which pushes the "experimental" procedure using Compton's 1923 methods in physics. But, a closer look by F&V show that Compton's experimental result was predated by Einstein 1917, using a "mathematical" procedure and providing principles without even making an experimental prediction. In light of this, F&V suggest that the scientific method of deriving facts from "first principles," such as that used within MP, is a valid and promising approach to understanding syntactic structures (as defined in *Syntactic Structures*).

Chapter 2 reminds the reader that "the mathematical perspective informs GP," and "because the MP is a particular implementation of GP [the Generative Program], the notion of perfection often invoked within MP is ultimately a mathematical notion, calling for a higher level of mathematical formalization in syntax" (p. 40; see also Chomsky 1995, 2004).

PART II: THE FORMAL SYSTEM

From Phonology to Syntax: A Formal Notion of *Occurrence* and *Chain* Is the Same in Both

A theory of metrical structure from Vergnaud's 2001–2004 line of thought (chapter 3) provides the roots of the grammatical architecture for both phonology (chapter 3) and syntax (chapter 3, section 8.4; developed in chapter 5). Vergnaud begins with a comparison of "clocks and number systems" to metrical structure, looking to the general mathematical notion of circular permutation, which he then uses to formalize metrical structure (and the notion of *chain*, which runs formally through both phonology and syntax). Vergnaud returns to the hypothesis that metrical structure and (syntactic) constituent structures are both hierarchical, and that the 'congruence' between the two is reduced to a correspondence between the two independently defined hierarchical structures. From this, chapter 3 looks to potential correspondence from clocks, and derives a notion of *occurrence* that allows for a formalization of chain in both metrical structure and syntactic structure. Each object used in a derivation (of stress, or of syntax), has two roles: that of a *goal* (chapter 3) or *item/interpretable* feature (chapter 5), or of a *source* (chapter 3), or *context/uninterpretable* feature (chapter 5). Then, a *checking* mechanism allows for the generation of strings and a single pronounced item, from the two roles it plays.

Formalizing the Notion of Occurrence: A Comparison of Circular Permutations and Metrical Structure

Vergnaud illustrates a useful relationship between 'beats' of metrical structure (syllables and stressed syllables) and a clock system with two hands (a big hand and a little hand). To do this, Vergnaud begins with a metrical grid for the word *nominee:*

(1)

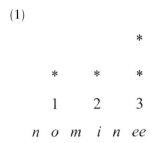

Here, the lower tier represents the syllable, and the higher tier represents the stressed syllable, at the level of the word. One could repeat the metrical grid periodically to create a 'beat' (imagine repeating the word *nominee* over and over):

(2)

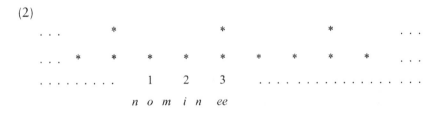

A *metrical constituent* is defined as a group of positions (syllables), and the stressed position is the *head* of the metrical constituent, representing the 'projection' of the head. This is the Hypothesis of Metrical Constituency (HMC), and it allows syntactic structure and metrical structure to be a correspondence between two *constituent structures* (Halle and Vergnaud 1987).

The pattern in (2) resembles a clock system, or a *circular permutation,* that repeats infinitely (of course, linguistic structure does not—but Vergnaud shows that the formal nature of these periodic structures is relevant to linguistic structure nonetheless). *Nominee* has 3 beats, so Vergnaud uses a clock with three numbers as an analogy. The bottom tier/syllable level corresponds to the big hand of a clock, and the top tier/word level corresponds to the little hand.

(3)

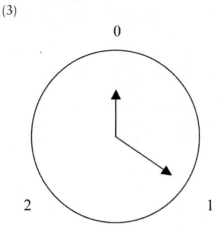

As the clock progresses, the little hand sits at 0 until the big hand makes a full revolution. When the big hand returns to 0, the little hand moves to 1, and sits at 1 until the big hand has made another revolution. This can be written out as in (4), with the bottom tier = big hand, and the top tier = little hand. This picture, in (4) resembles the metrical beat in (2).

(4)

		1			2			0
1	2	0	1	2	0	1	2	0
0	*1*	*2*	*3*	*4*	*5*	*6*	*7*	*8*	*9*

As Vergnaud points out, "In essence, a clock/number system defines a hierarchy of equivalence relations among numbers." The classes can be constructed by mapping the circular permutation displayed in (5) onto the linear set of numbers (as in the bottom tier of 4, above).

(5)

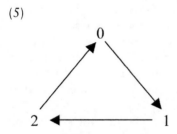

(5) can be notated using pairs of numbers, or *coordinates*. For example, the edge going from 0 to 1, above, can be written as the pair (0, 1)—where the left coordinate represents the initial number, and the right coordinate

represents the final number. In (0, 1), the clock hand starts at 0 and ends at 1. Here is the full permutation:

(6) (i)   (0, 1) (1, 2) (2, 0)

Mathematically, Vergnaud defines the pair as follows:

(ii) [*(x, y)* = $_{def}$ "*y is the image of x*"]: a circular permutation defined over the set {1, 2, 0}

The left coordinate, e.g. 0, *precedes* the right coordinate in a pair, e.g. 1. The clock hand starts at 0, and 0 *occurs first*, followed by the clock hand moving to 1, where 1 *occurs second*. So:

(iii) [*(x, y)* = $_{def}$ "*any **occurrence** of x precedes an **occurrence** of y*"]: a periodic distribution of 1, 2, and 0 defined over an infinite discrete linear set

The analogy Vergnaud draws between a metrical grid and a circular permutation is the beginning of his defining a formal notion of *occurrence* in linguistics, both in metrical structure and in syntax.

Notice, in (6), that each number occurs once as a left coordinate and once as a right coordinate. Similarly in (4), repeated here, the number 0 *occurs three times* in the bottom tier:

(7)

			1			2			0
	1	2	0	1	2	0	1	2	0
0	*1*	*2*	*3*	*4*	*5*	*6*	*7*	*8*	*9*

We can separate the *type* of object from the *instance*. The *type* of number 0, is an element of the set {0, 1, 2}, and it has some set of properties associated with it. There are three *instances* of 0 in (4)/(7), marked by the little hand of the clock: 0 occurs when the little hand is at 1, again when it is at 2, and again when it is at 0 (marked by positions *3*, *6* and *9*). Vergnaud defines a set of *occurrences* (e.g. of 0) as a *chain*. Here, the fact that 0 occurs three times is independent of the set of properties that define what 0 is; rather, it is based on the hands of the clock. Vergnaud calls ω the set of properties associated with some object (say, 0, or more linguistically, say, some grammatical object, e.g. T, which has a bundle of features), and he calls I the set of properties that can be freely associated with all objects, which can alternatively be called a set of *indices*—here, the system of the hands of the clock. Then, he defines an *occurrence* of ω (e.g. 0) as the pairing of ω with some element in I. However, the indices here are not arbitrary; rather, they arise from the properties of the clock itself: they arise from the properties of the *formal system.*

Vergnaud discusses the difference between the clock system/permutation and metrical structure, which is topological: the former is two-dimensional, and the latter is one-dimensional. One can convert the two-dimensional clock to one dimension (see chapter 3, section 5), and end up with the following:

(8) 0|1|2|0

The clock can be arranged linearly to generate any of the following sequences:

(9) (i)   0|1|2|0

  (ii)   1|2|0|1

  (iii) 2|0|1|2

Notice that, to preserve the effects of a permutation (or a circle) in one dimension, the ends must be repeated. To briefly illustrate, we can look to a circle such as that which follows. The circle is "topologically equivalent" to a line in which the two ends are "identified," or equal to one another:

(10) (i)

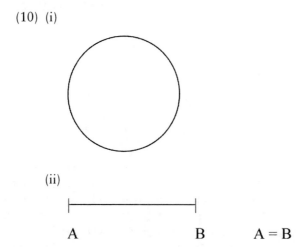

(ii)

A   B   A = B

Here, A and B are two *occurrences* of the same object (e.g. 0 in (9), above), and constitute a *chain.*

Returning to the two-dimensional permutation, we see that each object/ number occurs as a left coordinate and as a right coordinate:

(11) (i) (0, 1) (1, 2) (2, 0)

Vergnaud shows (chapter 3, section 5) that each *type* of object/number may be analyzed as a chain reflecting the two roles of the object (*two instances*): one as a left coordinate, and the other as a right coordinate. Vergnaud labels these *source* (left) and *goal* (right). There is an occurrence of each type of object as a source, in the domain, or as a goal, in the codomain. But, as introduced earlier, we can collapse this onto one dimension:

(12) 0|1|2|0

When we do this, we no longer 'see' that each of the numbers in the set $\{1, 2, 0\}$ form a chain—in fact, we can only allow ourselves to see *one* of the numbers that forms a chain (the endpoints)—and we must do this to preserve the topological equivalence Vergnaud discusses in (10), above. But, in two dimensions, it remains that each object occurs twice—once as a source and once as a goal—and so each object plays two *roles* in the structure. It is the linearization/collapsing onto one dimension where we collapse the two roles onto one object, or one "geometric point."

It is this notion of *occurrence* within this mathematical exploration of circular permutations that Vergnaud applies to linguistics, being reminded of two conjectures by Chomsky and Halle (resp.).

Applying the Notion of Occurrence to Linguistics: Metrical Structure

Reaching from mathematics to linguistics, Vergnaud identifies two conjectures about chaining, one by M. Halle and the other by N. Chomsky:

(13) Halle's conjecture (C_H)

Given a metrical grid M and some position *i* in M, the asterisks in the preceding column *i* form a chain.

(14) Chomsky's conjecture (C_C)

We could, for example, identify this [the full context of α in K-JRV] as K' = K with the occurrence of α in question replaced by some designated element OCC distinct from anything in K. (p. 43, note 64)

Vergnaud develops a theory that "vindicates" both conjectures, extending his formal notion of *chain* both to syntax and to metrical structure. The question is: how does one get from strings to circular permutations (as described earlier)? Vergnaud treats a string as a 'severed' permutation:

(15)

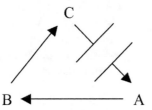

He replaces the notation A|B|C|A, notated subsequently, with a Δ represent-
ing a 'junction' or an edge of some constituent:

(16) a. ABC = {(A, B), (B, C), (C, Δ)}

   b. A|B|C|A = {(A, B), (B, C), (C, A)}

As with circular permutations, an object in a permutation (e.g. A) has two
roles. Taking Δ to be an instance of the OCC feature from Chomsky 1998, e.g.
{(X, Δ)} = <X, OCC>, we have one role for X—this is the *source* role, discussed
previously. The second role, <X, ID> represents X's ability to 'substitute' for Δ,
or, in other words, act as the *goal* for some {(Y, Δ)} pair (allowing us to recur-
sively create a string, e.g. XY). In creating the string XY, Vergnaud defines a
cochain, which exists with the identification of <X, OCC> with <Y, ID>.

(17) {<X, OCC>, <Y, ID>} is a *co-chain* iff. <X, OCC> = <Y, ID>

What this represents is the adjacency of X and Y in the string XY. We could
rephrase this and say that Y creates a context for X. We have a *chain* with
the elements <X, OCC> and <X, ID>—recall that these are two occurrences
of X as a *source* and as a *goal*—and we have a *cochain* with <X, OCC> and
<Y, ID>, which allows us to stitch together adjacency relations in chains.
Here is Vergnaud's example of the string ABC (see chapter 3, section 6.3
for details):

(18)

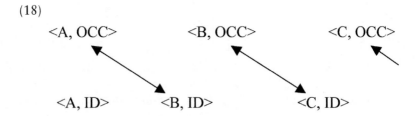

Returning to metrical grids, Vergnaud shows that the string in (18) can create
the metrical grid from (1). He demonstrates that this occurs, really, by a *checking* mechanism (in the minimalist sense): an OCC 'gesture,' or occurrence,
gets deleted when it is linked in a cochain with an ID 'gesture' (the arrows,

above). Essentially, an OCC-gesture is an uninterpretable feature in syntax, or in phonology, it means "that a stressed unit is defined as one that cannot be interpreted as a context for another unit"—stress as a *junctural mark*.

This is the core of Vergnaud's system as it relates to both phonology and syntax. While a clear picture of metrical grids occurs in chapter 3, it remains to be seen how it is worked out in syntax. Section 8.4 in chapter 3, and the entirety of chapter 5 develops this model.

The ideas in chapter 3 underpin the architecture proposed in chapter 5, as well as previewing Vergnaud's collaboration with Louis Goldstein in 2009 for a seminar at the University of Southern California linking gestural phonology with syntax, a realm which the 2009 seminar opened and one that remains open to investigation.

Algebra : Geometry :: Syntax : Phonology (or Vice Versa)

In chapter 4, Tommi Leung takes a broad perspective on the consequences of the approach Vergnaud proposes. He argues that Vergnaud's approach embodies the philosophy that parallels between syntax and phonology are not a matter of *collapsing* one field onto another, but rather looking to *domain-general principles* that may drive computation in both fields. To do this, Leung points out an analogy within the field of algebraic geometry (using algebra to explore geometry, and vice versa) to 'syntactic phonology': while there is a way to translate from one mathematical field to another (i.e. *coordinates*), linguists have not agreed on a translation between syntax and phonology. The central inquiry in chapter 3 is therefore the following: "To what extent can we reconstruct/reduce the two modules to abstract domain-general features, and the possible source of distinct properties?"

Chapter 4 goes on to recapitulate the important points of chain and occurrence, and instantiation vs. type—and then to generalize it to a larger clock, and larger chunk of syntactic structure. This more complex illustration should give the reader a clearer idea of the relationship Vergnaud was exploring between (mathematical) notions of periodicity and cyclic structure to linguistic computation. Leung's contribution serves to look at the formal components in chapter 3 with a more complex illustration, but perhaps more, serves as a discussion of the drive and purpose behind Vergnaud's line of thought in his final years. In the search for general mathematical principles to drive computation (following, quite seriously, the Minimalist Program), Leung projects that Vergnaud's desire to link levels of linguistic computation (e.g. syntax and phonology) is indeed universalist, a 'true discoverer' in the words of Henri Poincaré.

The Heart of the Formal System: The Items and Contexts Architecture (ICA)

The heart of the core formal system that stems from Vergnaud's thoughts in his final fifteen years of work is in chapter 5. Here, Vergnaud examines in close detail the major themes of this book. Chapters 2–3 are a precursor to the significant contribution in chapter 5, and chapters 6 and 7 explore empirical consequences of the system sketched there. Here, we provide an introductory window into the grammatical architecture and formal theory presented in chapter 5 of this volume, the *Items and Contexts Architecture* (ICA). We provide an overview and brief discussion of chapter 5, using Chomsky's Bare Phrase Structure and Baker's Mirror Principle as a basis for our discussion and interpretation of the ICA.

Under the Minimalist Program, linguistic theory has attempted to move toward a general set of computational principles, trying to disambiguate which principles are language specific and which are general (Chomsky 1995, 2004, et seq). Part of this program is to explore posited primitives and mechanisms that, while empirically motivated, remain stipulations. For example, binary branching, which was stipulated in X-bar theory, is derived in Minimalism. And the idea of government, which was central under the Government and Binding approach for a host of phenomena, has been dispensed with. Continuing in that tradition, Vergnaud's chapter 5 recharacterizes the grammatical architecture under Bare Phrase Structure (BPS) as a *matrix,* or a *graph,* dispensing of properties of the derivation that are only relevant for the interfaces (here, we discuss three) and allowing for a *more general phrase structure* that is used in *both* nominal and verbal contexts— by characterizing the primitives of phrase structure as playing dual roles (Manzini 1995, 1997), that of both an *item* and that of a *context.*

Various proposals throughout generative grammar embrace empirical parallelisms between the nominal and verbal domain (Chomsky 1970; Abney 1987; Szabolcsi 1989; Krifka 1989, 1992; Ogawa 2001; Megerdoomian 2002; Borer 2005, among many others) and attempt to provide a unified theory of structural parallels between nominal structure and verbal structure. For example, X-bar theory did account for the idea that both nominal and verbal categories have similar types of syntactic objects (XPs). However, while X-bar theory accounts for the parallels through the use of a similar primitive phrase structure template, the system in chapter 5 accounts for the parallel *hierarchy* that we see with certain linguistic features, based on observations by Lasnik and Uriagereka (2005) about clausal symmetry. In X-bar theory, this symmetry is represented by the order in which the XPs combine to form the verbal and nominal hierarchies, which remains a stipulation despite the use of XPs serving similar functions in both domains (i.e. classifier and aspect heads serving to represent the (same) abstract notion of 'end-point' in the nominal–mass vs. count nouns- and verbal–telic vs. atelic event– domains). Ever since Abney (1987), there is really no good way to represent selection of an argument by the verb, or local theta selection. A verb, e.g. *eat*, has no semantic relationship with D, alone—the D could be any type of D (*every, the, a,* etc . . .) (Lebeaux 1988, 1991, 2000, 2001; Sportiche 2005). What *eat* selects is the NP below the D—*apples,* but the NP is now embedded below a hierarchy of functional projections, and there is no way to encode this relationship locally.

Reaching out empirically, Vergnaud's paper proposes that the extended projection of the nominal and verbal domain are formed from "the same primitive formatives in the same hierarchical order" (chapter 5, p. 157) for the DP and the VP by having a single feature merged (*checked*) in two contexts: the N-category context, and the V-category context. In other words, Vergnaud's system takes the N/V parallels as a strong hypothesis, and his system derives exact parallels between the domains. It remains an empirical question whether or not this generalizes, but see chapter 7 for one example of an application across the N-V domains that resolves empirical problems to previous approaches, and that shows that even paradigms that don't appear on the surface to require parallels still do. Vergnaud works to derive the parallelisms in the hierarchies *across* nominal and verbal domains, such as the semantic relationship between V and N which both exist low in the hierarchies, from properties of the computation (narrow syntax) itself.

Vergnaud's formal contributions are no doubt difficult to read, but to ignore the formalism would be to miss his broad contribution, that formal mathematical principles must provide the basis for a computational model of linguistic theory. Even as a simple illustration, chapter 5 relates physical principles such as displacement of an object in a body of water (Archimedes' Principle), at an abstract level, to the general principle of grammatical structure mentioned earlier: the size of a specifier, measured in certain featural primitives, reflects the level of "displacement" in the verbal domain—the necessary number of verbal features must match that of the nominal domain. While this illustration is not to be taken as an attempt to relate the specifics of fluid displacement to the specifics of linguistics, it was Vergnaud's strong belief, in line with MP, that *general* physical and cognitive principles such as a notion of displacement also drive grammatical principles. It is recommended to the reader to carefully study the appendices to chapter 5, which deal directly with the formal notions discussed in the chapter itself.

The nature of this extended introduction is to recognize that this manuscript was left incomplete. The purpose of the publication of these manuscripts is not meant to be the capstone of a life's work, but rather the foundation of a new territory of grammatical theory—one that is meant to be explored and furthered by researchers. In this chapter, Vergnaud sets out a solid mathematical foundation for an exploration of constituent structure, broadening his contribution at the end of chapter 3 to a fully formal grammatical architecture. It is laid out and ready to be tested empirically, by linguists today, by us, to explore scientifically how these formal, mathematical, domain-general principles apply within various empirical domains (chapters 6 and 7 are two budding instances of such work).

Bare Phrase Structure and a Family of Trees

At the level of computation, Vergnaud's approach derives a family of *trees* from a syntactic representation that is a *2 x n matrix*—or, as is shown in

Appendices II–III to chapter 5, and in chapters 6/7, a *graph* (isomorphic to the matrix). In doing this, he takes narrow syntax to be a more abstract representation, from which constituent structure (represented as a tree or set of trees) is derived. From this, the family (or plurality) of trees computed from the matrix/graph in narrow syntax can be used at the interfaces for interpretation and linearization, at a second tier of analysis. This system, in the spirit of continued theoretical progress under the Minimalist Program, argues for a two-tiered architecture, which resolves concerns about computation that occurs at narrow syntax but instead is relevant only to interface properties.

This can be understood by looking to Bare Phrase Structure (Chomsky 1995). Here, merging α and β creates the set {α,{α,β}}. Then, merging another element δ builds the set to: {δ, {δ, {α,{α,β}}}}. This can be represented by the labeled tree in (19):

(19)

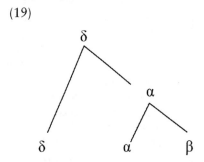

Notice, however, that at any 'level' of the derivation, or any 'level' of structure, one can see that α and β were merged originally. Here are the steps of the derivation so far:

1. Merge (α, β) = {α, {α, β}}

2. Merge (δ, {α, {α, β}}) = {δ, {δ, {α,{α, β}}}}

In both steps 1 and 2, one can see the 'history' of what has been merged—that is, the merging of α and β which took place originally. The derivation itself encodes *at every level* the history of the derivation, and at every step of the derivation there is a new tree. So, at the end of a long derivation, there are as many trees (representations of structure) that there are steps to the derivation. This set of trees, or 'family' of trees, that arises—and that is encoded in the derivation—is one way to think about Bare Phrase Structure. Vergnaud takes this perspective in chapter 4, and derives a family of trees for each derivation. This family of trees, or as Vergnaud puts it, is a *plurality of constituent structures.*

The family of trees can be represented by a series of dominance relations between labels (which, in chapter 5, Vergnaud aligns with Chomsky's 1981, 1986 notion of government). For example:

(20) δ ⟶ α ⟶ β

This graph represents the fact that α dominates β, and δ dominates α and everything that α contains, which here includes β. Two possible trees can be used to represent this structure:

(21)

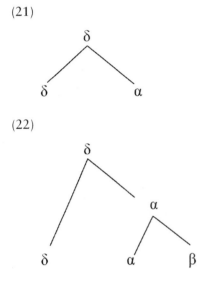

(22)

This is because α can represent/label the merge relationship for α and β. This is akin to telescoping, cf. Brody 1997, which Vergnaud refers to in chapter 5.[4] From these graphs that represent government relations between formatives, Vergnaud shows that several trees are possible—an *equivalence class, or plurality,* of trees arises, representing the different levels of structure that can be represented.

In chapter 5, Vergnaud introduces such graphs for both nominal and verbal domains, which can be schematized as follows:

(23) T ⟶ Asp ⟶ V ⟶ R(oot)

      T ⟶ Asp ⟶ N ⟶ R

Here, T is the standard tense formative, Asp is the aspect formative, V/N are categorical formatives, and R is the formative for the Root of the phrase. He takes, along the lines of Borer 2005 and others, Aspect and Tense to be found in the nominal domain as well (with their respective interpretations, i.e. Aspect representing the mass/count distinction and T the definite/indefinite distinction, possibly). He uses this clause structure throughout, though he acknowledges that the clause and nominal structure are much likely more complex than this illustration. However, the formal components of his system will remain despite possible modifications to the primitive grammatical formatives he uses in chapter 5, and left to future research (see chapter 7 for a possible modification regarding classifiers).

The family of possible trees, or possible constituent analyses (limited by the head projection relation), is a syntactic arrangement that Vergnaud calls an *Iterated Head-Complement* (IHC) structure. He argues that IHC structures make up the fabric of syntax, and are the primitive, or "minimal unit" of grammatical structure (citing Martin and Uriagereka 2000). This is an important point, because typically a derivation is represented by a single labeled tree. What Vergnaud illustrates is that using a single tree as the only representation of a derivation misses some properties rendered by Bare Phrase Structure that remain unaddressed—properties that come from a grammatical object occurring in two roles (as in chapter 3).

To compute the parallel nominal and verbal domains, pictured in the preceding graphs, Vergnaud departs from the standard notion of Merge as the simplest function. He proposes that there are two kinds of Merge, rather than a simple concatenation notion. One type of Merge forms *selectional* relationships–or builds hierarchical structure in an extended projection, Head-Merge. The second type of Merge forms *checking* relationships—allows for an N-context and a V-context to check one another, EPP-Merge. This differs from Chomsky 2004, who notes that the first Merge relationship creates a head-complement relationship, and further applications of Merge with the same head create what we call specifier relationships. Chomsky points out that it remains an empirical question whether this distinction is necessary or not, and proposes not to restrict the number of times a head can project (or the number of specifiers that can occur). Vergnaud departs from this concern, and permits one type of merge that allows for head-complement relationships (selection), and another type of merge that creates head-spec relationships (checking).

The parallel nominal and verbal domains that are created by EPP-Merge and Head-Merge, can be represented by a more abstract structure: a *2 x n* matrix, from which constituent structure (or Phrase-markers—or, standard *trees*) is derived. This is schematized as follows:

(24)

T	Asp	V	R
T	Asp	N	R

Here, we will take T = D, and Asp = Classifier/#, so we can revise the matrix as follows:

(25)

T	Asp	V	R
D	CL	N	R

The horizontal boxes represent Head-Merge, or selection, in the parallel domains (see chapter 5, p. 130 for details). The following arrows are illustrative of asymmetric Merge relations between items, construed as headedness/labeling, and are not meant to be formal graphs unlike those found in chapter 5.

(26)

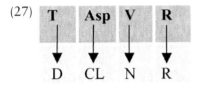

The vertical arrangement of boxes in the matrix represents EPP-Merge, or checking, across the nominal and verbal domains (N-related functional projections and V-related functional projections, respectively). This represents argument/specifier relationships:

(27)

T	Asp	V	R
↓	↓	↓	↓
D	CL	N	R

Notice that there is a direct, local relationship at every level of the clause. Vergnaud develops this further when he argues that each grammatical formative plays a role as an *item* and a *context* across dual domains (chapter 5, section 8), discussed below. This formal exploration opens the door to the chapter's main contribution: the Items and Contexts Architecture, which *derives* constituent structure from a more abstract grammatical representation. It provides an account of A-movement where feature-by-feature 'accretes' into the nominal and verbal domain *at the same time*: a parallel (nominal) specifier is paired with every verbal projection, and is of equal structural size. This leads to parallel growth of the nominal and verbal domain. More deeply, Vergnaud hypothesizes that, in the grammatical interface with the mental/cognitive brain system, the primitive objects of the *grammatical interface* are not lexical items, or grammatical items, but rather the *roles* played by these items. Each item has two roles: one role refers to an *object* in the mental system, and the other role relates to *being a context* in the mental system. Then, a grammatical structure is a set of mappings between items and contexts, the two types of roles of constituents.

The Mirror Principle

Vergnaud collapses Baker's Mirror Principle, the EPP, and checking under one formal mechanism. This predicts an empirical distinction between specifier creation and selection, which remains heterogeneous in the computation. Possible empirical consequences include predicting the existence of polysynthetic languages and deriving the (empirically observed) Mirror Principle.

Here, we introduce and explore the mechanism in detail, beginning with the Mirror Principle as stated informally in Baker 1985:

(28) Mirror Principle (Baker 1985)

Morphological derivations must directly reflect syntactic derivations (and vice versa).

Baker observes that certain morphological patterns are the mirrored order of syntactic patterns, more specifically in the linear ordering of these elements. Baker (1988) uses the head movement constraint (Travis 1984) to form agglutinative words via (syntactic) head-movement of morphological affixes. The morphological derivation *is* the syntactic derivation, and the mirrored order is created via affixation by cyclic, local head-movement.

Vergnaud's system takes the Mirror Principle to stem from the relationship between interpretable and uninterpretable pairs of features, paired e.g. across the nominal and verbal domains. Empirically, we observe that features that are uninterpretable in the verbal domain, e.g. person features under T, are interpretable in the nominal domain, i.e. under D. Vergnaud takes this to be a fundamental aspect of the computational component of human language, C_{HL}: some *uninterpretable* formative in the verbal domain is *interpretable* in a dual, nominal domain. He refers to an abstract categorical feature of the verbal domain (typically 'V') as O and the categorical feature of the nominal domain as O* (typically 'N'), as an abstraction away from standard theory, to illustrate the concept. Using Vergnaud's notation, where <O| is a *context* and |O*> is an *item,* he represents the uninterpretable verbal *contextual* formative as being under identity with the interpretable nominal *item* formative:

(29) <O| = |O*>

The verbal contextual feature *is* the nominal item feature, where the contextual features are *uninterpretable* and the item features are *interpretable.*

The notation that Vergnaud uses for *items (interpretable)* and *contexts (uninterpretable)* is the bra-ket notation used in quantum physics:

(30) <x|y>

where <x| is called a *bra-* and |x> is called a *–ket.* The *kets* are the items, and the *bras* are the contexts. This formal notation is only one of a few that Vergnaud introduces in the paper, as different ways of exploring the same idea, but it is one of the more intuitive ideas (and used pervasively throughout the formal consequences in the final sections of the paper, so we use it here).

From this, he derives a Mirrored template (under the Mirror Principle) by allowing a 'reversal' of which grammatical formatives act as *contexts* and which act as *items* from one domain to its dual. Essentially, we reverse, in each feature pair, which formative is the item and which is the context (this is based on the general feature identity, mentioned earlier):

(31) R = Root, V = categorical Verb feature, N = categorical Noun feature, A = Aspect, T = Tense, Ø = Edge feature, X = either V or N feature (a variable for a categorial feature)

Nominal Template, X = N:

{<ØlR>, <RlX>, <XlA>, <AlT>, <TlØ>}

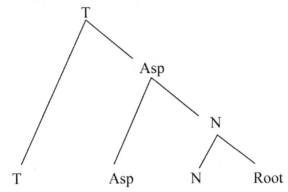

Notice that Vergnaud uses Edge features, Ø, for both T and Root features, to note that there is only a 'joker' feature creating an item for (context) Root, and context for (item) T (this is akin to Δ in chapter 3). We see here (and explained in chapter 5) that the –ket for each formative is akin to 'projecting' or labeling a head.

Then, taking <Ol = lO*>, or more specifically, reversing the each item-context pair in the nominal domain to create its dual (verbal) domain, derives a mirrored verbal template:

(32) Mirrored Verbal Template, X = V*:

{<RlØ>, <XlR>, <AlX>, <TlA>, <ØlT>}

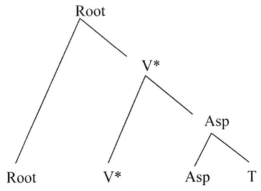

Notice that this tree represents the morphological linear ordering of a verbal root, with its affixes, crucially, taking the inverse of the features in the other domain.

What Vergnaud does here is pair two domains (defined as one instance of a template, as illustrated previously), where one 'checks' the other. He requires that there be dual domains, which is the same as requiring that any single template have a specifier—this is the essence of the EPP. By doing this, and by requiring the dual set to have a mirrored inverse as its dual, he *derives* the Mirror Principle. This comes from the single requirement that *the contextual/ uninterpretable features* of the nominal domain act as *items/interpretable features* in the verbal domain (and vice versa). This requirement is not given by a principle, but Vergnaud hints at the possibility of being an effect of Full Interpretation: if we have a set of grammatical formatives, then they must play both roles—as an item (interpretable) and as a context (uninterpretable).

This requirement about the duality of features, and the dual domains, is the essence of the ICA, and is how Vergnaud stitches together the fabric of syntax in an unexpected way—and this requirement allows the Mirror Principle, checking, and the EPP to be unified under one structural principle. This duality also allows for the nominal/verbal domains to be paired, and requires that each domain be the *same size* as its dual (specifiers are the same size as the constituent with which they are merged.), because each feature plays a role in both the nominal and verbal domains.

Dual Domains: Two Types of Merge

Here, let's return to the idea of parallel/dual nominal and verbal domains, looking to how Vergnaud creates these structures. He introduces the idea that there are two types of Merge: one that creates extended projections (what he calls Head-Merge), and one that creates checking relationships across domains (what he calls EPP-Merge). The role of sections 5–7 of chapter 5 is to pull together the notion of EPP-Merge and Head-Merge with the idea of the functional duality of a grammatical formative as both an item and a context. Notice that, to derive the Mirror Principle, Vergnaud required that some grammatical formative that is used as an interpretable *item* in one domain be used as uninterpretable *context* in a paired domain. However, we have necessarily skimmed over the idea that a given grammatical formative plays two roles *within a single nominal or verbal domain*. Let's return to the given structure for a verbal structure (notice that the template is always the same):

(33) Verbal Template, X = V:

{<∅|R>, <R|X>, <X|A>, <A|T>, <T|∅>}

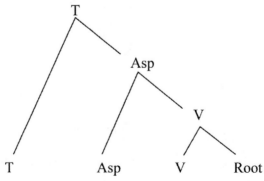

Recall that the feature T is an *item* in the pair <A|T>, and a *context* in the pair <T|∅>. This allows for selectional domains to be created, such as the verbal domain above (as we elaborate later).

Categorial Symmetry

In chapter 5, section 5, Vergnaud introduces the principle of Categorial Symmetry. From the notion of Head-Merge, he builds IHC structures to create extended projections, as in the preceding template, (33), and from EPP-Merge; he then pairs two IHC structures *in parallel*. Vergnaud links the idea of parallel IHC structures to the notion of symmetry in syntax from Lasnik and Uriagereka 2005, and proposes (a strong) principle to incorporate this notion of symmetry with that of IHC structures. This is the principle of Categorial Symmetry (CS), which states that *all* IHC structures are constructed from *the same grammatical formatives in the same hierarchical order*. Most importantly, the principle of CS implies that a noun phrase and a verb phrase (the parallel IHC structures linked by EPP-Merge) are made up of the same abstract components. This embodies observations in the literature that certain components of the verbal and nominal domains seem to play similar roles, such as aspect in the verbal domain being linked with count/mass distinctions, or *Div* (cf. Borer 2004) in the nominal domain. Essentially, an IHC structure with an N categorical feature will create a noun phrase, or if it is found in the context of a V categorical feature will create a verb phrase.

Given the IHC structure for a verb phrase set out in section 5 of chapter 5, in section 6 Vergnaud shows the template for a verb phrase, where each formative in (34) plays a role as an item (i.e. |X>) and as a context (i.e. <X|). As mentioned earlier, he notates the *ket* with a delta notation, where ΔX is equivalent to <X| (see p. 150, section 5), and represents the item X as creating a *context*. Then, to achieve the telescoping relation, each item is paired with a context. In *bra-ket* notation, the verb template is: (R = Root, A = Aspect, T = Tense, ∅ = Edge)

(34) {<∅|R>, <R|X>, <X|A>, <A|T>, <T|∅>}

Here, X is in the context of R (recall X = V or v), Aspect is in the context of X, and Tense is in the context of Aspect. The symbol ∅, as before, represents an Edge feature (so the R is found in the context of an 'edge,' and an 'edge' is found in the context of T of an IHC structure). The item/context notation is *crucially* represented in (34) as a directed edge of the graph, which expresses the *headedness/labeling* property of constituent structure. We see that Tense falls in the context of Aspect in (34) as well. Or, synonymously, Tense is the *label* of the constituent created when Aspect and Tense are Merged. Essentially, as Vergnaud states, headedness is the manifestation of a "mental/neural notion of *context*"—and this notion is what creates asymmetry in syntax. Vergnaud discusses the mental notion of context in chapter 5 (p. 149), which is a *symmetrical* one, and hypothesizes that a simplification creating an asymmetry is useful:

(35) *(p/q)* ⇔ *(q/p), where (x/y) is "x is in the context of y"*

Vergnaud hypothesizes that the computation can be simplified by only representing half of this relationship, citing Sauzet's 1993 concept of *attenance,* and argues that this *asymmetry* is computationally useful: "The syntactic relation of . . . *headedness* ultimately derives from the asymmetry of the mental/neural concept. That asymmetry is the basis of many features of the mind, such as the focus/background dichotomy."

A constituent is defined as any *bra-ket* pair, or *context* and *item* pair (see chapter 5, p. 150): <Q|P> = {Q, P} is a constituent. This relates the notion of context to that of constituent, and then we see that this is an asymmetric notion because if {Q, P} is a constituent, then it must be that either Q is a context *or* P is a context (either <Q|P> , or <P|Q>, but not both). In other words, either P or Q must be the label of a constituent.

To allow for recursivity, he adds a recursive rule that links two constituents:

(36) If *Q* is in the context of *P* and *R* is in the context of *Q*, then *R* is in the context of the couple *{Q, P}.*

(37) (Q, ΔP), (R, ΔQ) ⇒ (R, Δ{Q, P})

So items can be "nested" within constituents, allowing for more complex contexts. Then, the *item* in the *item-context* pair is the label/head for the pair, as mentioned previously.

Vergnaud puts all of the preceding axioms into a set of axioms called the Contextuality and Constituency Axioms, given in (159), repeated here:

(38) Contextuality and Constituency Axioms (CC Axioms)

Let *Q* and *P* be two constituents. Then:

a.   (Q, ΔP) ⇒ {Q, P} *is a constituent*

b.   {Q, P} *is a constituent* ⇒ (Q, ΔP) or (P, ΔQ)

c.   (Q, ΔP), (R, ΔQ) ⇒ (R, Δ{Q, P})

d.   (Q, ΔP) ⇒ *Q* is the *head* of the constituent *{Q, P}*

e.   A phrase with *label* Q is analyzed as a pair *{{Q, P}, (Q, ΔP)}.*

This set of axioms describes what is known in the literature as *Bare Phrase Structure,* and derives the intuitive idea of 'family of trees' which we discussed earlier.[5]

Vergnaud also addresses the derivational process in syntax in section 6, showing that the item-context pairs given in (34) can be selected Top-down, Bottom-up, or in any order. The same grammatical relations are encoded in any way. As long as the conditions are met, that every *ket* is paired with a *bra* that contains distinct formatives, and conversely, that every *bra* is paired with a *ket* that contains a distinct formative, and the mapping is one-one, then the structure is good.

Now, synthesizing the discussion of Bare Phrase Structure as creating *families* of constituent structures, and Sections 5–6, which set out the verb template v_X, we can see that the verb template is actually a family of possible constituent structures (or *tree structures*) that make up an equivalence class. This is represented by the bra-ket notation, and Section 7 formalizes the notion of how the mathematical interpretation of the domain, in bra-ket notation, relates to the notion of a family of constituent structure.

Phases and Cyclic Movement

In chapter 5, Vergnaud sets out a working hypothesis of the formatives that make up an IHC structure. A phase will be defined as the pairing of two IHC structures (one in the nominal, and one in the verbal domain), or 'dual domains.' As we have been utilizing in our earlier example, he proposes that the elements that make up a verb phrase are T, Asp, X, and R, where X = v/V distinction, and a noun phrase has T, Asp, X and R as well, with X = N. However, a clause is standardly made up of two verbal phases, a vP and a CP/TP phase. To do this with IHC structures, Vergnaud proposes that a clause is made up of two IHC structures, with two tenses, two aspects, a verbal v/V feature, and two R (root) features. Each of these IHC structures has a dual nominal projection. Essentially, as in Minimalism, two phases make up a transitive clause.

However, the mechanism for linking the lower (vP) phase and the higher (CP) phase remains incomplete. As we discuss later, Vergnaud has a mechanism for linking phases with *wh*-movement, focus, or other discourse-level properties, but this does not necessarily translate to linking a pair of CP and vP phases to build a transitive clause. As Vergnaud suggests in chapter 4, perhaps the right edge of the higher phase and the left edge of the lower phase are shared, although the formative that would partake in this role is not yet clear. The architecture presented by Vergnaud allows for many working hypotheses about the actual structure of a clause, and which formatives make up an IHC structure—he uses the formatives in chapter 5 for illustrative purposes, and acknowledges that the system will need to be richer than his initial proposal.

In section 9, Vergnaud defines a phase under this architecture as the pairing of a constituent with its dual ('mirror' from before, or *specifier*). So, the pair of nominal-verbal templates, repeated here, constitutes a phase:

(39) Verbal Template and Nominal Template:

$\{<\varnothing | R>, <R | V>, <V | A>, <A | T>, <T | \varnothing>\}$

$\{<\varnothing | R>, <R | N>, <N | A>, <A | T>, <T | \varnothing>\}$

However, one important function of phases is the edge position, which allows for cyclic movement to occur. Here, Vergnaud extends the architecture further and discusses how a category and its specifier may be linked by higher-order logical connectives that represent discourse-level functions (or functions commonly found in the C-domain). These connectives can only be used with a complete IHC structure, and signal the edge of a phase. There may be one '*focus*' per phase, or one set of linkers that connect the nominal and verbal domain. He extends this to *wh*-movement and complement clause embedding (see McKinney-Bock, to appear, for further discussion of complement clauses and a possible working out of the details of Vergnaud's theory). The details are not given explicitly in chapter 5, but we provide a basic introduction here, from Vergnaud's lecture notes and personal communication (the following is quoted from his notes):

"Human Language (HL) "quantifiers" are viewed as iterated logical connectives (in line with analyses found in the logical literature, such as in Skolem . . ., as well as in the linguistic literature, such as Harris . . .). To illustrate, English *every* and *each* arise from the iteration of ∧ (*and* in English), while English *any* arises from the iteration of some version of ∨ (*or* in English). Connectives are intrinsically binary, in the sense that a connective is an indissoluble pair of elements, of the form in (40), giving rise to the structure in (41) [and (42), added by KMB/MLZ, see also Liao 2011]:

(40) (K, k)

(41) Kx, ky, x, y phases

(42) $\text{K} \begin{cases} \{<\varnothing|R>, <R|V>, <V|A>, <A|T>, <T|\varnothing>\} \\ \{<\varnothing|R>, <R|N>, <N|A>, <A|T>, <T|\varnothing>\} \end{cases}$
$\text{k} \begin{cases} \{<\varnothing|R>, <R|V>, <V|A>, <A|T>, <T|\varnothing>\} \\ \{<\varnothing|R>, <R|N>, <N|A>, <A|T>, <T|\varnothing>\} \end{cases}$

Thus, a connective is a discontinuous lexical item. We elaborate later.

A connective can be *symmetrical*, with $K = k$, or *asymmetrical*, with $K \neq k$. The conjunctive connective and the disjunctive connective are symmetrical. The former is the pair *AND . . ., and . . .*, as in English *And Mary screamed and John cried*, typically realized as *Mary screamed and John cried*. The disjunctive connective is *OR . . ., or . . .*, as in *Or Mary screamed or John cried*, typically realized as *Mary screamed or John cried*. An asymmetrical connective is the connective *IF . . ., then . . .*. Another one is the *definiteness* connective. We slightly depart from Russell 1905 here in identifying definiteness as a particular *connective*, not as a particular *quantification*.

The defining property of a connected structure Kx, ky is:

(43) Connectedness is chaining (Cc)
Given the connective (K, k) in the structure Kx, ky, there must exist a constituent ∂ such that Kx and ky each contain a copy of ∂.

In the case of a symmetrical connective, Cc is trivially satisfied by taking ∂ to be $K = k$ [e.g. from chapter 7, there is an (OF, of) connective linking two noun phrases, OF = of.—KMB/MLZ]. In the case of an asymmetrical connective, there must be an independent ∂ that gives rise to a chain spanning the two halves of Kx, ky. [For example, in a relative clause (see chapter 6), there is an asymmetrical (D, C) connective which requires a shared noun phrase as its ∂ (the relativized noun). These connectives link *two phases* in the sense of complete, dual IHC nominal and verbal structures (x and y are variables representing two separate phases). Each contains a nominal and verbal counterpart—KMB/MLZ]."

Additionally, a short paper by Vergnaud in 2007 is included as an appendix in Chapter 5. Here, Vergnaud elaborates and develops the idea of a phase, looking at the equivalence of a label/head of a phrase and its constituent:

(44) Head(K) $\leftrightarrow$ K

(45) $(_{v\text{-}V}$ see$) \leftrightarrow (_{v\text{-}V}$ see him$)$

Vergnaud treats this equivalence as a generalized substitution transformation, which renders Transformation-markers (T-markers in the sense of Chomsky 1975) to be a 'system' of phases, each one depending on whether substitution of the entire constituent for the head has occurred (or not). Vergnaud expands the idea of phasal connectedness to adjuncts, and elaborates (as in the lecture notes, earlier) on *wh*-movement and phasal connectives.

To Conclude (and to Precede)

Chapter 5 builds, from formal mathematical concepts, a linguistic architecture that explores the consequences of a Minimalist system. Certain ramifications of the ICA appear radical, such as the idea that each phase is constructed of the same (nonrecursive) minimal feature hierarchy (an IHC structure). Others, however, simply reflect a mirror back towards what is currently being utilized in the field, possibly somewhat haphazardly at times, and gently challenges current theory (and theorists) to understand our computational formalisms and the consequences—for example, that of Bare Phrase Structure and labeling. Finally, the ICA contributes a deeper understanding of the empirical parallels between the nominal and verbal domains, and provides an architecture that can be used to further develop (a) the structure of the clause, as well as (b) laying out the framework to be able to explore how focus, *wh*- and discourse-level phenomena involving displacement (or multiple *contexts* for a single *item*) interact with basic clause structure.

The manuscript that is chapter 5 is, in parts, incomplete. It lays the foundation of a new territory of grammatical theory—one that is meant to be explored and furthered by researchers. In this chapter, Vergnaud sets out a solid mathematical foundation for an exploration of constituent structure, broadening his contribution at the end of chapter 3 to a fully formal grammatical architecture. Empirical extensions are given in chapters 6 and 7 (see also Leung 2007 for an empirical extension into free relatives) as a beginning to the research program outlined here, from Vergnaud's final fifteen years of linguistic thought.

PART III: EXTENSIONS/APPLICATIONS OF THE ICA

Chapter 6 builds off of the Items and Contexts Architecture in chapter 5, and looks to expand the architecture to relativization and A′ movement, which also continues thought about *the notion of occurrence* from chapter 3. Empirically, chapter 6 looks at a solution to split-antecedent relative clauses (Perlmutter and Ross 1970), which remain a difficulty for current theory.

(46) Mary met *a man* and John met *a woman* who know each other well.

McKinney-Bock and Vergnaud turn to a conflict in the Minimalist Program with the *source independence* of Merge and the Merge typology, and illustrate how different types of Merge (Internal and External) are only distinguishable by looking at a larger chunk of syntactic structure and not by local Merge. With this in mind, they explore cyclic copy-and-delete, and suggest that copying as a mechanism necessitates indexing and violates inclusiveness (Chomsky 1995). They conclude that movement should be represented as the sharing of a constituent in multiple local grammatical relationships, generalizing multidominance to all grammatical relationships within *graph theoretic syntax*.

Within graph theoretic syntax, headedness is represented by directionality on a graph rather than a 'projection' within a tree.[6] Merge creates an edge, intended here as a graph-theoretic notion of 'edge,'[7] with merged constituents the nodes. Two types of Merge are defined (along the edges of the graph): one is a checking relationship (EPP-Merge from chapter 5), and the other is selection (Selectional-Merge from chapter 5). Chapter 6 assumes the notion of symmetry from Chapters 5 and 7, where the DP is built in parallel with its VP (the argument is the same structural 'size' as the verb with which it merges). Then, trees are objects that are useful at PF for linearization and LF for interpretation/c-command, so it is shown how PF and LF trees are 'read' from the graphs at narrow syntax for interface purposes.

The empirical problem addressed in chapter 6 is that of split-antecedent relative clauses, which cannot be derived in current theory without construction-specific stipulations. McKinney-Bock and Vergnaud show that split-antecedent relative clauses are *predicted* within graph theoretic syntax as part of a family of coordinated structures with relative and matrix clauses, a natural consequence of how coordination interacts with relativization in this system. At a broader level, chapter 6 provides an explicit, generalized formalization of what it means for one object to 'share,' or, to *occur in multiple contexts.*

Chapter 7 takes a look into the structure of the DP in Chinese, and shows how the formal system presented in chapter 5 can unify the syntax of classifier constructions with those of N-of-N constructions present in nonclassifier languages. Liao and Vergnaud begin by presenting two possible analyses for classifier languages: the dual-constituent analysis and single-constituent analysis. They illustrate how analyses of English *of*-constructions from Kayne 2005/den Dikken 2006, both of which assume the presence of two copies of the functional item *of* (represented as {of, OF}), can be used to provide a syntax for Chinese classifier constructions. Furthering Kayne's and den Dikken's analysis, chapter 7 takes the idea of a pair of functional items and generalizes it within the ICA presented in chapter 5.

Liao and Vergnaud not only unify analyses of Chinese and English, but they argue that the formal system from chapter 5 can provide a representation of the DP that generalizes the notion of a pair of functional items, such that the Cartesian product of three pairs of items makes up the structure of the DP. This is represented graph-theoretically as a 'cube' to represent argument relations, functional-substantial grammatical relations, and the {of, OF} relations present in Kayne's and Den Dikken's work.

Chapter 7 touches on a breadth of hot empirical topics in the DP literature, including the mass/count distinction, plurality, quantificational adjectives such as *few/little* and *yi xie/yi dian,* and the implicational hierarchy of cross-linguistic representations of shape and number.

But perhaps the most potent empirical contribution is the account of *yi xie* and *yi dian* quantifiers in Chinese, which Liao and Vergnaud unify with Kayne's (2005) account of English *a few/a little.* Using empirical evidence from classifier reduplication and postverbal *yi* omission, Liao and Vergnaud argue that *xie* and *dian* are true syntactic classifiers, rather than bimorphemic quantifiers (such as *yi-qie* and *yi-ban*). From this, they argue that *yi-xie* and *yi-dian* are overt realizations of their (partially silent) English counterparts, few-NUMBER and little-AMOUNT. Then, using Merge-markers, they show that the sole difference between the Chinese classifiers *xie/dian* and their English counterparts, is that the Chinese classifiers select for the mass structure represented in the Merge-markers, while English selects for either count or mass.

Onward

In these manuscripts, Vergnaud's goal was not to radically depart from MP within generative grammar, but rather to take the underlying goal of the generative program and bring it to an even more general scientific level. The themes of *symmetry* and *periodicity* in this book reflect his goal of scientific progress in linguistics, and he has opened the doors to new exploration of old empirical problems in linguistics that may, someday, have deeper biological and physical explanations using his theory, which is grounded in general scientific inquiry.

NOTES

1. Chapter 2 was originally published by *Lingua* as J.-R. Vergnaud and R. Freidin, 2001, Exquisite connections: Some remarks on the evolution of linguistic theory, *Lingua* 111:639–666. Many thanks to Elsevier and *Lingua*. Chapter 3 was originally published by Mouton de Gruyter as J.-R. Vergnaud, 2003, On a certain notion of "occurrence": The source of metrical structure, and of much more, in *Living on the Edge*, ed. by S. Ploch. Many thanks to Mouton de Gruyter.
2. Chapter 4, while not directly in collaboration with Jean-Roger Vergnaud, was written as a companion piece to chapter 3 in 2011.
3. The notion of *symmetry* alluded to in this follows from a group theoretic notion that properties remain invariant under a series of transformations; see chapter 2 (p. 44) for a definition of *pronominal symmetry*, which states that the PF representation of *pro* remains constant no matter which representation is assigned to the NP component of the pronominal element.
4. Telescoping is also alluded to by Dependency Grammar and Word Grammar. See, e.g., Hudson (1984), Abney (1996), Robinson (1970).
5. As a note, Vergnaud interchanges several equivalent formal notations throughout the paper. For the reader's clarification, here is a list of notations used for *items* and *contexts*:

<X|Y>	*bra-ket* notation	<context|item>
(X, ΔY)	delta notation	(item, Δcontext)
X → Y	directed graph	context → item

6. As Tommi Leung (p.c.) points out, Word Grammar (Hudson 1984) and Relational Grammar (Blake 1990) also do without a projection. However, these grammars use a different type of graph than what chapter 4 assumes.
7. What is intended here is a graph-theoretic notion of *edge*. Take the graph G:

   X ⟶ Y

   The ordered pair <X,Y> denotes the edge connecting vertex X to vertex Y. G has the set of vertices {X, Y} and the set of edges {<X, Y>}. See Ch. 4, pg. 24 and Appendix III (also, e.g., Balakrishnan and Ranganathan 2000). This is distinct from the notion of 'edge' feature in Chomsky (1999, 2001, 2004, 2005), which is an EPP or OCC feature that permits raising to the phase edge (Chomsky 2004:15); see also chapter 5, p. 153.

REFERENCES

Abney, S. 1986. A grammar of projections. Ms.

————. 1987. The English noun phrase in its sentential aspect. Doctoral dissertation, MIT.

Baker, M. 1985. The Mirror Principle and morphosyntactic explanation. *Linguistic Inquiry* 16:373–415.

————. 1988. *Incorporation: A theory of grammatical function changing.* Chicago: University of Chicago Press.

Balakrishnan, R. and K. Ranganathan. 2000. *A Textbook of Graph Theory.* New York: Springer-Verlag.

Borer, H. 2005. *In name only. Structuring sense, Volume I.* Oxford: Oxford University Press.

Brody, M. 1997. Mirror theory. Ms., University College London.

Chomsky, N. 1957. *Syntactic Structures.* The Hague: Mouton.

————. 1970. Remarks on nominalization. In *Readings in Transformational Grammar*, ed. by R. Jacobs and P. Rosenbaum. Waltham, MA: Ginn.

————. 1981. *Lectures on Government and Binding.* Dordrecht: Foris.

————. 1986. *Barriers.* Cambridge, MA: MIT Press.

————. 1995. *The Minimalist Program.* Cambridge, MA: MIT Press.

————. 1998. Minimalist inquiries: The framework. In *Step by Step: Essays on Minimalist Syntax in Honor of Howard Lasnik*, ed. by R. Martin, D. Michaels, and J. Uriagereka. Cambridge, MA: MIT Press. [an early version appeared as *MIT Occasional Papers in Linguistics* 15, 1998]

————. 2004. Beyond explanatory adequacy. In *Structures and Beyond*, ed. by A. Belletti, 104–133. Oxford: Oxford University Press.

Compton, A. H. 1923. A quantum theory of the scattering of x-rays by light elements. *The Physical Review* 21:483–502.

den Dikken, M. 2006. *Relators and Linkers: The Syntax of Predication, Predicate Inversion, and Copulas.* Cambridge, MA: MIT Press.

Dirac, P. A. M. 1968. Methods in theoretical physics. In *From a Life of Physics; Evening Lectures at the International Center for Theoretical Physics, Trieste, Italy.* A special supplement of the International Atomic Energy Agency Bulletin, Austria.

Einstein, A. 1917. Zur Quantentheorie der Strahlung. *Physikalische Zeitschrift* 18:121–128. [First printed in 1916 in *Mitteilungen der Physikalische Gesellschaft Zürich* 16, 47–62]

Freidin, R. and J.-R. Vergnaud. 2001. "Exquisite connections: some remarks on the evolution of linguistic theory." *Lingua* 111, 639-666.

Halle, M. and J.-R. Vergnaud. 1987. *An Essay on Stress.* Cambridge, MA: MIT Press.

Hudson, R. A. 1984. *Word Grammar.* Oxford: Basil Blackwell.

Kayne, R. 2005. *Movement and Silence.* Oxford: Oxford University Press.

Krifka, M. 1989. Nominal reference, temporal constitution and quantification in event semantics. In *Semantics and Contextual Expression*, ed. by R. Bartsch, J. van Benthem, and P. van Emde Boas. Dordrecht: Foris.

————. 1992. Thematic relations as links between nominal reference and temporal constitution. In *Lexical Matters*, ed. by I. Sag and A. Szabolcsi. Stanford, CA: CSLI.

Lappin, S., R. Levine, and D. Johnson. 2000. The structure of unscientific revolutions. *Natural Language and Linguistic Theory* 18:665–671.

Lasnik, H., and J. Uriagereka. 2005. *A Course in Minimalist Syntax.* Maldin, Mass.: Blackwell.

Lebeaux, D. 1988. Language acquisition and the form of grammar. Doctoral dissertation, University of Massachusetts.

Lebeaux, D. 1991. Relative clauses, licensing, and the nature of the derivation. In *Perspectives on Phrase Structure: Heads and Licensing*, ed. by S. Rothstein. San Diego, CA: Academic Press.

———. 2000. *Language Acquisition and the Form of Grammar.* Philadelphia, PA: John Benjamins.

———. 2001. Prosodic form, syntactic form, phonological bootstrapping and telegraphic speech. In *Approaches to Bootstrapping: Phonological, Lexical, Syntactic, and Neurophysiological Aspects of Early Language Acquisition*, Vol. 2, ed. by J. Weissenborn and B. Höhle. Philadelphia, PA: John Benjamins.

Leung, T. 2007. Syntactic derivation and the theory of matching contextual features. Doctoral dissertation, University of Southern California, Los Angeles.

Liao, W.-w. 2011. The symmetry of syntactic relations. Doctoral dissertation, University of Southern California.

Manzini, M. R. 1995. From merge and move to form dependency. *UCLA Working Papers in Linguistics* 7:323–345.

———. 1997. Adjuncts and the theory of phrase structure. In *Proceedings of the Tilburg Conference on Rightward Movement*, ed. by D. Le Blanc and H. Van Riemsdijk. Amsterdam: John Benjamins.

Martin, R., and J. Uriagereka. 2000. Some possible foundations of the Minimalist Program. In *Step by Step: Essays on Minimalist Syntax in Honor of Howard Lasnik*, ed. by R. Martin, D. Michaels, and J. Uriagereka. Cambridge, MA: MIT Press.

McKinney-Bock, K. 2013. Building phrase structure from items and contexts. Doctoral dissertation, University of Southern California.

Megerdoomian, K. 2002. Beyond words and phrases: A unified theory of predicate composition. Doctoral dissertation, University of Southern California.

———. 2008. Parallel nominal and verbal projections. In *Foundational Issues in Linguistic Theory: Essays in Honor of Jean-Roger Vergnaud*, ed. by R. Freidin, C. P. Otero, and M. L. Zubizarreta. Cambridge, MA: MIT Press.

Ogawa, Y. 2001. *A Unified Theory of Verbal and Nominal Projections.* Oxford: Oxford University Press.

Perlmutter, D. M., and J. R. Ross. 1970. Relative clauses with split antecedents. *Linguistic Inquiry* 1:350.

Robinson, J. J. 1970. Dependency structures and transformational rules. *Language* 46:259–285.

Russell, B. 1905. On Denoting. *Mind* 14.56:479-493.

Sauzet, P. 1993. Attenance, gouvernement et mouvement en phonologie. Les constituants dans la phonologie et la morphologie de l'occitan. Doctoral dissertation, Université Paris 8. [Published in 1994, Montpellier: CEO/UPV]

Sportiche, D. 2005. Division of labor between merge and move: Strict locality of selection and apparent reconstruction paradoxes. In *Proceedings of the Workshop Divisions of Linguistic Labor, The La Bretesche Workshop.*

Szabolcsi, A. 1989. Noun phrases and clauses: Is DP analogous to IP or CP? In *The Structure of Noun Phrases*, ed. by J. Payne. Berlin: Mouton de Gruyter.

Travis, L. 1984. Parameters and effects of word order Variation. Doctoral dissertation, MIT.

2 Exquisite Connections
Some Remarks on the Evolution of Linguistic Theory

Robert Freidin and Jean-Roger Vergnaud[+][*]

Lappin, Levine, and Johnson's (2000) (*Natural Language and Linguistic Theory* 18: 665-671; henceforth LLJ) critique of the minimalist program raises three important issues: the relation between the MP and its predecessors (GB theory in particular), the empirical and conceptual motivation for the MP, and the relation (if any) of theoretical linguistics to the natural sciences. Sadly, LU's critique contributes virtually nothing to our understanding of these topics, as the following discussion will demonstrate.

1. MP VERSUS GB

As Chomsky and others have pointed out (see Chomsky 1995b; Freidin 1997a; Lasnik 1999), the MP is grounded in the principles and parameters framework, just like the GB theory it has to a large extent superseded. It shares at least three basic assumptions with virtually all of its predecessors within modern generative grammar. First and foremost, the mind/brain contains a language faculty, a component that interacts with other cognitive systems. Next, the cognitive system of language connects with performance systems via levels of linguistic representation, perhaps limited to only two external systems, one involving articulation and perception of the physical linguistic signal and the other involving the encoding or decoding of the meaning of the signal. Under this limitation there are only two interface levels, phonetic form (PF) and logical form (LF). Finally, performance systems do not differ across languages. Even at this fundamental level Chomsky (1995b:3) takes nothing for granted, noting that these assumptions are "not at all obvious."

As both the GB theory and the MP are grounded in the principles and parameters model, they share further specific assumptions (cf. Chomsky 1995b:170):

(i) regarding computational system for human language, C_{HL}, the initial state S_0 contains invariant principles and parameters (i.e., options restricted to functional elements)

(ii)   selection Σ of parameters determines a language

(iii) a language determines an infinite set of linguistic expressions (SDs), each pair (π, λ) obtained from the interface levels, PF and LF

(iv) language acquisition involves fixing Σ

(v)   the grammar of language states just Σ, lexical arbitrariness and the PF component aside

These shared assumptions have been standard for nearly two decades.

There is one further assumption articulated for the first time in Chomsky (1992), which could easily have been proposed prior to the MP. Chomsky offers as a narrow conjecture the suggestion that there is no variation in the overt syntax or the LF component. Ignoring PF options and lexical arbitrariness, Chomsky suggests that "variation is limited to nonsubstantive parts of the lexicon and general properties of lexical items," in which case "there is only one computational system and one lexicon," apart from the variation mentioned (Chomsky 1995b: 170).[1] Thus viewed at the appropriate level of abstraction, there is only one human language. Of course the truth or falsity of this bold conjecture remains to be established.

We come at last to the three assumptions that are unique to the MP: (1) that the interface levels LF and PF are the only relevant linguistic levels, in spite of apparent empirical evidence to the contrary (Chomsky 1995b:169), (2) that all conditions are interface conditions (p. 194), and (3) that a linguistic expression is the optimal realization of these conditions (p. 194). These three assumptions constitute what Chomsky (1999) calls the strong minimalist thesis. In contrast to the six basic assumptions that the MP shares with GB theory, the three assumptions unique to the MP do not add up to "a major paradigm change in the theory of grammar" as will become clear from the following discussion.

For LLJ the contrast between GB theory and the MP is that "the MP adds economy principles" "in addition to local constraints on operations and the structures they produce." While it is correct to highlight the role of economy in the development from GB to the MP, it is inaccurate to claim that economy conditions are an innovation unique to the MP.

The discussion of the role of economy in grammatical analysis begins with the advent of modern generative grammar, that is, Chomsky's *MMH* ([1951] 1979). There Chomsky identifies two kinds of criteria of adequacy for grammars—one for the correct description of the structure of the language under analysis, and the other for requirements imposed by its special purposes, "or, in the case of a linguistic grammar having no such special purposes, requirements of simplicity, economy, compactness, etc." (1). In a footnote, Chomsky supplies the following clarification:

> Such considerations are in general not trivial or 'merely esthetic.' It has been recognized of philosophical systems, and it is, I think, no less true

of grammatical systems, that the motives behind the demand for economy are in many ways the same as those behind the demand that there be a system at all (cf. Goodman 1943).

In other words, a grammar is not merely a description of a language; it is moreover an explanatory theory about the structure of a language, that is, why a language has the properties it does rather than other conceivable properties. It is in this context that considerations of economy, etc. first came into play.[2]

Applying economy conditions to the selection of derivations within each grammar represents a significant leap from applying them to the selection of grammars. Although economy conditions like Full Interpretation (FI) and Last Resort (LR) were not articulated in the earliest discussions, both were introduced as part of GB, the former in Chomsky (1986) and the latter in Chomsky (1991) (which first appeared in MITWPL #10 in 1989, three years prior to the advent of the MP). What happened in the 1990s, in a nutshell, was that certain economy conditions (e.g., FI) were interpreted in a way that made it natural for them to supplant a significant portion of the older GB principles.

Consider for example the Case Filter. It prohibits any phonetically realized nominal expression that is not marked for Case. Within GB, why this should be is just a matter of stipulation that appears to accord with the facts. From the point of view of economy, Case features are extraneous to interpretation at the LF interface at least and therefore should be eliminated from the derivation before LF. Otherwise, these uninterpretable features at the LF interface will violate FI, causing the derivation to crash. Thus legibility conditions imposed by the cognitive system that interfaces with C_{HL} determines how derivations proceed with respect to Case features. In this way FI and the Case Filter overlap in a way that FI subsumes the empirical effects of the Case Filter, but not conversely.[3] The preference for FI over the Case Filter is just the standard preference for the more general constraint, all things being equal.

In short, the heuristic of eliminating overlapping conditions, which has resulted in much fruitful research over several decades, is one of the central motivations for switching from the analysis of GB to that of the MP.[4]

The same logic provides one of the strongest motivations for eliminating the relation of government from current discussion. Consider the standard case of an ECP violation given in (1), where T stands for the functional category Tense and *t* is the trace of John.

(1) *John T is believed [that *t* T is happy]

Under MP analysis, (1) can be interpreted as a violation of FI in the following way. Suppose that the nominative Case feature of John is checked in the embedded clause by T, as is the nominative Case feature of T. When

John moves to the subject position of the matrix clause, Spec-T, only the D-feature of the nominal is available to check the D-feature of the matrix T. The nominative Case feature of *John* has been checked and thereby eliminated, so that the nominative Case feature of the matrix T remains, causing the derivation to crash at LF because of FI.[5] Thus the phenomena that fall separately under the Case Filter and the ECP within GB, are captured under a single principle within the MP analysis—moreover, one that functions as a natural legibility condition that regulates the interface between C_{HL} and other cognitive systems.[6]

Given the greater generality of FI, we would prima facie want to eliminate the ECP in favor of the more general principle.[7] Furthermore, this analysis, which explains deviance on the basis of legibility conditions imposed by cognitive systems that interface with C_{HL}, strikes us as a more promising explanatory account than the postulation of various constraints internal to C_{HL} that basically reflect the complexity of the phenomena in an essentially descriptive fashion.[8] Note incidentally that this approach is highly reminiscent of the one followed in Chomsky and Lasnik (1977). However, even if we discount impressions of what might be a more promising explanatory account, the methodological requirement to eliminate overlapping conditions whenever possible motivates the abandonment of much of the machinery of GB in favor of the MP analysis. Thus the change from GB to the MP is motivated by the same methodology that has always motivated changes in syntactic theory.

Another motivation for exploring the MP rather than continuing with GB concerns the central topic of phrase structure. The MP introduces bare phrase structure theory, which eliminates the ambivalent top-down and bottom-up view of phrase structure that has been characteristic of the field since the earliest formulations of X-bar theory in the late 1960s. With bare phrase structure there is only bottom up analysis of a specific kind.[9] The theory of bare phrase structure provides a derivational mechanism for syntactic representations, which has been missing from GB since the elimination of phrase structure rules (c. 1980) on the grounds that they are redundant given X-bar theory, the general principles of GB, and the specific properties of lexical items. Furthermore, bare phrase structure theory as incorporated within the MP cannot produce canonical D-structures, hence the elimination of D-structure as a level of representation follows from the nature of C_{HL} rather than a methodological stipulation.

Bare phrase structure eliminates in principle categorial distinctions for levels of phrasal projection, thereby conforming to the Inclusiveness Condition, which restricts computations solely to the elements (features) contained in lexical items. Given this condition, computations cannot introduce new elements such as bar levels, indices, or syntactic categories that are not already part of the lexical items computed.

Chomsky (1995b) is very clear that the Inclusiveness Condition provides one criterion for the "perfection" of C_{HL}. Although precisely what Chomsky intends by talking about language as a perfect system may not be totally clear in Chomsky (1995b), this discussion is clarified considerably in Chomsky (2000), written in 1998. Here the issue is represented in terms of the language faculty (FL) as a solution to legibility conditions imposed by the cognitive systems that interface with it. An optimal solution would encompass a C_{HL} restricted to just the properties of lexical items involved in computations plus just those few operations required for derivations that connect LF with PF (perhaps just the elementary operations of adjunction/concatenation (for Merge and Move) and deletion (for feature checking)). If the behavior of derivations is controlled solely by legibility conditions imposed by other cognitive systems at the interfaces, then C_{HL} can be reduced to these bare necessities, excluding additional internal machinery like the Case Filter and the ECP.[10] Thus in terms of simplicity, economy, and nonredundancy, the MP is clearly preferable to GB.

2.   ON CONCEPTUAL NATURALNESS

Appeal to general considerations of conceptual naturalness such as simplicity, economy, or nonredundancy is not unique to generative grammar.[11] It has been employed fruitfully in the more developed natural sciences— in particular, theoretical physics. The discussion of physics that follows attempts to elucidate this notion in a way that, ultimately, should illuminate its role in contemporary theoretical linguistics.

Consider, for example, Einstein's principle that all physical laws must be Lorentz invariant. As Putnam (1962) notes: "This is a rather vague principle, since it involves the general notion of a physical law. Yet in spite of its vagueness, or perhaps because of its vagueness, scientists have found it an extremely useful leading principle." This is because they have "no difficulty in recognizing laws:" a law of nature will be an equation relating "real magnitudes" that has "certain characteristics of simplicity and plausibility." In other words, determining whether Einstein's principle may be applied to any particular case will involve "general considerations of conceptual naturalness."

In a different area, Bohr's quantum mechanical Correspondence Principle (c. 1913) is arguably rooted in such considerations. It states that, in the classical limit, the results obtained from quantum mechanics should converge with those obtained from classical mechanics.[12] According to some physicists, the research work carried out during the years 1919–1925 that finally led to quantum mechanics may be described as systematic guessing guided by the Correspondence Principle. This is then a case where considerations of conceptual naturalness appear to have played a direct role in the progress of science.

The appeal to conceptual naturalness manifests itself also in the quest for mathematical beauty, which motivates many a theoretical physicist as Dirac (1968)[13] notes:

Theoretical physicists accept the need for mathematical beauty as an act of faith. There is no compelling reason for it, but it has proved a very profitable objective in the past. For example, the main reason why the theory of relativity is so universally accepted is its mathematical beauty.

In the natural sciences, while hypothesis formation may be guided by appeals to conceptual naturalness, any given hypothesis will carry weight only to the extent that it can be subjected to the inexorable test of experiment. This is the essence of the scientific method, which governs physics and linguistics alike. But there is no chosen method for elaborating the scientific hypotheses themselves. The scientific method is not concerned with that, nor could it be, for it is not possible to set up explicit rules or criteria in this area. This does not mean that "anything goes." But it does mean that there is a lot of diversity in the ways scientists deal with problems and arrive at solutions.

Dirac discusses this diversity of methods in theoretical physics:

One can distinguish between two main procedures for a theoretical physicist. One of them is to work from the experimental basis. For this, one must keep in close touch with the experimental physicists. One reads about all the results they obtain and tries to fit them into a comprehensive and satisfying scheme.

The other procedure is to work from the mathematical basis. One examines and criticizes the existing theory. One tries to pinpoint the faults in it and then tries to remove them. The difficulty here is to remove the faults without destroying the very great successes of the existing theory.

There are these two general procedures, but of course the distinction between them is not hard-and-fast. There are all grades of procedures between the extremes. (Dirac 1968)

Dirac designates the two types of procedures as "experimental" and "mathematical," respectively. He then proceeds to give several examples of the mathematical procedure:

Maxwell's investigation of an inconsistency in the electromagnetic equations of his time led to his introducing the displacement current, which led to the theory of electromagnetic waves. . . . Einstein noticed a difficulty in the theory of an atom in equilibrium in blackbody radiation and was led to introduce stimulated emission, which has led to the modern lasers. [this is Einstein 1917; RF&JRV] But the supreme example is Einstein's discovery of his law of gravitation, which came from the need to reconcile Newtonian gravitation with special relativity. (Dirac 1968)[14]

Dirac's notions also apply to the founding work in quantum mechanics between 1913 and 1925. The following description is striking:

Whether one follows the experimental or the mathematical procedure depends largely on the subject of study, but not entirely so. It also depends on the man. This is illustrated by the discovery of quantum mechanics.

Two men are involved, Heisenberg and Schrödinger. Heisenberg was working from the experimental basis, using the results of spectroscopy, which by 1925 had accumulated an enormous amount of data. Much of this was not useful, but some was, for example the relative intensities of the lines of a multiplet. It was Heisenberg's genius that he was able to pick out the important things from the great wealth of information and arrange them in a natural scheme. He was thus led to matrices.

Schrödinger's approach was quite different. He worked from the mathematical basis. He was not well informed about the latest spectroscopic results, like Heisenberg was, but had the idea at the back of his mind that spectral frequencies should be fixed by eigenvalue equations, something like those that fix the frequencies of systems of vibrating springs. He had this idea for a long time, and was eventually able to find the right equation, in an indirect way. (Dirac 1968)

The "mathematical procedure" typically arises in what Husserl has called the "Galilean style of science," in recognition of its origins in the work of Galileo. Weinberg (1976) characterizes this style as follows:

. . . we have all been making abstract mathematical models of the universe to which at least the physicists give a higher degree of reality than they accord the ordinary world of sensation.

More generally, one can define Galilean science as the search for mathematical patterns in nature.[15] As Chomsky notes, implementing the Galilean style entails a "readiness to tolerate unexplained phenomena or even as yet unexplained counterevidence to theoretical constructions that have achieved a certain degree of explanatory depth in some limited domain, much as Galileo did not abandon his enterprise because he was unable to give a coherent explanation for the fact that objects do not fly off the earth's surface" (1980: 9–10).

A significant feature of the Generative Revolution in linguistics has been the development of a Galilean style in that field. And, to a great extent, the recent developments within MP must be viewed in this light—specifically, as Dirac's mathematical procedure (method) at work within linguistics. Dirac has identified two main methods within the mathematical procedure itself: one is to remove inconsistencies, the other, to unite theories that were previously disjoint (see Dirac 1968). In linguistics, the inconsistencies primarily concern overlapping grammatical conditions, as discussed earlier, which conflict with the basic assumption that C_{HL} has an optimal design. Note further that this assumption itself relates directly to the quest for mathematical beauty, which informs the Galilean style.

One aspect of Dirac's mathematical procedure as applied in linguistics involves the effort to extend and deepen the mathematical formalism used to express syntactic concepts and syntactic principles. We will refer to this facet of the Minimalist endeavor as the "Generative Program" for the study of language (GP) because it originates in Chomsky's foundational work in the fifties and sixties and has been essential to the development of the Galilean style in linguistics.[16] However, it should be obvious that linguistics and physics are at very different stages of mathematical maturation. From this perspective, it is useful to distinguish the "Galilean character" of an area, that is, how much of the subject matter can be analyzed mathematically, from what one could call its "Pythagorean character," how much of mathematics is put to use in the Galilean treatment. Linguistics and physics have the same Galilean character, although they obviously differ in Pythagorean character.[17]

The difference in mathematical status between physics and linguistics partly reflects the more general difference between physics and biology—especially from the perspective that generative grammar is ultimately a branch of theoretical biology, more specifically, of theoretical developmental biology. In biology, the genetic code rather than mathematics has been the tool of choice for explaining life.

This, however, appears to be a historical accident, not the result of some principled difference between biology and the physical sciences. Mathematics has a central explanatory role to play in biology, as discussed in Stewart (1998), whose title, *Life's other secret,* is intended as contrapuntal to "life's first secret," which is the genetic code:

> The mathematical control of the growing organism is the *other* secret—the second secret, if you will—of life. Without it, we will never solve the deeper mysteries of the living world—for life is a partnership between genes and mathematics, and we must take proper account of the role of *both* partners. This cognizance of both secrets has run like a shining thread through the history of the biological sciences—but it has attracted the mavericks, not the mainstream scientist. Instead of thinking the way most biologists think, these mavericks have been taking a much different approach to biology by thinking the way most physical scientists and mathematicians think. This difference in working philosophy is the main reason why understanding of the deeper aspects of life has been left to the mavericks. (Stewart 1998:xi)

The main message of d'Arcy Thompson, one of the great mavericks in biology, is that "life is founded on mathematical patterns of the physical world."[18] Thus one role of theoretical biology is to identify such mathematical patterns and elucidate the way they function in organisms:

> The role of mathematics [in biology] is to analyze the implications of models—not 'nature red in truth and complexity,' as Tennyson did not

quite say, but nature stripped down to its essence. Mathematics pursues the necessary consequences of certain structural features. *If* a planet can be considered a uniform sphere, what would its gravitational attraction be like? . . . *If* the movement of cells in some circumstances is controlled by physical forces and does not greatly depend on complicated internal features such as mitochondria, what will the cells do? From this point of view, the role of mathematics is not to explain biology in detail, but to help us separate out which properties of life are consequences of the deep mathematical patterns of the inorganic universe, and which are the result of more or less arbitrary initial conditions programmed into lengthy sequences of DNA code. (Stewart 1998:243–244)

It is worth noting at this point that Chomsky was aware that both approaches, separately or jointly, might account for the human language faculty. In criticizing the empiricist view of language acquisition in the first chapter of Chomsky 1965 (written in 1958–1959, as mentioned in Huybregts and van Riemsdijk 1982), he notes:

. . . there is surely no reason today for taking seriously the position that attributes a complex human achievement entirely to months (or at most years) of experience, rather than to millions of years of evolution or to principles of neural organization that may be even more deeply grounded in physical law. . . . (59)

However, twenty years later, Chomsky is openly skeptical of a purely genetic approach to evolution.

It does seem very hard to believe that the specific character of organisms can be accounted for purely in terms of random mutation and selectional controls. I would imagine that biology of 100 years from now is going to deal with evolution of organisms the way it now deals with evolution of amino acids, assuming that there is just a fairly small space of physically possible systems that can realize complicated structures. (Huybregts and van Riemsdijk 1982:23)

From this point of view, the more promising approach is "d'Arcy Thompson's attempt to show that many properties of organisms, like symmetry, for example, do not really have anything to do with a specific selection but just with the ways in which things can exist in the physical world" (Huybregts and van Riemsdijk 1982:23).[19]

The mathematical perspective informs the Generative Program (GP), in effect, "the study of language's other secret." Thus Chomsky's mathematical work defines a central facet of GP, beginning with his construction of the foundations of modern generative grammar in Chomsky (1951; 1955–56).[20]

Because the MP is a particular implementation of GP, the notion of perfection often invoked within MP is ultimately a mathematical notion, calling for a higher level of mathematical formalization in syntax.[21] The Minimalist conjecture that C_{HL} is a "perfect system" is a tentative claim about the form and the complexity of each computation. The claim is (i) that each computation can be represented as an abstract mathematical structure completely defined by interface (output) conditions and (ii) that this structure is an extremum in some mathematical space. A natural metric for the comparison of computations is their complexity as measured by their length. Note that, if the only constraints on C_{HL} are those that follow from legibility conditions at the interfaces, then it is unavoidable that some notion of computational cost should be part of the definition of "effective" computations, since, within such a system, it is always possible to combine a computation with a "vacuous one" (i.e., one that has a null effect). The unidirectionality of movement (if it is a fact) would then be a particular design feature aimed at reducing the likelihood of vacuous steps.

Considerations of economy have a long standing legitimacy in the physical sciences. It was in physics that an economy principle of any depth was first advanced.[22] This was the *principle of least time,* discovered by Fermat circa 1650.[23] That principle states that, out of all possible paths that it might take to get from one point to another, light takes the path which requires the *shortest time.*[24] Fermat's principle is a particular instance of the general physical principle of least action. Another important economy principle of physics is "the idea that the inorganic world is fundamentally lazy: it generally behaves in whatever manner requires the least energy" (Stewart 1998:16). That idea was for Thompson (1942) a central principle underpinning the mathematics of growth and form found in living organisms.

Comparing Fermat's principle with Snell's theory of light,[25] Feynman notes that such economy principles have a special philosophical character distinct from causal explanations of phenomena.

> With Snell's theory we can 'understand' light. Light goes along, it sees a surface, it bends because it does something at the surface. The idea of causality, that it goes from one point to another, and another, and so on, is easy to understand. But the principle of least time is a completely different philosophical principle about the way nature works. Instead of saying it is a causal thing, that when we do one thing, something else happens, and so on, it says this: we set up the situation, and light decides which is the shortest time, or the extreme one, and chooses that path. (Feynman, Leighton, and Sands 1963:26–27)

Feynman's observation extends to all economy considerations developed in the natural sciences. Economy principles fall under what seventeenth- and eighteenth-century philosophers called "final causes," as opposed to "efficient causes."[26] Efficient causes are essentially mechanistic in nature like those invoked in a Newtonian account of the dynamics of a point particle, for example, or Snell's account of refraction as des cribed by Feynman earlier. Final causes involve a deeper level of understanding, as Feynman notes:

> Now in the further development of science, we want more than just a formula. First we have an observation, then we have numbers that we measure, then we have a law which summarizes all the numbers. But the real *glory* of science is that *we can find a way of thinking such that the law is evident.* (Feynman, Leighton, and Sands 1963:26–33)

Thus, the distinction between efficient and final causes is locally one of levels of analysis and globally one of levels of explanation.

The notion "level" (of analysis, of explanation) is evidently crucial. The natural sciences provide instances where successful explanatory theories that had been developed at a certain level were later unified with theories at some other level. This is the case for classical thermodynamics, which is deducible from statistical mechanics (hence a reduction). Also the unification of structural chemistry with physics was made possible by the development of quantum mechanics, which provided a common foundation (for discussion, see Chomsky 1995a; Smith 1999). However, the explanatory import of a theoretical principle at some given level L is in general relatively independent of the possibility of unifying L with other levels. A case in point is that of the principle of least action mentioned earlier (the general principle subsuming Fermat's principle of least time), which is reducible to other principles in every area where it applies (for discussion, see Jourdain 1913; Lanczos 1970). Thus, it applies in classical mechanics, where it is known as Hamilton's principle. And, indeed, Hamilton's principle is an alternative formulation of classical mechanics, equivalent to the Newtonian formulation. As it turns out, though, the Hamiltonian formulation has desirable features not found within the Newtonian formulation. For example, the Hamiltonian formalism can be generalized to all types of coordinates and, furthermore, is more convenient than Newton's equations when the system is complex. But the real importance of the Hamiltonian formalism arises from the fact, both, that it can be generalized to classical electricity and magnetism (with an appropriate Lagrangian) and that it constitutes the point of departure for the quantization of physical systems (e.g., see the discussion in Cohen-Tannoudji, Diu, and Laloë 1996:1476–1491).

There may be deep reasons for this remarkable generality. The following excerpt from Toffoli (1999) is intriguing in that respect:

> We are taught to regard with awe the variational principles of mechanics [such as Hamilton's principle RF-JRV]. There is something miraculous about them, and something timeless too: the storms of relativity and quantum mechanics have come and gone, but Hamilton's principle of least action still shines among our most precious jewels.

But perhaps the reason that these principles have survived such physical upheavals is that after all they are not strictly *physical* principles! To me, they appear to be the expression, in a physical context, of general facts about *computation*, much as the second law of thermodynamics is the expression, in the same context, of general facts about *information*. More specifically, just as entropy measures, on a log scale, the number of possible microscopic *states* consistent with a given macroscopic description, so I argue that action measures, again on a log scale, the number of possible microscopic *laws* consistent with a given macroscopic behavior. If entropy measures *in how many different states you could be in detail* and still be substantially the same, then action measures *how many different recipes you could follow in detail* and still behave substantially the same. (349–350)

If this is on the right track, the computational significance of the Hamiltonian formalism supersedes any deduction of it in any particular subdomain.[27]

The computational nature of economy considerations provides a link between physics and linguistics, at least metaphorically. Whether it is stronger than that will have to be determined by a future neuroscience that can validate the physical approach to complex mental structures as suggested by Chomsky, extending the views of d'Arcy Thompson. In any event, economy considerations contribute substantially to what constitutes the "perfection" of the computational system in both domains. Whether these considerations for each domain turn out to be related or the same remains an empirical question for the future.

In linguistics, there are several ways the "perfection" of C_{HL} could be manifested in terms of economy conditions. Shortness of derivation is only one symptom of perfection. Another manifestation, possibly equivalent in some cases, would be the existence of symmetries across levels of analysis, given that such symmetries enhance the economy of computations.

To illustrate, consider the following well-known contrast in anaphoric interpretation for the paradigm in (2):[28]

(2) a. Mary thinks she solved the problem.

   b. She thinks Mary solved the problem.

While *Mary* in (2a) may be construed as anaphoric with *she*, this is not a possible construal for (2b). Exactly how we account for this depends crucially on what representations are available. Prior to the Minimalist Program these anaphoric representations would be given in terms of co-indexing generated by a rule of Index NP (for discussion, see Freidin and Lasnik 1981). Thus the construals under discussion would be given as (3a) and (3b) respectively, where the viable construal of (2b) is given as (3c).

(3) a. Mary$_i$ thinks she$_i$ solved the problem.

    b. *She$_i$ thinks Mary$_i$ solved the problem.

    c. She$_j$ thinks Mary$_i$ solved the problem.

However, given the Inclusiveness Condition (4), which we take to be central to the Minimalist Program, indices are not legitimate elements of representations.

(4) *Inclusiveness Condition*

    "Outputs consist of nothing beyond properties of the lexicon (lexical features)" (Chomsky, 1995b: 225)

Therefore the construals of (2) indicated in (3) will have to be represented another way. We shall assume that a definite pronoun is a definite description with a silent NP component (cf. Postal 1966; Brody 1982). Specifically, we posit the following underlying representation for a pronoun:

(5) $[_{DP}$ *[+def]* φ ~~NP~~*]*, with φ the agreement features of the nominal expression and ~~NP~~ the silent NP component.[29]

For example, the pronoun *she* has the representation in (6):

(6) $[_{DP}$ [+def] [3rd person, singular, feminine] ~~NP~~]

The form *she* is taken to be the PF realization of the morphosyntactic representation in (7):

(7) $[_{DP}$ [+def] [3rd person, singular, feminine]]

The NP component of the pronoun determines its interpretation: two different interpretations of a pronoun reflect two distinct underlying representations of that pronoun. For example, the sentence in (2a) is represented as in (8) when *she* is construed as anaphoric with *Mary*, but as in (9) when *she* is construed as referring to *Clea*:[30]

(8) Mary thinks *[[+def] [3rd pers., sg., fem.]* ~~Mary~~*]* solved the problem.

(9) Mary thinks *[[+def] [3rd pers., sg., fem.]* ~~Clea~~*]* solved the problem.

We propose to relate the interpretive contrast in (2) to symmetries in the representations of the structures involved.

    The defining property of a pronominal element like *she* in (2) is that its PF representation is invariant under substitution of its NP component. Call this the *pronominal symmetry*:

(10) *Pronominal Symmetry*

Let *pro* be some singular pronoun analyzed as $[_{DP} [+def] \varphi$ ~~NP~~$]$. The PF representation of *pro* is invariant under the substitution in (i):

(iii) NP → NP′

No matter what representation is assigned to NP, the PF representation of pro remains constant. We formalize this as in (11):

(11) Let *pro* be some occurrence of a pronominal item in a structure Σ:

(i) pro = $[_{DP}$ [+def] [nth person, α number, β gender] ~~NP~~].

Define *pro(NP′)* to be the pronominal element obtained by substituting *NP′* for *NP* in (i). Define the *range of pro*, denoted by <*pro*>, to be the set of all pronouns *pro(NP′)* for which *NP′* has the same agreement feature specifications as *NP*. Note that <*pro*> includes *pro* itself. It also includes such descriptions as *pro(scientist that discovered radioactivity)*, *pro(Clea)*, *pro(trigger-happy officer)*, etc.[31]

Thus all elements in the range of *pro* share the same PF representation.

Now, there is a general principle in grammar that items in a structure are not interpreted in isolation, but always with respect to some larger domain. Technically, grammar constructs an interpretation of the head and of the specifier of *x* only at the level of some constituent properly containing *x*. Call this the *Generalized Phase Conjecture*, in reference to the analysis proposed in Chomsky (1999):

(12) *Generalized Phase Conjecture (GPC)*

Given some constituent *C*, the head of *C* and its specifier are interpreted at the level of a constituent $[_P \ldots C \ldots]$, where *P* properly contains *C*. *P* is called the *phase for C*.

Chomsky (1999) considers a notion of phase that seems appropriate for the interpretation of expressions involving displacements. We conjecture that a different notion of phase exists for the assessment of anaphoric relations. Specifically, the phase for a pronominal expression *pro* is its c-command domain.[32]

Considering now the paradigm in (2), let us call P_{she} the phase for the pronoun *she*. For the form in (2a), P_{she} is the embedded TP *[she solved the problem]*. The pronominal symmetry associated with *she* carries over to P_{she} : the PF representation of the phase of *she* is invariant under substitution of NP in the representation of *she*, quite obviously. We assume this to be a general requirement for phases, stated as (13):

(13) *The Principle of Phasal Coherence (PPC)*

Given some structure Σ containing constituent x, let P_x be the phase for x (i.e., the minimal phase containing x). Then, every interpretive symmetry of x must also be a symmetry of P_x.

Given the PPC, the PF invariance of a pronoun *pro*, which constitutes the pronominal symmetry, must in general carry over to the phase of *pro* P_{pro}. We evaluate satisfaction of the PPC by extending the notion of range to P_{pro}:

(14) In a structure Σ, let *pro(NP)* be some occurrence of a pronominal item and let P_{pro} be the phase of *pro(NP)* in Σ. Denote by $P_{pro}(NP')$ the constituent obtained from P_{pro} by substituting *NP'* for *NP* in *pro(NP)*. Define the *range of P_{pro} relative to pro*, denoted by $<P_{pro}$, *pro>*, to be the set of all constituents $P_{pro}(NP')$ for which *NP'* has the same phi-feature specifications as *NP*. Note that $< P_{pro}$, *pro>* includes P_{pro} itself.

Accordingly, the range of *pro* in (15a) establishes the set of parallel structures in (15b):

(15) a. $\text{<pro>} = \cup_i \{[_{DP} \text{[+def]} \varphi \text{ NP}_i]\}$

b. $\text{<}P_{pro}, \text{pro>} = \cup_i \{P_{pro}([_{DP} \text{[+def]} \varphi \text{ NP}_i])\}$

Then:

(16) The pair (*pro*, P_{pro}) satisfies the PPC only if all structures in $<P_{pro}$, *pro>* share the same PF.

In this way, (2a) satisfies the PPC.[33]

Consider next whether (ii) satisfies the PPC. In that structure, the phase P_{she} is the matrix TP containing in addition to the pronoun a second DP which could, but need not, relate to the interpretation of the pronoun. In the case where *she* in (2b) is interpreted as *Mary*, the corresponding representation is that in (17) (with the phi-features *[3rd person, singular, feminine]*):

(17) [[[+def] φ ~~Mary~~] thinks *Mary* solved the problem]

The structure in (17) contains the accidental chain in (18):

(18) (~~Mary~~, Mary)

The set of parallel structures established by the range of *pro* in this case includes one structure in which a pair of expressions are anaphorically linked, to wit the structure in (17). This conformation is subject to the Parallelism Principle[34] as formulated in (19):

(19) *Parallelism Principle for anaphora*

Let $\{\Sigma_i\}_{i \in I}$ be a set of parallel structures and let (N, pro) be a pair of nominal expressions with *pro* a pronoun such that N and *pro* are anaphorically linked in Σ_P, $p \in I$. Then, either (i) the anaphoric link remains constant across all structures in $\{\Sigma_i\}_{i \in I}$ (the case of "sloppy identity") or (ii) the value of *pro* remains constant across all structures in $\{\Sigma_i\}_{i \in I}$.

Given the definition of the range of *pro*, case (ii) doesn't apply to the set of parallel structures $<P_{pro}, pro>$. The application of case (i) amounts to revising the definition of the range $<P_{pro}, pro>$ as follows:

(20) In a structure Σ, let *pro(NP)* be some occurrence of a pronominal item and let P_{pro} be the phase of *pro(NP)* in Σ. Denote by $P_{pro}(NP'[i])$ the constituent obtained from P_{pro} by substituting *NP'* for some occurrence *NP[i]* of *NP* in P_{pro}. The range of P_{pro} relative to *pro*, denoted by $<P_{pro}, pro>$, is defined as *the maximal set of structures* $P_{pro}(NP'[i])$ *that verifies (i)–(iii):*

(i) *NP'* has the same phi-feature specifications as *NP*

(ii) $<P_{pro}, pro>$ includes P_{pro}

(iii) $<P_{pro}, pro>$ obeys the Parallelism Principle.

If we apply this definition to the structure in (17), then, the range of P_{she} relative to *she* includes such structures as those in (21):

(21) $<P_{she}, she>$:

(i) [[[+def] φ ~~Clea~~] thinks *Clea* solved the problem]

(ii) [[[+def] φ ~~Susan~~] thinks *Susan* solved the problem]

(iii) Etc.

Because the set $<P_{she}, she>$ in (21) is not PF invariant, the PPC is violated.[35] In this way, the construal (3b) of (2b) is excluded. Note that, in the case of the construal in (3c), the range of P_{she} may not include the structure in (17)—the structure where *she* is anaphoric with *Mary*—by (ii) and (iii) of (20). It is easy to check that (2b), under construal (3c), satisfies the PPC: no matter the value of *pro* within the admissible range, the pronoun and its phase will both remain PF invariant. In essence, Principle C reflects a conflict between Parallelism and Phasal Coherence: in the case of a structure such as (17), there is no coherent definition of "range of a phase" that can satisfy both principles.[36]

To summarize, Principle C follows from the interaction of the Principle of Phasal Coherence, related to QR, with the Parallelism Principle.[37] This account immediately extends to the contrast in (21) if the chunk *him* in *himself* is treated as a pronoun falling under the preceding analysis:

(22) a. Clea believes Luc$_i$ to have introduced himself$_i$ to Mary.

b. Clea believes himself$_i$ to have introduced Luc$_i$ to Mary.

The preceding account also extends to the following paradigm from French:

(23) a. Le juriste$_i$ sait très bien qu'il$_i$ est en difficulté.

'The jurist$_i$ knows very well that he$_i$ has a problem'.

b. *Il$_i$ sait très bien que le juriste$_i$ est en difficulté.

'He$_i$ knows very well that the jurist$_i$ has a problem'.

c. Il$_i$ sait très bien que le juriste qu'il$_i$ est est en difficulté.

'He$_i$ knows very well that the jurist that he$_i$ is has a problem'.

d. Pierre$_i$ sait très bien que le juriste qu'il$_i$ est est en difficulté.

'Peter$_i$ knows very well that the jurist that he$_i$ is has a problem'.

e. *Il$_i$ sait très bien que le juriste que Pierre$_i$ est est en difficulté. ·

'He$_i$ knows very well that the jurist that Peter$_i$ is has a problem'.

f. *Le juriste qu'il$_i$ est sait très bien que Pierre$_i$ est en difficulté.

'The jurist that he$_i$ is knows very well that Peter$_i$ has a problem'.

g. Le juriste que Pierre$_i$ est sait très bien qu'il$_i$ est en difficulté.

'The jurist that Peter$_i$ is knows very well that he$_i$ has a problem'.

h. Le juriste qu'il$_i$ a nommé sait très bien que Pierre$_i$ est en difficulté.

'The jurist that he$_i$ appointed knows very well that Peter$_i$ has a problem'.

(23a–b) show the standard contrast for disjoint reference under c-command as in (2). In surprising contrast, (23c) allows the coreferential interpretation between the pronominal matrix subject and the complement subject via the pronoun in the relative clause. The same anaphoric behavior obtains when pronominal matrix subject is replaced by an R-expression, as in (23d). However, disjoint reference obtains again if the pronoun in the relative clause in (23c) is replaced by an R-expression, as illustrated in (23e). Note that (23f) results from transposing the matrix and complement subjects in (23d) and thus this pair is exactly parallel to (23a–b). This analysis extends to the pair (23e–g). The example in (23h) is grammatical as expected, in contrast to (23f).

The paradigm in (23) shows that the constituent *[le juriste que DP est]* 'the jurist that DP is' has the same anaphoric behavior as the DP in it. For the purpose of applying Principle C, it behaves as a pronoun when DP is a pronoun and as a name otherwise.[38] DP in turn behaves as if it occupied the position of the head modified by the relative clause. Noting that the predicate *juriste* and its subject *DP* within the restrictive relative clause construction *[le juriste que DP est]* share the same set of phi-features φ we shall assume that the notion of symmetry extends to such pairs of constituents:

(24) Let (C, C') be a pair of constituents in Σ that share the same phi-features. Let S be some interpretive symmetry that holds of the pair (C, C'). The PPC is extended to such a case, requiring that S also hold of the minimal phase for (C, C').

Consider in this light the form *[le juriste que pro(NP) est]*, with *pro(NP)* a pronoun. The PF of the pair *(juriste, pro(NP))* remains invariant under the substitution of *NP'* for *NP* in the pair *(juriste, pro(NP))*. By the preceding extension, *pro(NP)* establishes a range not only for its own phase, but also for the phase of the raised predicate *le juriste,* since *pro(NP)* and *juriste* share the same phi-features. The PPC gives rise to the contrast between (23g) and (23h). Note that (24) entails that, in a similar fashion, the notion of symmetry may be extended to the pair *(Mary, she)* in the structure in (3a), since the DP *Mary* and the pronoun *she* share the same phi-features. However, in that case, if an *NP* different from *Mary* is substituted for *Mary* within the pair *(Mary, ~~Mary~~)*, the PF of the pair is altered (we assume that the substitution takes place across the board). No PF invariance obtains and the PPC is then not relevant to the pair *(Mary, she)*.

To the extent that the kind of analysis proposed earlier is viable, it provides a modest illustration of what is being referred to as the "perfection" of the grammatical system. The possibility then arises that the abstract analytical principles involved in the formal definition of a computation turn out to have exactly the right empirical consequences.[39] This is an exciting prospect, which, combined with that of potentially rich mathematical developments, is stirring imaginations. The authors of this note understand the excitement, and share in it. Uriagereka's *Rhyme and reason* is a particular expression of that entirely natural and legitimate reaction. In essential respects, linguistics is no different from other fields in natural sciences at comparable stages of development.[40]

3.   METHODOLOGICAL ISSUES

But apart from prospects for any line of research, there is the more concrete methodological question of how to proceed. LLJ propose as a model Arthur Holly Compton's Nobel Prize–winning work on the quantum theory of the scattering of X-rays and γ-rays by light elements. Compton discovered that, when X-rays of a given frequency are scattered from (essentially) free electrons at rest, the frequency of the scattered X-rays is not unaltered, as the classical theory would predict, but decreases with increasing scattering angle. He described this effect by treating the rays as relativistic particles of energy *hv* and momentum *hv/c,* and by applying the usual energy and momentum conservation laws to the collision. One could characterize Compton's contribution as an instance of Dirac's "experimental procedure," working from the empirical data to arrive at the theoretical conclusions.[41] This is in contrast with the general style of the MP, which tends to operate in the reverse direction using the mathematical procedure.

The actual history of the quantum theory of radiation–matter interaction provides a more complicated picture, though. It is not just a story about the triumph of the experimental procedure, but also one that involves the triumph of the mathematical procedure as well. In fact, Compton (1923) is preceded by an article by Einstein (1917), cited in Dirac (1968) as an example of the "mathematical procedure," see the quote in section 2). This article indeed "addresses questions of principle without offering any new experimental conclusion or prediction" (Pais 1982:chapter 21). By general admission, this article was a fundamental contribution, which has served as a basis for subsequent research on absorption, emission and dispersion of radiation (with the notable exception of Compton).[42] One of its central results concerned the exchange of momentum in radiation–matter interactions. This result can be stated as follows:

(25) In conditions of thermal equilibrium, an exchange of energy *hv* between radiation and matter that occurs by a transition process (between two stationary states of an atomic system) is accompanied by an exchange of momentum of the amount *hv/c,* just as would be the case if the transition were accompanied by the starting or stopping of a small entity moving with the velocity of light *c* and containing the energy *hv* (adapted from Bohr, Kramers, and Slater 1924).

This conclusion constituted a fundamental innovation, a conceptual "mutation," since, by associating momentum quanta with energy quanta, it amounted to defining light-quanta as particles, on a par with, e.g., electrons: light-quanta, like electrons, were taken to be entities endowed both with energy and momentum. Previous discussions of the interaction between radiation and matter had solely been concerned with the exchange of energy (cf., e.g., Einstein 1905).[43]

This central result in Einstein (1917) anticipates Compton's account. Conversely, Compton's discovery helped clinch the argument in Einstein's article for ascribing a certain physical reality to the theory of light-quanta.[44] The mathematical and experimental procedures are, in the best circumstances, mutually reinforcing.

Thus there are several complementary facets to the story of the quantum theory of radiation–matter interaction. (To tell the story properly, one would need the combined talents of the author of *The Alexandria Quartet* and of the author of *Blackbody Theory and the Quantum Discontinuity, 1894–1912.*) Theoretical strands and contributions are intertwined in a complex pattern of interactions that are hard to disentangle. What is sure is that a conceptual "mutation" happened, by which the light quantum postulated by Planck in 1900 and in Einstein (1905) was granted the fundamental attributes of particles, namely energy and momentum. Several strands of work contributed to that mutation. It would be nonsensical to single out any of them as the most representative. What we really have here is a kind of "ecological system."

The development of scientific hypotheses can actually be advantageously compared to the evolution of species. New hypotheses are put forward and concepts created, which are then subjected to selection. Normally only the fittest survives. Selectional pressure, e.g., in the form of such an experiment as Compton's, is then crucial to the development of successful hypotheses and theories. At the same time, selection is not the "exclusive means of modification."[45] Quite obviously, there must exist a source of new hypotheses (i.e., scientific "mutations"). So we are led to distinguish two types of scientific events: "selectional events" (often, but not exclusively, experiments) and "mutational events."[46] Analogously, we can distinguish between "selectional contributions" and "mutational contributions." If we follow Dirac (1968), "mutational contributions" in turn would be of two types, "experimental" (i.e., like Heisenberg's, which was based on the experimental data) or "mathematical." Note that the distinction between "selectional contributions" and "mutational contributions" is one of roles, not essences, relative to scientific situations. The same contribution might count as selectional or mutational depending on the set of hypotheses considered.[47]

Compton's Nobel Prize–winning contribution was both a selectional and a mutational one.[48] However, it was obviously quite different in character and in scope (see note 41) from that of the fundamental "mutational contributors" to quantum mechanics, including Bohr, Born, Dirac, Einstein, Heisenberg, Jordan, Planck, Pauli, and Schrödinger. While Compton was initially busy defending classical physics, they were building an alternative framework, often with few certainties at hand. From the evolutionary point of view of earlier, both approaches were necessary to ensure the required level of "ecological diversity." One cannot emphasize this point too much. Science needs a diversity of styles for its continued progress. This applies as much to linguistics as to physics, perhaps more so given the relative immaturity of the field.

Chomsky's work on the MP has been from the outset grounded in the mathematical procedure he employed so successfully to launch modern generative grammar in the early 1950s. In essence it constitutes a distillation of the mathematical procedure applied to linguistic theory that Chomsky envisioned in the opening paragraph of *Syntactic Structures*: "The ultimate outcome of these investigations should be a theory of linguistic structure in which the descriptive devices utilized in particular grammars are presented and studied abstractly, with no specific reference to particular languages." From one perspective, the MP offers the most promising approach to this goal, far off though it still remains. Nonetheless, based on the considerable empirical successes of its predecessor, which to a large extent are still incorporated under current proposals, there is good reason to continue exploring the MP to discover whatever insights it can provide as well as whatever its actual limitations may be.

NOTES

+ This chapter was originally published by Lingua as J.-R. Vergnaud and R. Freidin, "Exquisite Connections: Some Remarks on the Evolution of Linguistic Theory," Lingua 111 (2001):639–666. Many thanks to Elsevier and Lingua.

* Authors' note: We would like to thank Noam Chomsky, Carlos Otero, Maria Rita Manzini, Martin Prinzhorn, Johan Rooryck, Alain Rouveret, Andrew Simpson, Neil Smith, and Maria Luisa Zubizarreta for discussions.

1. References are to the version of Chomsky (1993) reprinted as chapter 3 of Chomsky (1995b).

2. It is worth pointing out here that in *MMH* Chomsky's notion of simplicity bears some general similarity to the more current discussions of economy.

> "For the formulation of any relative precise notion of simplicity, it is necessary that the general structure of the grammar be more or less fixed, as well as the notations by means of which it is constructed. We want the notion of simplicity to be broad enough to comprehend all those aspects of simplicity of grammar which enter into consideration when linguistic elements are set up. Thus we want the reduction of the number of elements and statements, any generalizations, and, to generalize the notion of generalization itself, any similarity in the form of non-identical statements, to increase the total simplicity of the grammar. As a first approximation to the notion of simplicity, we will here consider shortness of grammar as a measure of simplicity, and will use such notations as will permit similar statements to be coalesced." (Chomsky [1951] 1979:5)

> To avoid circularity, the notation must be fixed in advance and neutral to any particular grammar.

> "Given the fixed notation, the criteria of simplicity governing the ordering of statements are as follows: that the shorter grammar is the simpler, and that among equally short grammars, the simplest is that in which the average length of derivation of sentences is least." (Chomsky [1951] 1979:6)

> In current work, the "shortness" of grammars and of derivations is driven by substantive principles of UG.

> A notion of economy is also mentioned in the literature of structuralist linguistics. Hymes and Fought (1981) cite the following from Hockett:

> "A model must be efficient: its application to any given language should achieve the necessary results with a minimum of machinery." (Hockett 1954:233)

> However it is doubtful that Chomsky's notion of economy was influenced by structuralist linguistics in any significant way. *MMH* predates Hockett's formulation by at least three years. Moreover, Chomsky's discussion cites the work of philosopher Nelson Goodman as the source of his ideas, not work in structuralist linguistics.

3. FI prohibits superfluous symbols in general, ruling out vacuous quantification for example, where Case is not an issue.

4. For a detailed discussion of the rationale that has guided the evolution of generative syntactic theory, see Freidin (1994).

5. Under the system of analysis in Chomsky (1999), the φ-features of the matrix T in (1) would not be checked because the N *John* would be

frozen in place in the complement clause (see Chomsky 1999:5). Therefore φ-features of the matrix T would violate FI at LF, rather than a Case feature of that T, which may be an unnecessary postulation. Thus (1) is prohibited because it would involve a single DP entering into two independent Spec-head agreement relations. We assume that such configurations are generally excluded. Whether *John* could actually move to the matrix subject position of (1) is a separate issue. Given that matrix T has a D-feature (EPP) that normally drives movement, then *John* would move to matrix SpecTP. If it does, then somehow its agreement features must be unavailable for checking the matching features of matrix T, even though they are interpretable at LF and therefore not erased. For evidence that NP-movement may be motivated solely by a D-feature of T as well as further discussion of this issue, see Lavine and Freidin (2001).

6. The example in (1) is also ruled out by the Case uniqueness requirement of the Chain Condition. Therefore, we might also want to investigate whether the empirical coverage of the Case uniqueness requirement can be subsumed under FI as well. Notice also that certain violations of the θ-uniqueness of chains also fall out from FI with respect to unchecked Case features. For example, in the simplest case (i) the Case feature of T will not be checked.

(i) *Bill T mentioned *t*.

Because the Case feature of Bill is checked in VP, there is no Case feature to check the nominative Case feature of T.

7. Whether this is feasible depends on a demonstration that other cases of ECP violations can be subsumed in a similar fashion under FI or some other general condition. However, it is a reasonable and promising line of investigation.

8. The fact that that the level of complexity of the analysis mirrors the complexity of the data constitutes yet another argument against the ECP analysis. This analysis functions more like a technical description of the data than an explanatory account of the phenomena under analysis.

9. The top-down analysis instantiated via phrase structure rules actually became suspect within GB when it was realized that phrase structure rules function as language specific stipulations of properties that were already accounted for by general principles in conjunction with the specific properties of lexical items. Therefore, given the redundant character of phrase structure rules, it was assumed that they existed neither in individual grammars nor in UG. However, without phrase structure rules in GB, there appears to be no explicit way to derive phrase structure representations, though there were explicit conditions on the form of such representations (i.e., *X*-bar theory). Thus bare phrase structure answers the crucial question: if not via phrase structure rules, then via what? For this reason alone, the MP constitutes an important alternative to GB.

10. At present this bare necessities view does not account for locality conditions on movement, which appear to be conditions internal to C_{HL} itself rather than the effects of legibility conditions imposed on C_{HL} by other systems that interface with it.

11. Chomsky (1995b:1) observes that one question that has motivated the work in generative grammar is that of the conditions that are imposed on the language faculty by virtue of "general considerations of conceptual naturalness that have some independent plausibility, namely, simplicity, economy, symmetry, non-redundancy, and the like."

12. More precisely, the principle states that the classical theory is in agreement with the experiments for processes which depend on the statistical behavior of a large number of atoms and which involve states where the difference between neighboring states is comparatively little.

A more specific formulation is found in Bohr (1913) for the emission and absorption of spectral lines. There, the principle is taken to postulate a general conjugation of each of the various possible transitions between stationary states with one of the harmonic oscillation components in which the electrical moment of the atom can be resolved.

The Correspondence Principle has been a staple of textbooks on quantum mechanics. However, recent experiments have shown it to be incorrect.

13. P. A. M. Dirac shared the 1933 Nobel Prize for physics with E. Schrödinger.

14. One could add to this short list Dirac's own discovery of the correct laws of relativity quantum mechanics, which was arrived at simply by guessing the equation (see Feynman 1965:57).

15. Of course, there are many different types of mathematical patterns: algebraic, geometrical, analytical, topological, etc.

16. See Chomsky (1955, 1957, 1965). Following standard practice, we view language as one component of the human mind. Thus the study of language via GP concerns human cognition, and human biology more broadly.

17. Considering that modern mathematics with its dazzling complexity evolved in great part from the study of numbers, it is to be expected that a science that is concerned with quantitative relations like physics will tend to make maximal use of the structures found in mathematics. This is all the more so since there exist many connections between the different parts of mathematics.

18. See Stewart (1998:243). Stewart's book, which features a quotation from Thompson (1942) at the beginning of each chapter, constitutes a contemporary commentary on Thompson's seminal ideas.

19. See Jenkins (2000) for further discussion.

20. In the early 1950s Chomsky had developed a mathematical understanding of natural language, which he then brought to bear on current issues in automata theory—in particular, demonstrating the inadequacy of finite state automata as a model of natural language (Chomsky 1956, 1959) and investigating more broadly the relation between automata and grammars. The famous "Chomsky Hierarchy" of formal grammars (and corresponding formal languages) is due to him (Chomsky 1959), and so are the proofs of associated central theorems about regular grammars (Chomsky and Miller 1958) and context free grammars (Chomsky 1962), all results that have ever since been a staple of textbooks in computer science. Chomsky (1962), for example, establishes the equivalence of context-free languages and push-down automata (which was proved independently by M. P. Schützenberger and by J. Evey). For additional clarification concerning the context of Chomsky's contributions to computer science, see Otero (1994).

21. We stress "ultimately" because the MP is a research program based on specific conjectures, not a theory or even a framework. As Chomsky (1998:119–120 has noted, "there are minimalist questions, but no specific minimalist answers." It should go without saying that whatever minimalist answers we might discover will only be found by actively pursuing the questions posed by the MP. Furthermore, it should be noted that Chomsky has been quite clear about the provisional nature of the MP, saying explicitly that it could turn out to be wrong, or equally problematic, premature (i.e., in much the same way that Einstein's search for a unified field theory was premature, though not wrong if developments in string theory succeed; see Greene 1999).

22. The first 'economy principle' acknowledged within the Western intellectual tradition actually is the maxim known as Ockham's razor: *Entia non sunt multiplicanda praeter necessitatem*. The prominent fourteenth-century philosopher and logician William of Ockham (c. 1295–1349) has traditionally

been credited with this principle (hence the name). However, the historical record suggests otherwise. We quote from Kneale and Kneale (1962): "No doubt this [the maxim RF-JRV] represents correctly the general tendency of his philosophy, but it has not so far been found in any of his writings. His nearest pronouncement seems to be *Numquam ponenda est pluralitas sine necessitate,* which occurs in his theological work on the *Sentences* of Peter Lombard" (243). See also Boehner (1958).

23. Fermat had been preceded by Hero of Alexandria, who had stated that the light travels in such a way that it goes from a point to a mirror and then to another point in the shortest possible *distance.*

24. Actually, as Feynman points out, the principle as stated is incorrect, since it would predict that light emanating from a point in front of a mirror should avoid the mirror! There is a more exact formulation that avoids this problem and coincides with Fermat's original formulation in the case of refraction of light. See Feynman, Leighton, and Sands (1963:chapter 26).

25. Willebrord Snell, a Dutch mathematician, found the formula describing the change of angle of a ray of light that goes from one medium into another.

26. See the discussion in Thompson (1942:chapter 1).

27. In the light of this discussion, the following statement (LLJ:666) appears to be profoundly in error:

> "Finally, one may suggest that the notion of perfection that Chomsky has in mind is based upon an analogy with the minima and maxima principles of physics. So, for example, air pressure in a soap bubble produces a spherical shape as the optimal geometric design for distributing this pressure. Similarly, light reflecting of a mirror takes the path of least time between two points. If this is, in fact, the sort of optimality that Chomsky has in mind, then it has no place in the theory of grammar. Minimization/maximization principles are derived from deeper physical properties of the particles (waves, vectors, etc.) which satisfy them. They follow from the subatomic structure and attributes of these particles, and are not themselves basic elements of the theory. Hence they have no independent explanatory status within physics, but are reducible to other principles. By contrast, the MP takes economy conditions to be essential elements of the grammar and the optimality which they encode to be one of its defining properties."

LLJ claim that because the empirical content of a principle X is deducible from other more elementary considerations, X has "no independent explanatory status." They suggest that this applies to linguistics as well as physics and therefore that the economy principles discussed in linguistics cannot legitimately be considered part of the theory of language. In the case of linguistics, this suggestion is moot because as yet no deductive relation with more elementary considerations has been established. Therefore it is both natural and rational to consider economy conditions as fundamental. In the case of physics, the point appears to be mistaken as the text above indicates.

28. The discussion of Principle C follows from Vergnaud (1998), which is a handout for a lecture given at UCLA, explores various notions of "multiplicity of representations."

29. The DP constitutes a definite description where the head D is indicated by the feature [+def]. At this point whether the agreement features φ are associated with D or N is left open.

30. Questions arise in the case of such structures as that in (i) (discussed in Jacobson 1977):

(i) [the man who loved her$_2$]$_1$ kissed [his$_1$ wife]$_2$

We have the following descriptions for the constituents *his wife* and *her* in (i):

(ii) a. $[his_1 \text{ wife}]_2 = [[[+\text{def}] \, \varphi_1 \textit{ man}]\text{'s } \varphi_2 \text{ wife}]$, with φ_1 and φ_2 the agreement features for *man* and *wife*, respectively

     b. $her_2 = [[[+\text{def}] \, \varphi_1 \textit{ man}]\text{'s } \varphi_2 \text{ wife}]$.

We assume that:

(iii) The DP "the man's wife" is [+def] for the same reason that "a man's wife" is [-def] (technical details aside).

(iv) The structure $[[[+\text{def}] \, \varphi_1 \textit{ man}]\text{'s } \varphi_2 \text{ wife}]$ in (iib) is ambiguously realized as *his* or as *her*.

(v) In (iv) above, *his* is the PF realization of $[+\textit{def}] \, \varphi_1\text{'s}$ and *her*, of $[+\textit{def}] \, \varphi_2$.

Independent principles (having to do with contrast at surface structure) determine which one of the alternative forms in (v) is realized. An important fact discovered by P. Jacobson is that *her* in (i) must be analyzed as a copy of the whole antecedent *his wife*, and not merely as a copy of $[+\textit{def}]$ *wife*. In other words, *her* in (i) must be described as in (iv). Call this the *Principle of Anaphora Interpretation*:

(vi) Definite anaphora only holds between complete DPs.

An analogous principle was postulated in Vergnaud (1974). The principle in (vi) entails the ungrammaticality of (vii) on the indicated reading (see Brody 1982):

(vii) $[his_2 \text{ employer}]_1$ respects $[her_1 \text{ secretary}]_2$

The constituents *his employer* and *her secretary* in (vii) are described as in (viii):

(viii) a. $[his_2 \text{ employer}]_1 = [[[+\text{def}] \, \varphi_2 \textit{ secretary}]\text{'s } \varphi_1 \textit{ employer}]$

     b. $[her_1 \text{ secretary}]_2 = [[[+\text{def}] \, \varphi_1 \textit{ employer}]\text{'s } \varphi_2 \textit{ secretary}]$

Note that the above assumptions require that the head of the relative clause construction in (i) (the man) be analyzed as a DP. The impossibility of (ix) is presumably related to that of (x):

(ix) *$[\text{The President}]_i$ said that $[\text{he}]_i$ that had been elected could not resign

(x) *$[\text{A man}]_i$ came in. $[\text{The man}]_i$ that looked tired sat down.

The example (x) contrasts with (xi):

(xi) $[\text{A man}]_i$ came in. $[\text{The man}]_i$ sat down.

31. The range of an expression is more than a mere list. To wit, it is a semi-lattice structure (see Vergnaud and Zubizarreta 2000). Note that the range of an expression may also include descriptions outside the linguistic modality, e.g., visual descriptions (see Vergnaud and Zubizarreta 2000).

32. For the purpose of that discussion, we assume that c-command is reflexive, so that the c-command domain of x contains x.

33. Observe that, in a different domain, the rule of Quantifier Raising (QR) can be taken as a manifestation of the PPC. QR ensures that the inherent variable interpretation associated with a quantified expression QNP is carried over to the phase of QNP. The existence of such symmetries among linguistic representations might suggest an approach to the study of the underlying neural system very much in the spirit of that pioneered by Stewart (1998, 1999) for the study of animal locomotion (e.g., see Stewart 1998:chapter 9).

34. Introduced by Chomsky in class lectures during the mid-1970s.

35. By contrast, no violation of the PPC occurs in the case of (2a) because P_{she} is the embedded TP and therefore does not contain an accidental chain, even though the matrix TP does. The notion of range introduced in the text analysis could be developed so as to provide an account of the anaphoric interpretation of pronouns in the spirit of that of Lasnik (1976), where there is no specific rule of grammar that establishes an anaphoric reading between a pronoun and an antecedent.

36. A fundamental aspect of the account of Principle C proposed in the text is that it centrally relies on the PF distinction between the full-fledged nominal expression *[[+def] φ NP]* and its pronominal counterpart *[[+def] φ NP]*. The prediction is then that Principle C is inoperative in elided constituents such as deleted VPs. The prediction appears to be correct, as shown by the grammaticality of the construal in which *he* is anaphoric with *John* for the form in (i) (see Fiengo and May 1994:220):

(i) Mary loves John, and he thinks that Sally does, too.

Indeed, the representation of pronouns proposed in the text would obviate the need for any "vehicle change" in the sense of Fiengo and May (1994; see also Lappin 1991; Lappin and McCord 1990). Note however the contrast between (ii) and (iii):

(ii) Mary believes that John is eligible and Sally claims he does, too.

(iii) Mary believes John to be eligible and Sally claims he does, too.

The pronoun *he* may be construed as anaphoric with *John* in (ii), but not in (iii). This suggests that an independent LF constraint is at work in the case of (iii), presumably the Principle of Disjoint Reference (see Chomsky 1976). If this is on the right track, then the behavior of Principle C with respect to reconstruction phenomena needs to be reconsidered.

37. Given the representation of pronouns postulated, the text account reduces Principle C to the law that states that only the most c-commanding element in a chain may be realized at PF. Conversely, one can take that law to be a subcase of Principle C.

Note that the Parallelism Principle itself can be described as a principle of symmetry preservation. The relevant symmetry in that case is the invariance of LF interpretation under the permutation of anaphorically linked expressions.

38. Technically, the generalization encompasses other cases—e.g., (i).

(i)   *Pierre$_i$ sait très bien que le juriste que Pierre$_i$ est est en difficulté.
      'Peter$_i$ knows very well that the jurist that Peter$_i$ is has a problem'

(i) has the same anaphoric behavior as (ii).

(ii)   *Pierre$_i$ sait très bien que Pierre$_i$ est en difficulté.
      'Peter$_i$ knows very well that Peter$_i$ has a problem'

Surprisingly, (iii) is not as deviant as (ii) or (i).

(iii)   ?Le juriste que le Pierre$_i$ est sait très bien que le Pierre$_i$ est en difficulté.
      'The jurist that the Peter$_i$ is knows very well that the Peter$_i$ has a problem'

(iii) may constitute an exception to this generalization. However, the coreferential interpretation of a pair of R-expressions may not be within the purview of Principle C under the appropriate formulation. See Lasnik (1991) and Freidin (1997b) for some discussion.

39. Some intriguing proposals in this area are put forth by Jenkins (see, e.g., Jenkins 2000:151–170). See also Fukui (1996) for another line of investigation into these topics.

40. Perhaps linguistics is, in this regard, roughly comparable in character to structural chemistry in the years preceding its unification with physics (see Chomsky 1995a for important remarks on structural chemistry in connection with the issue of 'reductionism'), or with the initial development of quantum physics prior to the Heisenberg/Schrödinger formulations.

41. In that sense, both Heisenberg's research and Compton's Nobel Prize–winning work belong in the same "Diracian category," i.e., the "experimental procedure." However, one cannot stress enough the difference in scope between the contributions of the two scientists. Compton was concerned with the interpretation of a particular experiment. Heisenberg was a theoretician trying to construct a general account of all the spectroscopic data available at the time in order to get a better understanding of the laws of nature. Heisenberg ended up constructing a new physics.

42. It seems that Compton was unaware of Einstein's results at the time he was developing his theory. His only reference to Einstein in connection to the question of the interaction between radiation and matter is to Einstein (1905). Compton presented his theory at the 1 December 1922 meeting of the American Physical Society held at the University of Chicago. It is somewhat surprising that he would not have known of Einstein's (1917) article at the time, since there was really a free flow of information and ideas in physics between Europe and the U.S. at the beginning of the 1920s. Thus, Debye could learn quickly about Compton's experimental results, as did Einstein. There were also common channels of publication (e.g., *The Philosophical Magazine*, in which A. Compton had previously published, as had many major contributors to quantum mechanics). More surprisingly, nowhere in his whole work does he refer to Einstein's 1917 paper.

One may surmise that Compton arrived at his result by a different route, namely, from classical electrodynamics (as it turns out, in conjunction with O. W. Richardson, Compton's first research advisor at Princeton University). Within classical electrodynamics, an electromagnetic wave carries momentum, giving rise to "radiation pressure." This is how it works. Suppose an electromagnetic wave is acting on an electric charge. The electric component in the wave makes the charge oscillate. This oscillation in turn interacts with the magnetic component of the wave, creating a force in the direction of the propagation of the wave. The value of the induced momentum is equal to the energy absorbed by the charge divided by the speed of light c. The division by c merely reflects the fact that the strength of the magnetic field associated with the wave is that of the electric field divided by c (see, e.g., Feynman, Leighton, and Sands 1963: Chapter 34, Sections 10 & 11). A particular instance of radiation pressure is that of an atom emitting an energy W in some direction. Then, according to classical electrodynamics, there is a recoil momentum $p = W/c$.

There is a big leap between the classical theory and the quantum hypothesis put forth in Einstein (1917), in Compton (1923), and in Debye (1923), though. The classical relation is a statistical relation, defined over averages of fluctuating quantities. More seriously, it only applies to directional waves. In case of a spherical wave, there should be no recoil. Einstein's fundamental insight was to consider that every exchange of energy was accompanied by an exchange of momentum. Correlatively, he was led to assume that the radiation was always directional, even in, e.g., the case of spontaneous emission, which was classically described as a spherical wave. Einstein assumed that that was a case where direction was only determined by "chance."

43. Einstein's article included several other far-reaching assumptions, from which Einstein was able to derive both Planck's radiation law and Bohr's frequency condition, among other results. Indeed, one of the article's central

contributions was to establish a bridge between blackbody radiation and Bohr's theory of spectra.

44. Debye, who knew about Compton's evidence against the classical theory, independently derived the equations describing the scattering of a photon off an electron at rest (Debye 1923). We note that, in his article, Debye expressed his indebtedness to Einstein's 1917 theory.

45. Cf. the introduction to Darwin (1859), where the last sentence reads as follows:

   (i) "Furthermore, I am convinced that Natural Selection has been the main but not exclusive means of modification."

46. One issue of importance is how one recognizes a "mutational event." For example, was the atomism of Leucippus and Democritus a mutational scientific hypothesis? Of course, a preliminary question is whether it was a scientific hypothesis at all. Given that one could not really conceive of any serious experimental testing of the (rather vague) philosophy of the Greek atomistic school, it would not qualify as a scientific hypothesis. In general, there are various criteria by which one may evaluate and compare mutational hypotheses. One factor is the "likelihood" of an hypothesis, i.e., the degree of expectation of the hypothesis given the state of the knowledge at the time. We could call this the "originality" of the hypothesis. Thus, when the Danish astronomer Roemer proposed that the apparent discrepancies between the measured movement of the moons of Jupiter and Newton's Law were merely an observational illusion due to the noninstantaneous character of light propagation, this was an original hypothesis at the time. Another criterion in evaluating an hypothesis is its complexity, i.e., how much mathematical or conceptual elaboration it involves, and how much revision of the existing system of knowledge it requires.

47. It should be clear that such notions as "scientific mutation" or "scientific selection" are intended to apply to all sciences, not only to Galilean sciences. Thus, Darwin's hypothesis concerning natural selection and evolution qualifies as a mutational hypothesis.

48. It was a selectional contribution in two distinct ways. It established the reality of the light quantum as a true particle. But also, because it could not account for the angular dependence of the scattered X-ray intensities, the total scattering cross-section as a function of energy, or the exact state of polarization of the Compton scattered X-rays, it emphasized the need for a more basic quantum mechanics, to be soon developed by Born, de Broglie, Dirac, Heisenberg and Schrödinger.

REFERENCES

Boehner, P. 1958. *Collected Articles on Ockham,* ed. by E.M. Buytaert. St. Bonaventure, NY: Franciscan Institute.

Bohr, N. 1913. On the constitution of atoms and molecules. *Philosophical Magazine* 26:1–25, 476–502, 857–875.

Bohr, N., H.A. Kramers, and J.C. Slater. 1924. The quantum theory of radiation. *Philosophical Magazine* 47:785–802. [A German version appeared in *Zeitschrift fur Physik* 24:69–87 (1924)]

Brody, M. 1982. On circular readings. In *Mutual Knowledge,* ed. by N.V. Smith. New York: Academic Press.

Chomsky, N. (1951) 1979. *Morphophonemics of Modem Hebrew.* Repr., New York: Garland.

————. (1955) 1975. *The Logical Structure of Linguistic Theory*. Repr., New York: Plenum.

————. 1956. Three models for the description of languages. *IRE Transactions on Information Theory* 2:113–124.

————. 1957. *Syntactic Structures*. The Hague: Mouton.

————. 1959. On certain formal properties of grammars. *Information and Control* 2:137–167.

Chomsky, N. 1962. Context-free grammar and pushdown storage. *Quarterly Progress Report* 65:187–194.

————. 1965. *Aspects of the Theory of Syntax*. Cambridge, MA: MIT Press.

————. 1976. Conditions on rules of grammar. *Linguistic Analysis* 2:303–351.

————. 1980. On binding. *Linguistic Inquiry* 11:1–46.

————. 1986. *Knowledge of Language*. New York: Praeger.

————. 1991. Some notes on the economy of derivation and representation. In *Principles and Parameters in Comparative Grammar*, ed. by R. Freidin. Cambridge, MA: MIT Press.

————. 1992. A minimalist program for linguistic theory. Cambridge, MA: *MIT Occasional Papers in Linguistics*, 1. [reprinted in Chomsky 1995b]

————. 1993. A minimalist program for linguistic theory. In *The View from Building 20*, ed. by K. Hale and S. J. Keyser. Cambridge, MA: MIT Press.

————. 1995a. Language and nature. *Mind* 104:1–61.

————. 1995b. *The Minimalist Program*. Cambridge, MA: MIT Press.

————. 1998. Minimalist inquiries: The framework. In *Step by Step: Essays on Minimalist Syntax in Honor of Howard Lasnik*, ed. by R. Martin, D. Michaels, and J. Uriagereka. Cambridge, MA: MIT Press.

————. 1999. Derivation by phase. *MIT Occasional Papers in Linguistics* 18.

————. 2000. *New Horizons in the Study of Language and Mind*. New York: Cambridge University Press.

————, and H. Lasnik. 1977. Filters and control. *Linguistic Inquiry* 8:425–504.

————, and G. A. Miller. 1958. Finite-state languages. *Information and Control* 1:91–112.

Cohen-Tannoudji, C. B. Diu, and F. Laloë. 1996. *Mécanique Quantique*. Paris: Hermann.

Compton, A. H. 1923. A quantum theory of the scattering of X-rays by light elements. *The Physical Review* 21:483–502.

Darwin, C. 1859. *On the Origin of Species by Means of Natural Selection*. London: John Murray.

Debye, P. 1923. Zerstreuung von Röntgenstrahlen und Quantentheorie. *Physikalische Zeitschrift* 24:161–166.

Dirac, P. A. M. 1968. Methods in theoretical physics. In *From a Life of Physics: Evening Lectures at the International Center for Theoretical Physics, Trieste, Italy*. A special supplement of the International Atomic Energy Agency Bulletin, Austria.

Einstein, A. 1905. Über einen die Erzeugung und Verwandlung des Lichtes betreffenden heuristischen Gesichtspunkt. *Annalen der Physik* 17:132–148.

————. 1917. Zur Quantentheorie der Strahlung. *Physikalische Zeitschrift* 18:121–128.

Feynman, R. 1971. *The Character of Physical Law*. Cambridge, MA: MIT Press.

————, R. B. Leighton, and M. Sands. 1963. *The Feynman Lectures on Physics*. Vol. 1. Reading, MA: Addison-Wesley.

Fiengo, R., and R. May. 1994. *Indices and Identity*. Cambridge, MA: MIT Press.

Freidin, R. 1994. Conceptual shifts in the science of grammar: 1951–1992. In *Noam Chomsky: Critical Assessments*, vol. 1, ed. by C. P. Otero. London: Routledge.

————. 1997a. Review article: N. Chomsky. The minimalist program. Cambridge, MA: MIT Press. 1995. *Language* 73:571–582.

————. 1997b. Binding theory on minimalist assumptions. In *Atomism and Binding*, ed. by H. Bennis, P. Pica, and J. Rooryck. Dordrecht, Netherlands: Foris.

———, and H. Lasnik. 1981. Disjoint reference and wh-trace. *Linguistic Inquiry* 12:39–53.

Fukui, N. 1996. On the nature of economy in language. *Cognitive Studies* 3:51–71.

Goodman, N. 1943. On the simplicity of ideas. *Journal of Symbolic Logic* 8:107–121.

Greene, B. 1999. *The Elegant Universe: Superstrings, Hidden Dimensions, and the Quest for the Ultimate Theory.* New York: W. W. Norton.

Hockett, C. 1954. Two models of grammatical description. *Word* 10:210–234.

Huybregts, R., and H. van Riemsdijk. 1982. *Noam Chomsky on the Generative Enterprise.* Dordrecht, Netherlands: Foris.

Hymes, D., and J. Fought. 1981. *American Structuralism.* The Hague: Mouton.

Jacobson, P. 1977. The syntax of crossing coreference sentences. Doctoral dissertation, University of California, Berkeley.

Jenkins, L. 2000. *Biolinguistics.* Cambridge: Cambridge University Press.

Jourdain, P. E. B. 1913. *The Principle of Least Action.* Chicago Open Court.

Kneale, W., and M. Kneale. 1962. *The Development of Logic.* Oxford: Oxford University Press.

Lanczos, C. 1970. *The Variational Principles of Mechanics.* 4th ed. Toronto: University of Toronto Press.

Lappin, S. 1991. Concepts of logical form in linguistics and philosophy. In *The Chomskyan Turn*, ed. by A. Kasher. Oxford: Blackwell.

———, R. Levine, and D. Johnson. 2000. The structure of unscientific revolutions. *Natural Language and Linguistic Theory* 18:665–671.

———, and M. McCord. 1990. Anaphora resolution in slot grammar. *Computational Linguistics* 16:197–212.

Lasnik, H. 1976. Remarks on coreference. *Linguistic Analysis* 2:1–22.

———. 1991. On the necessity of binding conditions. In *Principles and Parameters in Comparative Grammar*, ed. by R. Freidin, 7–28. Cambridge, MA: MIT Press.

———. 1999. *Minimalist Analysis.* Malden, MA: Blackwell.

Lavine, J., and R. Freidin. 2001. The subject of defective T(ense) in Slavic. *Journal of Slavic Linguistics* 10:253–289.

Otero, C. 1994. Chomsky and the cognitive revolution of the 1950s: The emergence of transformational generative grammar. In *Noam Chomsky: Critical Assessments*, vol. 1, ed. by C. P. Otero. London: Routledge.

Pais, A. 1982. *"Subtle Is the Lord . . . ": The Science and Life of Albert Einstein.* Oxford: Oxford University Press.

Postal, P. 1966. On so-called "pronouns" in English. In *Report of the Seventeenth Annual Round Table Meeting on Linguistics and Language Studies*, ed. by F. Dinneen, 177–206. Washington, DC: Georgetown University Press.

Putnam, H. 1962. The analytic and the synthetic. In *Minnesota Studies in the Philosophy of Science*, III, ed. by H. Feigl and G. Maxwell. Minneapolis: University of Minnesota Press.

Smith, N. 1999. *Chomsky: Ideas and Ideals.* Cambridge: Cambridge University Press.

Stewart, I. 1998. *Life's Other Secret.* New York: John Wiley.

———. 1999. Designer differential equations for animal locomotion. *Complexity* 5:12–22.

Thompson, D. W. 1942. *On Growth and Form: A New Edition.* Cambridge: Cambridge University Press.

Toffoli, T. 1999. Action, or the fungibility of computation. In *Feynman and Computation*, ed. by A. J. G. Hey. Reading, MA: Perseus Books.

Vergnaud, J.-R. 1974. French relative clauses. Doctoral dissertation, MIT.

———. 1998. On two notions of representations in syntax. Ms.

———, and M. L. Zubizarreta. 2000. Intervention effects in French wh-in-situ construction: Syntax or interpretation? Ms., University of Southern California.

Weinberg, S. 1976. The forces of nature. *Bulletin of the American Academy of Arts and Sciences* 29:13–29.

3 On a Certain Notion of Occurrence
The Source of Metrical Structure and of Much More[1,2]

Jean-Roger Vergnaud

1. THE METRICAL HYPOTHESIS

Consider such an English word as *nominee*. The primary stress in *nominee* is located on the last vowel. This stress contour is standardly represented as in (1):[3]

(1)

```
                      *
      *        *      *
      1        2      3
   n  o   m    i   n  ee
```

The notation in (1) has been referred to as a *metrical grid*. It was originally developed in M. Liberman's work (see, e.g., Liberman 1975), and subsequently adapted in Halle and Vergnaud 1987. In essence, the metrical notation identifies a stress contour with a particular period in some beat. For *nominee*, the correspondence is indicated in (2):

(2)

```
. . .           *              *              *           . . .
. . .   *       *      *       *      *       *      *       . . .
. . . . . . . . 1      2       3      . . . . . . . . . . . . . . . .
                n  o   m    i   n  ee
```

The underlying hypothesis is that a stress contour is a rhythmic organization of constituents. Call this the *metrical hypothesis*.

(3) The metrical hypothesis (MH)

A stress contour for the linguistic expression LE is a rhythmic organization of constituents of LE.

Thus, an asterisk on the bottom tier in (1)–(2) denotes the time position of a syllable, or, more generally, of a "stress-bearing unit" (SBU). As for the asterisk on the higher tier at position 3 in (1)–(2), it indicates that the stroke in the period of the beat identified with *nominee* is aligned with the last SBU in that word. Assuming MH, two distinct, but related, questions arise:

(4)

    (a) Given a linguistic expression LE, what are the constituents of LE in terms of which the rhythmic/metrical structure of LE is defined?

    (b) Is the correspondence between metrical grids and beats exemplified in (1)–(2) a principled one, i.e., is it inherent in the formal definition of the metrical grid?

This article is concerned with the second question in (4). We will argue that a proper formalization of metrical structure indeed leads to a positive answer to that question. To start with, we briefly recapitulate some relevant points relating to the first question.

    In general, more than one type of constituent may serve as the basis for the rhythmic organization of any linguistic category across languages. To take but one example, the rhythmic structure of words is defined over syllables in a large number of languages, but one also finds languages in which it is defined over a subclass of the syllables, or over a subclass of the vowels (see Halle and Vergnaud 1987). Invariably, though, the rhythmic organization of linguistic expressions is congruent with the constituent structure independently defined by the grammar.[4] We state this in (5):

(5) The Congruence Principle (CP)
    The rhythmic organization of linguistic expressions is congruent with the underlying constituent structure. Specifically, each tier in a metrical grid is associated with a certain level of constituency, and the hierarchy of tiers reflects a scale of constituent sizes.

In the case of (1)–(2), the bottom tier is taken to correspond to the syllabic level, with each asterisk identifying a syllable, while the top tier corresponds to the level of words. So, the asterisks on the bottom tier scan the syllables while those on the top tier do the words. The congruence of stress and constituent structures is a cornerstone of the generative theory in Chomsky and Halle 1968. Note that CP is a guiding principle, really, more than an actual generalization or a law. As stated, it is admittedly rather vague, in particular since the notion of constituent is not uniform across the various components of grammar (phonology, morphology, syntax) and since different modes of combination may apply in these various components. Yet in spite of its vagueness, or perhaps because of its vagueness, linguists have found it an extremely useful leading idea.

There are evident violations of CP, in which a stress contour departs from the ideal pattern and fails to respect the underlying constituent structure. However, such discrepancies can in general be analyzed as perturbations caused by independent nongrammatical preferences, e.g., the preference for more balanced patterns or for simpler phonological phrases (see Chomsky and Halle 1968). Both adherence to CP and departure from it can be naturally analyzed by adopting the following approach. A sequence of abstract positions such as 1|2|3 in (1)–(2) is described as a *metrical constituent* (MC) and the stressed position in it, as the *head* of MC in the sense of X-bar theory (see, e.g., Chomsky 1995). Call this the *Hypothesis of Metrical Constituency* (HMC). Thus, by HMC, the sequence 1|2|3 in (1)–(2) is a metrical constituent whose head is position 3 on the bottom tier. An MC on some tier n is *labeled* by an abstract position $L(MC)$ on the next higher tier $n+1$. $L(MC)$ is aligned with the head of MC and is described as the *projection* of that head. For the constituent 1|2|3 in (1)–(2), the label $L(1|2|3)$ is the position on the top tier aligned with 3.

HMC is central to the theory in Halle and Vergnaud 1987. Given HMC, the congruence between rhythmic structure and underlying constituent structure reduces to a correspondence between two independently defined constituent structures (see Halle and Vergnaud 1987). Furthermore, the hierarchy of tiers in a rhythmic organization such as (2) defines an autonomous scale of metrical units. Interestingly, this provides a lead toward answering the question in (4ii). For, when it is interpreted in accordance with HMC, a rhythmic pattern such as (2) bears some resemblance to structures generated by clocks or number systems. We discuss this aspect subsequently.

2. ON METRICAL GRIDS, CLOCKS, AND NUMBER SYSTEMS

Assuming HMC, a sequence of three consecutive positions on the bottom tier in the rhythmic grid in (2) is an MC. This MC is labeled by an asterisk on the top tier aligned with its head. Thus, the asterisks on the bottom tier correspond to SBUs and those on the top tier, to MCs. This is reminiscent of the dial of a clock with two hands, in which the smaller units of time are scanned by the big hand and the bigger ones, by the little hand. For the grid in (2), the corresponding clock has three positions. This is shown in (6), where the three positions are denoted by 0, 1 and 2 (corresponding, respectively, to positions 3, 1 and 2 in (2)):

(6)

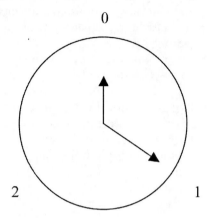

In the clock represented in (6), a full revolution of the big hand from position 0 through positions 1 and 2 back to position 0 triggers a movement of the little hand from one position to the next. The behavior of the clock in (6) over a period of time corresponding to a full revolution of the little hand can be represented by the grid of numbers in (7) or, equivalently, by the simplified variant in (8):

(7)

	0	0	1	1	1	2	2	2	0
	1	2	0	1	2	0	1	2	0
0	*1*	*2*	*3*	*4*	*5*	*6*	*7*	*8*	*9*

(8)

			1			2			0
	1	2	0	1	2	0	1	2	0
0	*1*	*2*	*3*	*4*	*5*	*6*	*7*	*8*	*9*

The bottom line in (7) and (8) represents the time axis, formalized as a sequence of evenly spaced time points with origin $t = 0$. Either grid (7) or (8) should be read as indicated in (9), where l_H denotes the first tier of numbers above the time axis and l_b, the next tier above:

(9) A number on tier l_H (resp. l_b) above t on the time axis represents the clock position to which the big (resp. little) hand moves at t.

The representation in (7)–(8) brings to light the common nature of a clock like that in (6) and of a number system with fixed base 3. By definition, such a number system has only three distinct symbols to represent numbers, say 0, 1 and 2, ordered as in the decimal system. For example, the number represented as 16 in the decimal system will be represented as 121 in the system with fixed base 3, as shown by the factorizations in (10):

(10) $(1 \times 10) + (6 \times 1) = (1 \times 3^2) + (2 \times 3) + (1 \times 1)$

The representation 121 for decimal 16 can be read from the grid in (11) or, equivalently, from the simplified variant in (12):

(11)

0	0	0	0	0	0	0	0	1	1	1	1	1	1	1	1
0	0	1	1	1	2	2	2	0	0	0	1	1	1	2	2
1	2	0	1	2	0	1	2	0	1	2	0	1	2	0	1
0	*1*	*2*	*3*	*4*	*5*	*6*	*7*	*8*	*9*	*10*	*11*	*12*	*13*	*14*	*15*	*16*

(12)

								1							
	1			2				0			1			2	
1	2	0	1	2	0	1	2	0	1	2	0	1	2	0	1
0	*1*	*2*	*3*	*4*	*5*	*6*	*7*	*8*	*9*	*10*	*11*	*12*	*13*	*14*	*15*	*16*

The rhythmic grid in (2) is thus comparable to the clock grid in (7)–(8) or the number grid in (11)–(12). These grids all share a defining feature, which is their periodic structure, arising from the repetition of a basic motif. At the same time, they differ in a significant respect. The hierarchy of periods in a clock/number grid is unbounded. By contrast, a rhythm grid only involves one level of periodicity per grammatical category.[5] In the end, linguistic rhythm is not a counting device. Nevertheless, it is useful to compare the two types of structures, because an analysis of clock/number systems will provide insight into the formal nature of periodicity, thus illuminating the question in (4b). We want eventually to argue for the following thesis:

(13) Given the proper formalization of metrical grids, the relation between a metrical grid such as (1) and the corresponding beat in (2) is comparable to that between the clock in (6) and the associated grid in (7)–(8).

There is an informal interpretation of the metrical grid in (1) according to which the grid provides instructions for the gesture producing the beat in (2). This gesture is analyzed into two components. One, call it A, defines the regular amplitude of the gesture occurring at every time point. The other, call it a, defines an increase in the amplitude of the gesture, which occurs on the last time point in the grid. Then, one may speculate that A corresponds to the big hand in the clock in (6) and a, to the little hand. This still falls short of establishing the conjecture in (13). As observed earlier, metrical structure is far removed from number systems. However, we shall see that the informal interpretation just proposed relates to a formal description that actually yields the required analysis of the metrical grid. We now turn to a more detailed discussion of the relation between the clock in (6) and the associated grid in (7) or (8).

3. ON PERIODICITY

In essence, a clock/number system defines a hierarchy of equivalence relations among numbers. In the case of a system with fixed base 3, the equivalence relation at the bottom of that hierarchy is constituted by the set of three classes in (14):[6]

(14)

    (a) the numbers of the form $3n$, i.e., the numbers that are exact multiples of 3

    (b) the numbers of the form $3n+1$, i.e., the numbers that leave the remainder 1 when divided by 3

    (c) the numbers of the form $3n+2$, i.e., the numbers that leave the remainder 2 when divided by 3

Let us denote by $0°$, $1°$ and $2°$ the classes in (14a), (14b) and (14c), respectively:

(15)

    (a) $0° =_{\text{def}}$ the class of numbers of the form $3n$

    (b) $1° =_{\text{def}}$ the class of numbers of the form $3n+1$

    (c) $2° =_{\text{def}}$ the class of numbers of the form $3n+2$

The set of classes $\{0°, 1°, 2°\}$ constitutes a finite set of "supernumbers" that displays the same arithmetic properties as the set of natural numbers. For example, one can define an "addition" of classes with the same properties as standard addition.[7] The addition table for classes is as in (16):

(16)

	0·	1·	2·
0·	0·	1·	2·
1·	1·	2·	0·
2·	2·	0·	1·

The preceding table is constructed by the rule in (17):

(17) Let $r°(n)$ be the class of n (r is the remainder left when n is divided by 3). Then:

(i) $r°(n) + r°(m) = r°(n+m)$

Mathematically, the classes in (15) can be constructed by mapping the circular permutation displayed in (18) onto the linear set of numbers.

(18)

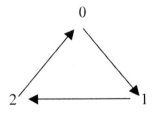

The circular permutation in (18) is formalized in (19a), with (x, y) defined as in (19b):[8]

(19)
(a) (0, 1), (1, 2), (2, 0)
(b) $(x, y) =_{\text{def}}$ "y is the image of x"

Consider now the bottom tier in (7) or (8), repeated in (20):

(20)

	1	2	0	1	2	0	1	2	0
0	*1*	*2*	*3*	*4*	*5*	*6*	*7*	*8*	*9*

The array in (20) may be taken to represent the mapping that pairs each number n with the remainder left by n when divided by 3. In other words, the array in (20) identifies the equivalence classes $0°$, $1°$, $2°$ defined in (15). The periodic distribution of 1, 2, and 0 in (20) can be described by the pairs in (19a), repeated later in (21a), if (x, y) is construed as in (21b):

(21)

    (a) (0, 1), (1, 2), (2, 0)

    (b) (x, y) = $_{def}$ "any *occurrence* of x precedes an *occurrence* of y"

The periodic distribution on the bottom tier in the grids (7) and (8) (or (11) and (12) for that matter) is then formalized as an alternative interpretation of the permutation in (18), one according to which this permutation applies to variable *occurrences* of the numbers 1, 2, and 0 along an infinite axis. This is summarized in (22):

(22)

    (a) (0, 1), (1, 2), (2, 0)

    (b) $[(x, y)$ = $_{def}$ "y is *the image of* x"]: a circular permutation defined over the set {1, 2, 0}

    (c) $[(x, y)$ = $_{def}$ "*any* occurrence *of* x *precedes an* occurrence *of* y"]: a periodic distribution of 1, 2, and 0 defined over an infinite discrete linear set

Evidently, the crucial concept in the characterization in (22) is that of "occurrence" of an object. We now turn to a discussion of that notion.

4. ON THE NOTION OF 'OCCURRENCE'

The arithmetic nature of the domain of objects in (22) suggests the following approach. Given any number n, the quotient q and the remainder r when n is divided by 3 are uniquely determined. The number n can then be identified with the pair $<r, q>$:

(23) $<r, q>$ = $_{def}$ the number n such that $n = 3q + r$

Given the identification $<r, q>$ = n, we call r the "first projection" of n, denoted by $\pi^1(n)$, and q, its "second projection," denoted by $\pi^2(n)$:

(24) $n = <r, q> \leftrightarrow r = \pi^1(n), q = \pi^2(n)$

The objects under consideration are the possible remainders. We define an *occurrence* of the remainder r as a pair $<r, m>$, m some integer, i.e., as the number $3m + r$:

(25) *An occurrence of $r =$* def $3m + r = <r, m>$, *for some m*

A *chain* is a set of occurrences of an object, i.e., a set of pairs sharing the same right "coordinate." For example, each division class $r°$, $r = 0, 1, 2$, defined in (15) constitutes a chain in that structure. With these definitions, the set of occurrences of the remainders 0, 1, 2 is represented by the grid in (26):

(26)

	0	0	1	1	1	2	2	2	3 ...
	1	2	0	1	2	0	1	2	0 ...
0	*1*	*2*	*3*	*4*	*5*	*6*	*7*	*8*	*9* ...

The structure in (26) is reminiscent of the clock grid in (7) or (8) and of the bottom tiers in the number grid in (11) or (12). The occurrences of the remainders 0, 1, 2 are defined as the integers on the bottom line in (26). For example, the number 8 on that line is the occurrence <2,2> of the remainder 2.

As it turns out, then, the right "coordinate" in (23) is treated as an indexing of the left 'coordinate' for the purpose of defining the notion of occurrence. This indexing is not arbitrary, though, but arises from the very formalization of the objects. We take this formalization to exemplify the general notion of occurrence:

(27) Let O be some class of objects and let ω be an element of O. An occurrence of ω is an element of the Cartesian product $I \times O$, where I is a set of features that naturally combine with each object in O.

The notion of chain is generalized accordingly:

(28) A set of occurrences of ω is a *chain*.

The formalization in (27) implicitly involves a distinction between two kinds of properties of entities, those properties that identify the *type* of an entity and those that are used to identify an *instance* of that type. Denote by ω a set of properties defining some type. The set ω is what we have called an "object." The properties in ω are said to be intrinsic to the object ω. By contrast, the properties that define an instance of ω are not intrinsic to it, but can be freely associated with all objects. Denote by I the set of such properties. An occurrence of ω is then identified with the pairing of ω with some elements in I.

In addition to introducing the notion of occurrence, the alternative definition in (21ii) specifies a particular interpretation of the mapping (x, y), namely "x precedes y." We argue that this specification does not have to be stipulated independently, but merely follows from the extension of the mapping (19) to the set of occurrences of remainders. Call S the mapping in (19).

Quite obviously, the set of remainders {0, 1, 2} may be endowed with the same algebraic structure as the set of equivalence classes defined in (15). In particular, one can define the addition table in (29) for the remainders, identical to the table for the corresponding classes in (16):

(29)

	0	1	2
0	0	1	2
1	1	2	0
2	2	0	1

The preceding table is constructed by the rule in (30), which is the same as that for the equivalence classes in (17):

(30) Let $r(n)$ be the remainder left when n is divided by 3. Then:

(i) $r(n) + r(m) = r(n+m)$

Given the structure in (29), the mapping S in (19) can now be identified with the operation Add 1:

(31) $S(x) =_{\text{def}} x+1$

This mapping is naturally extended to the pairs $<r, q>$ defined in (23)–(25) as shown in (32):

(32) $S(<r, q>) =_{def} <S(r), \pi^2(S(3q+r))>$, with $\pi^2(n)$ defined as in (24)

The extension in (32) is consistent with the identification $<r, q> = 3q+r$ in (23):

(33) If $<r, q>$ is equated with $n = 3q+r$, then $S(<r, q>)$ is equated with $S(n)$.

The construction in (32)–(33) defines the relation "x precedes y." It thus provides the underpinning for the informal characterization in (22) of the relation between the notions of circular permutation and of periodic distribution in the case of natural numbers.

We now return to the clock in (6):

(6)

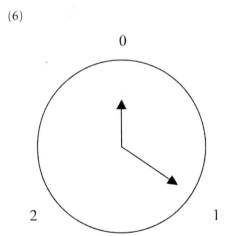

The activity of the big hand in that clock can clearly be identified with the circular permutation in (18). We then have a description of the relation between that particular component of the clock and the bottom part of the clock grid in (7) or (8). This description can be generalized to all the components of the clock. We state this in (34):

(34)
    (i) The activity of a hand in a clock is formalized as a circular permutation of the corresponding dial points.

    (ii) The hand can be interpreted as scanning a periodic distribution of numbers over time by taking the dial points to denote variable occurrences of numbers along the time axis.

Again, the crucial, but elusive, notion in this rather obvious statement is that of occurrence. In (34ii), an "occurrence" is identified in terms of the particular algebraic structure postulated for the set of numbers and the corresponding set of indices (the set I in (27)) is just a facet of that structure. Note however that the notion of occurrence defined in (27) is essentially a relative notion, to be interpreted within a particular formal context. Concretely, the set of indices I in the general characterization (27) depends on the formal structure in which it is embedded. As we are now going to see, a notion of occurrence different from that exemplified earlier applies in the case of the relation between (1) and (7)–(8).

5.   PRESENTATIONS OF CIRCULAR PERMUTATIONS

We repeat the conjecture in (13):

(13) Given the proper formalization of metrical grids, the relation between a metrical grid such as (1) and the corresponding beat in (2) is comparable to that between the clock in (6) and the associated grid in (7)–(8).

Note that an important difference between the metrical grid in (1) and the clock in (6) or the diagram for the circular permutation in (18) has to do with the topology of the medium. The representation in (1) is embedded in a one-dimensional medium (a line), while those in (6) and (18) are embedded in a two-dimensional medium (a plane). As a step toward making (1) comparable with (6) or (18), we shall convert the "two-dimensional" representation in (6) or (18) into a "one-dimensional" one. To that end, we introduce the notation in (35a) and the convention in (35b):

(35)
    (a) Let (x, y) be the relation in (19ii). The left (resp. right) "coordinate" is denoted by $x|$ (resp. $|y$). We call $x|$ the *source component* and $|y$ the *goal component*.

    (b) In a linear arrangement, a sequence of two identical symbols ww is replaced by w. The symbols that fall under that convention are: any number, any letter, the vertical bar $|$.

To illustrate, consider the linear arrangement in (36) of the sequence of pairs in (19i):

(36) (0, 1) - (1, 2) - (2, 0)

By (35a), this arrangement can be rewritten as (37):

(37) 0|1 - 1|2 - 2|0

By (35b), the arrangement in (37) reduces to (38):

(38) 0|1|2|0

Then, the set of pairs in (19a) can be arranged in a linear array in such a way as to yield any one of the sequences in (39):

(39)
    (i)   0|1|2|0

    (ii) 1|2|0|1

    (iii) 2|0|1|2

Assuming the addition table in (29), the representations in (39) have the general form in (40):

(40) $n \mid (n+1) \mid (n+2) \mid n$

The linear representation in (40) can be described as the "projection" of the circular representation in (18) or in (6) into a one-dimensional medium. That projection displays a repetition of its initial (resp. final) element at the end (resp. the beginning). This can be viewed as a topological effect: if the topological properties of a circular arrangement such as (18) or (6) are to be preserved under projection into a one-dimensional space, the projection must have repeated ends. This is a well-known, and easily established, mathematical result (see, e.g., Godbillon 1971). Thus, a circle such as that in (41a) is topologically equivalent to a segment in which the two ends have been identified, such as the segment *AB* in (41b):

(41)

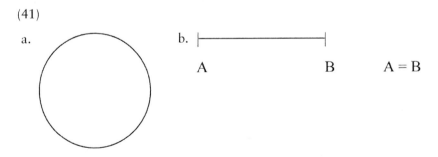

a.   b.

                                     A   B   A = B

Intuitively, one can see that a pointer that simulates the movement of a hand in a circular clock by describing some sequence of positions $\{1, 2, \ldots\}$ embedded in a one-dimensional space must be able to return to a position immediately preceding 1 once it has reached the right end of the sequence. Introducing a copy of the last position 0 (resp. first position 1) before 1 (resp. after 0) accomplishes just that: with the copying, the last and the first positions become equivalent and the desired effect obtains. Of course, to identify some part A in a representation R with some other part B of R is the same thing as stating that A and B constitute two occurrences of the same object, i.e., constitute a chain in the sense of (27)–(28):

(42) The two ends in (41b) constitute a chain.

Similarly, the two ends of the representational sequence in (40) constitute a chain:

(43) In the linear representation $n|(n+1)|(n+2)|n$ of the circular arrangement in (18) or (6), the two ends $n|$ and $|n$ constitute a chain.

However, the relevant notion of occurrence here is different from that found in (22) and (25). This difference merely reflects the fact that the object examined is not the circular permutation in (18)–(19) proper, but rather what one would call "presentations" of that circular permutation. Such presentations constitute formal objects in their own right, which can be defined in abstract terms and, in particular, independently of the nature of the domain of the permutation. Let us then replace the numbers 0, 1, 2 in the preceding discussion by three distinct arbitrary symbols A, B, C (the distinctness of the symbols is obviously crucial). The representation in (19) becomes (44):

(44)
   (i) $(A, B), (B, C), (C, A)$
   (ii) $(x, y) =_{\text{def}}$ "y is the image of x"

Similarly, the representations in (18) and (39) become (45) and (46), respectively:

(45)

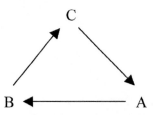

(46)
   (a) $C|A|B|C$
   (b) $A|B|C|A$
   (c) $B|C|A|B$

A general formula for the linear representations in (46) is:

(47) Z|X|Y|Z

We shall now compare the various representations in (44)–(47).

We can derive the relation between (45) and (47) by elementary considerations, without recourse to general theorems of topology. By definition, a one-one mapping from the set $\Sigma = \{A, B, C\}$ onto itself is a particular subset of the Cartesian product $\Sigma \times \Sigma$ which, in particular, includes two occurrences of each symbol A, B, C. An occurrence of a symbol is identified as a position of that symbol in the set-theoretic definition of the mapping. Specifically, a symbol can be described as an element of the *domain* or of the *image* (*codomain*), i.e., as the "x" or as the "y" in the relation (x, y) in (44ii). We introduce the notation in (48), where S denotes the mapping in (44):

(48)

    a. $<X, S> =$ ₍def₎ the symbol X viewed as a member of the domain, i.e., as the left factor in a pairing $(X, \ldots)$

    b. $<X, S^*> =$ ₍def₎ the symbol X viewed as a member of the image (codomain), i.e., as the right factor in a pairing $(\ldots, X)$

We have the following correspondence between the preceding notation and the notation in (35a):

(49)

    a. $<X, S> = X|$

    b. $<X, S^*> = |X$

The two roles $<X, S>$ and $<X, S^*>$ of the symbol X in (48) are what we have called in (35a) the "source component" and the "goal component," respectively. These two roles/components count as two occurrences of X by the general definition in (27). They form a chain by (28). To present the mapping (44) within some medium MED, one needs to provide a MED presentation of each occurrence of each symbol. Assuming a one-one mapping into MED (with each occurrence represented as a different point), one can present the relation (x, y) in (44ii) as a symmetric adjacency relation within MED. This is in essence the proposal in Sauzet 1993, 1994, where the relation within MED is denoted by the French term *attenance*. We translate *attenance* as NEXT-TO (ℵ). Thus, we have the presentation in (50), with (X, Y) defined as in (44ii):

(50) $(X, Y) \approx X_S \, ℵ \, Y_{S^*}$

Minimally, a presentation of (44) must then include the relations in (51), where X_u is the presentation of $<X, u>$:

(51) $A_S \ltimes B_{S^*}$

　　　$B_S \ltimes C_{S^*}$

　　　$C_S \ltimes A_{S^*}$

Let us introduce the notation in (52) and the associated definitions in (53):

(52) $[X] =_{def}$ the ordered chain $\{<X, S^*>, <X, S>\} = \{X_1, X_2\}$

(53)
　　a. the first coordinate of $\{X_1, X_2\} =_{def} X_1 = <X, S^*>$ (the goal component)
　　b. the second coordinate of $\{X_1, X_2\} =_{def} X_2 = <X, S>$ (the source component)

For obvious reasons, the medium chosen to present a mapping like (44) usually is a common geometric one, such as a plane or a line. This is the case in (45) and (47). In actual practice, chains are maximally collapsed into single geometric points, thus contravening the bijective character of the presentation assumed in the earlier discussion. This is really the sense of the simplification convention in (35b). Obviously, any presentation of a circular permutation must respect the distinctness of the symbols involved. At the least, distinct chains must be presented as distinct points. For example, each geometric point A, B, C in the "circular" presentation in (45) represents a chain as indicated in (54), where X is the presentation of the chain $[X]$ and X_u, that of the component $<X, u>$ as in (51):

(54) The "circular" presentation in (45):
　　a. Geometric point $A = A = \{A_{S^*}, A_S\}$
　　b. Geometric point $B = B = \{B_{S^*}, B_S\}$
　　c. Geometric point $C = C = \{C_{S^*}, C_S\}$

In accordance with the two-dimensional nature of the medium in (45), each point X corresponding to the chain $[X]$ may be described as a pair of coordinates. Each coordinate of X is the projection of X onto an "axis" within the geometrical frame of reference for the points, and it may be taken as a presentation of the corresponding component of $[X]$.

The collapsing of chains into single geometric points requires that the relation $\ltimes$ in (50) be extended to images of chains. This can be done in the manner indicated in (55) (note that the extension of $\ltimes$ to chains is no longer a symmetric relation):

(55) $X \ltimes Y$ iff. $X_S \ltimes Y_{S^*}$

Now, in the case of a two-dimensional medium as in (45), $\aleph$ may be consistently extended to all chains. For, even though a chain is presented as a single point, its two components ("coordinates" in the sense of (53)) remain distinguishable given that a point in a two-dimensional medium indeed has two coordinates; cf. (54). The relation $\aleph$ has an abstract interpretation, applying so to speak "across the two dimensions." Specifically, it applies between points located on distinct axes. There is then no sense in which a point could "intervene" between two adjacent points, and there can be no issue of conflicting adjacency requirements. Concretely, one constructs a graph representing a circular permutation by assigning a point P_X to each chain $[X]$ so that no three points are aligned. Then, one defines a pair (P_X, P_Y) as a directed edge of the graph whenever the relation $X \aleph Y$ holds (the resulting graph does not have to be a convex polygon). By contrast, within a one-dimensional medium as in (47), the collapsing of chains drastically affects the realization of $\aleph$. The relation $\aleph$ has to encompass both components of a chain identified with a given point, with the implication in (56):

(56) $(X_S \aleph Y_{S^*}) \Rightarrow \{ (X_S \aleph Y_S)$ and $(X_{S^*} \aleph Y_{S^*})$ and $(X_{S^*} \aleph Y_S) \}$

Assuming that $\aleph$ is interpreted in the usual sense, it is not possible to collapse all chains into single points, because a point that is adjacent to two points P and Q must be located between P and Q. At least one chain must be mapped onto two distinct points. In the case of the circular permutation in (44), we have the presentation in (47). In the latter, the "source/goal asymmetry" is presented as the left/right asymmetry: given the relation $X_S \aleph Y_{S^*}$, the point representing $[X]$ or the occurrence X_S of X is to the left of the point representing $[Y]$ or the occurrence Y_{S^*} of Y.

To summarize, a symbol X that figures in a circular permutation is analyzed into two components, $<X, S^*>$ and $<X, S>$ in this order, as indicated in (48). The $<X, S>$ component (the second component), called the source component, denotes the role of the symbol as a member of the domain of the circular permutation. The $<X, S^*>$ component (the first component), called the goal component, denotes the role of the symbol as a member of the image (codomain) of the circular permutation. These two components count as occurrences of the symbol in the general sense of (27) and form a chain in the sense of (28). A representation of a circular permutation is analyzed as a presentation of that permutation within some medium MED. Assuming that each occurrence of a symbol is mapped onto a different point in MED, the relation (x, y) in (44ii) may be presented as a symmetric adjacency relation called NEXT-TO and denoted by $\aleph$. The correspondence between the mapping (x, y) and $\aleph$ is described in (50). In actual practice, chains are maximally collapsed into single geometric points, thus contravening the bijective nature of the rendering just assumed. This requires the relation $\aleph$ to be extended as in (55). The extension can be carried over to all chains in the case of a medium with more than two dimensions, but not in the case of a one-dimensional medium. In the latter case, at least one chain must be presented as two distinct points, each one representing a different component of the chain, i.e., a different occurrence of the corresponding symbol. It appears that the dimensional contrast ultimately reflects the fact that the two components of a chain collapsed into a single point P remain distinguishable as projections or coordinates of P when the medium has more than one dimension, but not otherwise.

The linchpin of the preceding analysis is the observation that each symbol X in a circular permutation S of the set Σ may be analyzed as a chain $[X]$ of two functions reflecting the two roles of Σ in the mathematical definition of S, namely, that of being the domain of S and that of being the image of S. By definition, each role of X counts as an occurrence of X. We take the emergence of a chain in the translation of the two-dimensional presentation (45) into the one-dimensional presentation (47) as direct evidence for the appropriateness of this approach. Then, given some set of symbols Σ and a circulation permutation S of Σ, we have the fundamental equation:

(57) $X = \{<X, S^*>, <X, S>\}, X \in \Sigma$

In the present context, the fundamental equation in (57) evokes two conjectures, one by Noam Chomsky and one by Morris Halle. We now turn to a presentation and a discussion of these two conjectures.

6.   THE METRICAL GRID RECIPE: A CONJECTURE BY NOAM CHOMSKY PLUS A CONJECTURE BY MORRIS HALLE

6.1.   Two Relevant Conjectures

In a lecture given in the fall of 1982, Morris Halle made the proposal that the asterisk on the higher tier in such a representation as (1) should be viewed as the *copy* of the one below it, in the same sense that the fronted occurrence of *what* in the structure in (58) is analyzed as a copy of its primordial occurrence (*what*) in the object position of *do* (see Chomsky 1993).

(58) One wonders *what* he will do (*what*) next

According to Halle's conjecture, then, the two asterisks in the preceding column 3 in (1) form a *chain* in the standard sense of syntactic theory: they share all attributes but their height and, thus, count as two occurrences of the same object. The general formulation of the conjecture is given in (59):

(59) Halle's conjecture (C_H)

Given a metrical grid M and some position i in M, the asterisks in the column above i form a chain.

Clearly, the import of the conjecture ultimately depends on what attributes an asterisk has in a metrical representation such as (1). We explore this subsequently.

The central question is what defines an "occurrence" of an asterisk or, more generally, of a linguistic expression. The original proposal in Chomsky (1955) 1975, adapted from Quine's (1951) *Mathematical Logic,* was to take an occurrence of α in K to be the full context of α in K. This proposal surfaces in various guises in subsequent developments, for example in Chomsky 1981:45, in Chomsky 1995:251–252), in Chomsky 1998, in Chomsky 1999, and in Chomsky 2001. Chomsky 1998 suggests the following:

(60) Chomsky's conjecture (C_c)

We could, for example, identify this [the full context of α in K-JRV] as $K' = K$ with the occurrence of α in question replaced by some designated element OCC distinct from anything in K. (45n64)

Chomsky 2001 identifies OCC with the EPP-feature (the feature that requires the presence of a specifier). Given category K with label OCC, OCC must be checked by external or internal Merge. OCC clearly falls in the same class as what we have called the "source component" or the "goal component" of a symbol figuring in a permutation S (see (35i)). Both properties are contextual features:

(61)
    a. the source (goal) component of X in S = [X—]
    b. the feature OCC on K = [K—]

We refer to the approach sketched in the preceding sections as the "present approach" (PA). There is a difference between PA and the "Chomsky–Quine approach" (CQ):

(62) Within CQ the feature [K—] identifies the context of K, while it identifies an occurrence of K within PA.

The characterization in (62) is somewhat terse and will be qualified later. But it brings to light the reciprocal nature of C_c and PA. Since PA is embedded within the general theoretical framework developed in Chomsky (1955) 1975, 1995, 1998, 1999, 2001 and borrows central concepts and hypotheses from the latter work, we shall refer to it as the *dual of* C_c (C_c^*).

C_c^* has been developed to provide an account of circular permutations and their representations. But an LE viewed as a string of atoms/symbols is clearly no circular permutation. The question is then how C_c^* should be revised in order to be applied to LEs and to be linked to C_c and to C_H. As we are going to see, though, a string of symbols of the kind used to describe LEs comes close to being a circular permutation.

6.2. The Mapping Representation of Strings

Consider the string of three symbols in (63):

(63) *ABC*

This string may be described as the relation "*A* precedes *B*" and "*B* precedes *C*." This is formalized in (64):

(64)

    (i) $\{(A, B), (B, C)\}$

    (ii) $(x, y) =_{\text{def}}$ "*x* precedes *y*"

The properties we are going to discuss only depend on the form of the mapping in (64), not on its interpretation. Accordingly, we generalize (64) to (65):

(65)

    (i) $\{(A, B), (B, C)\}$

    (ii) $(x, y) =_{\text{def}}$ "*y* is the image of *x*"

The string *ABC* is then identified as a particular relation/mapping defined over the set $\{A, B, C\}$. A mapping must meet certain conditions in order to be interpretable as a string. Quite obviously, it must be injective. Furthermore, it must contain no cycle in the following sense:

(66) Let Σ be a set and let S be an injective mapping on Σ. For S to be interpretable as a string over Σ, there can be no pair (n, X), n an integer, $X \in \Sigma$, such that $S^n(X) = X$.

When Σ is finite (the case relevant to the present discussion), a mapping S on Σ that meets (66) is necessarily a partial mapping:

(67) A mapping S on a finite set Σ may represent a string only if it is undefined for at least one element in Σ.

This indeed holds of the mapping in (65). For strings that are descriptions of LEs, the property in (67) may be represented in a way that mirrors an LE's characteristic ability to combine with other LEs. Call this ability the *recursivity* of LEs (RLE). RLE implies that a relation/mapping S on Σ that formalizes a string necessarily includes a "juncture," i.e., an "open' pair, represented as (x, Δ) or (Δ, y), where Δ is a placeholder. Accordingly, we augment (65) to (68), with (C, Δ) the juncture:

(68)

      (i) $\{(A, B), (B, C), (C, \Delta)\}$

      (ii) $(x, y) =$ _{def} "y is the image of x"

Whether (x, Δ) or (Δ, y) is selected to represent the juncture is a matter of convention. Thus, the following format could be selected instead of (68):

(69)

      (i) $\{(\Delta, A), (A, B), (B, C)\}$

      (ii) $(x, y) =$ _{def} "y is the image of x"

We call the format illustrated in (68) the *right juncture format* and that in (69), the *left juncture format*. In this discussion, we shall use the right juncture format. Note that incorporating a juncture into the representation of a mapping S on Σ is tantamount to adding the juncture symbol Δ to Σ, subject to the interpretation in (70a) and to the restriction in (70b):

(70) Let S be a string mapping on the finite set of symbols Σ.

      (a) Δ is a "joker," i.e., is nondistinct from X, X any symbol in Σ or outside Σ.

      (b) Δ is not part of the domain of S, but only belongs to the co-domain of S.

To summarize so far:

(71) A relation/mapping S on a finite set Σ represents a string iff:

      (a) S is injective.

      (b) S contains no cycle, i.e., there is no pair (n, X), n an integer, $X \in \Sigma$, such that $S^n(X) = X$; cf. (66). In particular, S is a partial mapping; cf. (67).

      (c) S includes a juncture, i.e., a pairing of the form(x, Δ) or (Δ, y).

A relation/mapping that meets the conditions in (71), we shall call a "string relation/mapping."

Assuming the preceding formalization, the concatenation of two strings can be identified with the product of the corresponding string mappings in the standard sense. To illustrate, consider the concatenation of *ABC* with the string *PQ* described in (72):

(72) $\{(P, Q), (Q, \Delta)\}$

The string mapping *PQ* can be composed with *ABC* as a left or as a right factor; that is, *PQ* can precede or follow *ABC* in the composition operation. Consider the case where *PQ* is a right factor. By (70a), the image of *ABC* shares exactly one element with the domain of *PQ*, namely the variable that shows up in the juncture (C, Δ). Define the following reduction transformation for mappings:

(73) The reduction transformation Λ

Let ψ be a relation/mapping on Σ containing a pair (X, Δ). A reduced form of ψ with respect to X is a relation/mapping obtained from ψ by substituting Y for Δ in (X, Δ), where Y belongs to the domain of ψ. The class of reduced forms of ψ for X is denoted by $\Lambda_X(\psi)$.

In general $\Lambda_X(\psi)$ has more than one element. Take the union $ABC \cup PQ$ of the two string mappings *ABC* and *PQ* and consider the class of reduced forms $\Lambda_C(ABC \cup PQ)$. From this class, select the mapping that meets the conditions in (71), i.e., the one that is a string mapping. Denote by $ABC \times PQ$ that particular mapping. It is easy to check that $ABC \times PQ$ is a mapping representation of the concatenation *ABCPQ*. We define a mapping representation of the concatenation *PQABC* in a symmetrical fashion. We then have the commutative diagram in (74), where $S(\omega)$ is the mapping representation of the string ω:

(74)

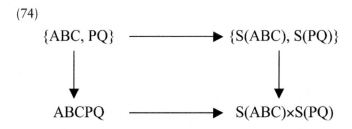

We now see that a circular permutation is a reduced form of a string in the sense just defined. For example, the circular permutation $A|B|C|A^9$ is a reduced form of the string mapping *ABC*, to wit that obtained by substituting A for Δ in the juncture (C, Δ). This is illustrated in (75):

(75)
  a. $ABC = \{(A, B), (B, C), (C, \Delta)\}$
  b. $A|B|C|A = \{(A, B), (B, C), (C, A)\}$

Thus, one can view a string in general as a "severed circular permutation." This is illustrated in (76) in the case of the string *ABC*:

(76)

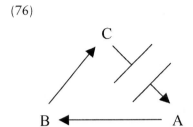

This analogy suggests that the description of circular permutations in section 5 which has led to $C_c{}^*$ may be adapted and generalized to strings. We argue that a mental symbol may be analyzed as a chain of two roles, albeit with a different interpretation from the case of circular permutations.

6.3. Mental Symbols As Chains of Functions

A string such as ABC is defined as the concatenation of *A*, *B* and *C* in this order. The commutative diagram in (74) then yields the equation in (77), where $S(X)$ is the mapping representation of *X*:

(77) $S(ABC) = S(A) \times S(B) \times S(C)$

The representation $S(X)$ of a single symbol *X* is as in (78):

(78) $S(X) = \{(X, \Delta)\}$

The "virtual mapping" associated with *X* in (78) merely expresses the RLE property (the Recursivity of LEs) in the case of an individual symbol. Specifically, RLE entails that each individual symbol is endowed with a contextual feature that represents its ability to combine with other symbols. The virtual mapping $\{(X, \Delta)\}$ in (78) can obviously be identified with the feature OCC introduced in Chomsky 1998 (see section 6.1):

(79) The feature OCC on $X = \{(X, \Delta)\}$

We denote OCC on *X* as <*X*, OCC>:

(80) The feature OCC on $X = \{(X, \Delta)\} = <X, OCC>$

Keeping to the spirit of the analysis of the earlier circular permutations properly adapted to the case of strings, we analyze the symbol *X* into two roles. One role is represented as the feature <*X*, OCC> in (80). The other role corresponds to X's "mirror ability" to substitute for Δ in a pair $\{(Y, \Delta)\}$ = $<Y, OCC>$. We denote that second role by $<X, ID>$. We equate X with the chain constituted by these two roles:

(81) The fundamental equation for mental symbols

$$X = \{<X, ID>, <X, OCC>\}$$

By definition, each component of the chain in (81) is an occurrence of X. The equation in (81) is similar to the fundamental equation in (57). The two components $<X, ID>$ and $<X, OCC>$ correspond to the goal role and to the source role in section 5, respectively.

We assume that collocations are built up from the primitive mental relation $\aleph$ (NEXT-TO; cf. Sauzet 1993, 1994):

(82) X NEXT-TO $Y = X \aleph Y$

For the purpose of this argument, we assume furthermore that a symbol may be related to at most two other symbols by $\aleph$. This is not a logical necessity. In fact, mental computations in general manipulate structures in which symbols may be connected to multiplicities of adjacent symbols. This is not the case for LEs, because of the physical limitations at the PF interface (see Kayne 1994). Within the framework just outlined, a string is constructed by identifying the component $<X, OCC>$ of some symbol X in a set with the component $<Y, ID>$ of another symbol Y in the same set. We call such an identification a *cochain*:

(83) $\{<X, OCC>, <Y, ID>\}$ is a *cochain* iff. $<X, OCC> = <Y, ID>$

A cochain is interpreted as follows. Given the finite set of symbols Σ, we take the feature $<X, OCC>$ to denote the choice function on Σ that picks out the symbol next to X in the string under consideration, and we take the feature $<Y, ID>$ to denote the choice function that picks out the symbol Y itself. Then, the identity $<X, OCC> = <Y, ID>$ represents the adjacency of X and Y in the string XY. This is illustrated in (84):

(84) Description of the string ABC
   a. Chains: $\{<U, ID>, <U, OCC>\}, U = A, B, C$
   b. Cochains:
      (i) $\{<A, OCC>, <B, ID>\}$
      (ii) $\{<B, OCC>, <C, ID>\}$
      (iii) $\{<C, OCC>\}$

The degenerate cochain (biii) in (84) corresponds to the pairing (C, Δ) in the representation in (68). The formalization in (84) is pictured by the diagram in (85). In this diagram, the components of a chain are aligned vertically, while a cochain is indicated by a double-headed arrow, or by a simple arrow when it is degenerate:

(85)

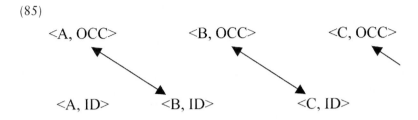

We argue that the metrical grid in (1) can be described as an interpretation of the diagram in (85).

6.4. The Metrical Grid As an Interpretation of Functional Chains and Cochains

We adopt the informal interpretation sketched in (13) in section 2. Specifically, we assume that:

(86)
    (i) Each symbolic role in a diagram such as (85) is manifested as a discrete instruction for some gesture.

    (ii) The timing of the gestures is read from the "horizontal axis" in the diagram.

Furthermore, we postulate the following:

(87)
    (i) Each $<X, ID>$ component is associated with a gesture.

    (ii) Each cochain is associated with a gesture.

    (iii) The number of gestures is minimal.

It is easy to check that, when each discrete gesture is represented as an asterisk, (87) yields the grid in (1) when applied to (85). Note that the logic of the algorithm in (87) is really that of checking in the sense of minimalist syntax. Thus, we may suppose that a primitive algorithm assigns one gesture per symbolic function. So we get both "*ID*-gestures" and "*OCC*-gestures." A "checking" mechanism then ensures that an *OCC*-gesture gets deleted when it is linked to the same cochain as an *ID*-gesture. Within this analogy, an *OCC*-gesture has the same status as an uninterpretable feature in minimalist syntax. Applied to the case of a phonological grid such as (1), this means that a stressed unit is defined as one that cannot be interpreted as a context for another unit. This is the traditional interpretation of (primary) stress as a junctural mark.

A question arises concerning the timing of the additional OCC-gesture associated with the last symbol in (85). One could reason as follows. The feature <C, OCC> is really identified with a virtual element following C. So any gesture associated with the cochain <C, OCC> should be timed after the *ID*-gesture of C. In fact, this is what happens in the case of the other symbols in the string. Such reasoning misses an important point, though. A contextual feature such as <C, OCC> may give rise to an "anticipatory gesture." Such anticipation is an important component of phonological strings. When the anticipatory gesture may develop into a complete gesture, it loses its autonomous status, its planning being incorporated with that of the complete gesture. Otherwise, it counts as an independent gesture. This elementary model is essentially the one adopted for the description of glides in Klein 1991. It expresses a basic intuition originally found in the analysis of French liaison in Encrevé 1983, 1988. Assuming this model, we now have a natural interpretation of the grid in (1).

6.5.   Some Consequences

Call the preceding approach the *Neo-Theory of Metrical Structure* (NMS). If true, NMS vindicates both C_H (cf. (59)) and C_C (cf. (60)). In the case of C_c, an extension to syntax must obviously be provided. We very briefly turn to this later. Recall that a central concern in this paper is the conjecture in (13), repeated here:

> (13) Given the proper formalization of metrical grids, the relation between a metrical grid such as (1) and the corresponding beat in (2) is comparable to that between the clock in (6) and the associated grid in (7)–(8).

We have seen earlier that a circular permutation such as $A|B|C|A$ may be analyzed as a reduced form of the string ABC (cf. (75)–(76)). Accordingly, the beat in (2) may be viewed as arising from the reduction of the metrical grid in (1) in the sense of (73). The additional asterisk corresponding to the stress-bearing unit remains because the algorithm (86)–(87) applies to the original string, not to the reduced forms.

7.   A VERY BRIEF DISCUSSION OF LOCALITY

Consider again the string in (88):

(88) *ABC*

A central question is how such a string should be represented to reveal the local character of the adjacency relation at play within it. The problem is that, by representing the string as in (88), we implicitly introduce global nonlocal relations. For example, non only does the representation in (88) states that C is contextually connected with B, but it also states that it is contextually connected with A, namely it is in the context AB—:

(89) C is in the contexts B—, AB—

The same is true of A in (88). Locality by definition requires that a given element be only connected with its immediate, i.e., *adjacent*, neighbors. Then, the problem is to reconcile the locality requirement with the global nature of the string, for the string after all is more than a collection of binary bonds. It has a global structure that derives from the fact that any given element may be shared by two bonds. As it turns out, the model illustrated in (84)–(85) provides a solution of this dilemma. In the structure (84)–(85), the locality of the connections between each element and its neighbors derives from the fact that each bond (cochain) is established using distinct symbols.

The fact that there is a global structure to the string ABC, i.e., that it is an individual object in its own right which is more than a mere collection of disconnected bonds is then described by independently identifying symbols across relations as chains of occurrences.

It appears that the observance of locality leads one to a condition on symbols that can be stated roughly as follows:

(90) Two distinct relations in a given representation may not share any symbol.

The condition in (90) is reminiscent of the *Obligatory Contour Principle* (OCP) in phonology (see Leben 1973; Goldsmith 1976). Indeed, we shall identify the two conditions and refer to the condition in (90) as the OCP:

(91) Obligatory Contour Principle
      Two distinct relations in a given representation may not share any symbol.

So, we have:

(92) Locality ↔ OCP

It is easy to see why we should have the equivalence in (92). Informally, locality implies that any given element must be identifiable by "local coordinates," i.e., its "local context." But that will be feasible if and only if all elements in the relevant domain are distinct. To illustrate consider (93):

(93) *tafata

      tafaka

      kafata

This of course requires that we adopt a "nonlocal" approach to OCP (see Pierrehumbert 1993; Frisch 1996).

8. SOME SHORT REMARKS AND CONJECTURES

8.1. Stress and Movement

Consider again the structure in (84)–(85). A reduced form of that structure is the circular permutation $C|A|B|C$ in which the chain for C is split, with the contextual occurrence $<C, OCC>$ preceding the chain for A. If the algorithm (86)–(87) is applied to that reduced form instead of the original string, the two occurrences of the symbol C are positioned at different points in time, one at the beginning and one at the end of the string, providing a representation of movement. Which leads to the following conjecture:

(94) Movement and Nuclear Stress apply in opposite directions.

Thus, applying Nuclear Stress to some constituent on the right is like moving it covertly to the left.

8.2. Reduplication and Phonological Processes

A string appears to be the pairing of two strings really, the actual one and a ghost one. Reduplication may be viewed as the surfacing of the ghost string within the actual string. So construed, this process is much more general than usually assumed. It may explain, e.g., the fine structure of Semitic morphophonology (see Guerssel and Lowenstamm 1996; Ségéral 1995).

8.3. The Theory of Stress

The model developed earlier supports the approach put forward in Halle and Idsardi 1995.

8.4. Syntax

We apply this structure as follows. All syntactic categories are analyzed in terms of the same features. To illustrate, consider a primitive system with the three features in (95):

(95) Determiner, Aspect/Classifier, Category

These features correspond to the three symbols A, B, C. We can identify the categorial features V and N as the features ID and OCC, respectively. A string such as ABC then represents a pair of right-branching trees of categories V and N that are matched feature by feature. This is the EPP. A specifier is a case of complete reduplication. Note that such a feature as OCC may be interpreted at several levels. If it gets a PF interpretation in addition to its syntactic interpretation within (84)–(85), we have the case of "strong EPP" in the sense of Chomsky 1995. Note also that, by this formalization, the specifier and the object must be on opposite sides of the head.

The approach to syntactic structure shown here has certain implications. Thus, an elementary chain cannot have more than two elements. So, the kind of derivational approach developed in Chomsky 1999, 2001 is required. More generally, it may lead to an understanding of the general principles that govern the ordering of categories across linguistic levels.[10]

NOTES

1. Central parts of this paper have been inspired by conversations with N. Chomsky and M. Halle in the late 1970s and early 1980s. I have also benefited from discussions with A. Arnaiz, R. Belvin, S. Bromberger, F. Dell, E. Dresher, P. Encrevé, B. Freidin, J. Hawkins, J. Kaye, M. Klein, J. Keyser, P. Martin, C. Otero, M. Prinzhorn, H. van Riemsdijk, A. Rouveret, P. Sauzet, and M. L. Zubizarreta.

2. This chapter was originally published by Mouton de Gruyter as J.-R. Vergnaud, "On a Certain Notion of 'Occurrence': The Source of Metrical Structure, and of Much More," in *Living on the Edge*, ed. by S. Ploch. Berlin: Mouton de Gruyter, 2003. Many thanks to Mouton de Gruyter.

3. As stated in the text, only primary stress is represented in (1). There is a secondary stress on the first syllable of *nominee* (see, e.g., Chomsky and Halle 1968; Halle and Vergnaud 1987). A complete representation of the stress pattern of *nominee* must then posit three distinct levels of stress, as indicated in (i):

   (i)

   ```
                     *
       *             *
       *      *      *

     n  o  m  i  n  ee
   ```

   The argument in the text is only concerned with primary stress. We shall then ignore subsidiary stresses.

4. At least in the case of primary stress. Nonprimary stress obeys distinct principles. See, e.g., Dresher 1994.

5. We are talking here about the "virtual" periodicity exemplified in (19) in the text. There is some restricted counting in the case of alternating stress patterns. But this does not affect the main point, which is that linguistic rhythm does not display the unbounded hierarchy of periods central to any number system.

6. Note that a circular analog clock of the standard kind defines a number system with changing bases (60 and 12).

7. Indeed, the set $\{0°, 1°, 2°\}$ is a ring in the sense of algebra; see, e.g., Birkhoff and Mac Lane 1997:25–31.

8. A standard representation of the circular permutation in (i) is the table in (i), where the element under n is its image (see, e.g., Aigner 1997:20–25):

   (i) 0 1 2
       1 2 0

9. The form *A*|*B*|*C*|*A* is a presentation of the circular permutation in (i) in the sense of section 5 in the text (cf. (44)–(46)).

(i) (A, B), (B, C), (C, A)

10. See Carstairs-McCarthy 1999; Kaye, Lowenstamm, and Vergnaud 1990.

REFERENCES

Aigner, M. 1997. *Combinatorial Theory*. Berlin: Springer.

Birkhoff, G., and S. Mac Lane. 1997. *A Survey of Modern Algebra*. Wellesley, MA: A. K. Peters.

Carstairs-McCarthy, A. 1999. *The Origins of Complex Language*. Oxford: Oxford University Press.

Chomsky, N. (1955) 1975. *The Logical Structure of Linguistic Theory*. New York: Plenum.

———. 1981. *Lectures on Government and Binding*. Dordrecht, Netherlands: Foris.

———. 1993. A minimalist program for linguistic theory. In *The View from Building 20*, ed. by K. Hale and S. J. Keyser. Cambridge, MA: MIT Press. [reprinted in Chomsky 1995].

———. 1995. *The Minimalist Program*. Cambridge, MA: MIT Press.

———. 1998. Minimalist inquiries: The framework. In *Step by Step: Essays on Minimalist Syntax in Honor of Howard Lasnik*, ed. by R. Martin, D. Michaels, and J. Uriagereka. Cambridge, MA: MIT Press.

———. 1999. Derivation by phase. *MIT Occasional Papers in Linguistics* 18.

———. 2001. Derivation by phase. In *Ken Hale: A Life in Language*, ed. by M. Kenstowicz. Cambridge, MA: MIT Press.

———, and M. Halle. 1968. *The Sound Pattern of English*. New York: Harper and Row.

Dresher, E. 1994. The prosodic basis of the Tiberian Hebrew system of accents. *Language* 70:1–52.

Encrevé, P. 1983. La liaison sans enchaînement. *Actes de la Recherche en Sciences Sociales* 46:39–66.

———. 1988. *La liaison avec et sans enchaînement: Phonologie tridimensionnelle et usages du français*. Paris: Le Seuil.

Frisch, S. 1996. Similarity and frequency in phonology. Doctoral dissertation, Northwestern University.

Godbillon, C. 1971. *Eléments de topologie algébrique*. Paris: Hermann.

Goldsmith, J. 1976. Autosegmental phonology. Doctoral dissertation, MIT.

Guerssel, M., and J. Lowenstamm. 1996. The derivational morphology of the classical Arabic verbal system. Ms., Université du Québec à Montréal/Université Denis Diderot.

Halle, M., and W. Idsardi. 1995. General properties of stress and metrical structure. In *A Handbook of Phonological Theory*, ed. John Goldsmith. Oxford: Basil Blackwell.

———, and J.-R. Vergnaud. 1987. *An Essay on Stress*. Cambridge, MA: MIT Press.

Kaye, J., J. Lowenstamm, and J.-R. Vergnaud. 1990. Constituent structure and government in phonology. *Phonology* 7:193–231.

Kayne, R. 1994. *The Antisymmetry of Syntax*. Cambridge, MA: MIT Press.

Klein, M. 1991. Vers une approche substantielle et dynamique de la constituance syllabique, le cas des semi-voyelles. Doctoral dissertation, Université Paris 8.

Leben, W. 1973. Suprasegmental phonology. Doctoral dissertation, MIT.

Liberman, M. 1975. The intonational system of English. Doctoral dissertation, MIT.

Pierrehumbert, J. 1993. Dissimilarity in the Arabic verbal roots. *Proceedings of the North East Linguistics Society* 23:367–381.

Quine, W. V. 1951. *Mathematical Logic.* Cambridge, MA: Harvard University Press.

Sauzet, P. 1993. Attenance, gouvernement et mouvement en phonologie. Les constituants dans la phonologie et la morphologie de l'occitan. Doctoral dissertation, Université Paris 8.

———. 1994. Extensions du modèle a-linéaire en phonologie: syllabe, accent, morphologie. Mémoire d'Habilitation à diriger des recherches, Paris VII.

Ségéral, P. 1995. Une théorie généralisée de l'apophonie. Doctoral dissertation, Université Paris 7.

Acronyms

C_c: Chomsky's conjecture ((60))
C_H: Halle's conjecture ((59))
CP: the Congruence Principle ((5))
CQ: the Chomsky-Quine approach to the notion of 'occurrence' (cf. (62))
HMC: the Hypothesis of Metrical Constituency (second paragraph on p.63)
LE: linguistic expression
L(MC): the label of MC
MC: metrical constituent
MED: medium (see (49))
MH: the Metrical Hypothesis (see (3))
NMT: the Neo-Theory of Metrical Structure (section 6.5)
RLE: the recursivity of LEs (see (66))
SBU: stress-bearing unit

4 Generalizing the Notion of Occurrence

Tommi Leung

1. VERGNAUD'S MANIFESTO

In 2003, Jean-Roger Vergnaud published his last phonology paper (chapter 3 of this volume). The paper starts by stating the "metrical hypothesis" in which a stress contour of a linguistic expression is a rhythmic organization of constituents of that expression. In particular, Vergnaud questions the formal correspondence between metrical grids and stress-bearing units, an issue which was discussed in varying degrees of depth since Liberman (1975), Liberman and Prince (1977), Halle and Vergnaud (1987a and 1987b), and Hayes (1995), among others. The whole inquiry leads Vergnaud to delve into the formalization of metrical structure. He stresses that observations as diverse as metrical structure, clocks, and other analogous rhythmic systems can be conceptually unified given a domain-general notion of occurrence. One goal of Vergnaud (2003) is that occurrences and the notion of "chains" as a set of occurrences can be fully instantiated across cognitive and computational domains. To Vergnaud, any cognitive domain can be described by listing the inventory of basic formatives along with their operations, and in this regard, it is the occurrence which defines or restricts how operations generally apply. The entire vision that any grammatical system can be adequately defined by the interaction between elements and contexts is termed by Vergnaud as "Items and Contexts Architecture" (ICA) (chapter 5 of this volume). The main purpose of this chapter is to revisit and expound the notion of occurrence as one major primitive of the ICA, and moreover to suggest possible empirical extension for further verification.

Represented in chapter 3 is Vergnaud's overall research philosophy with respect to the notion of symmetry. In particular, chapter 3 (and this chapter as well) expounds the thesis of "symmetry in a broad sense," e.g., the symmetry between syntax and phonology, and moreover the symmetry between language and other cognitive systems, using "occurrence" as a point of departure. On the other hand, it is more common for syntacticians to exercise the thesis of "symmetry in a narrow sense." One current practice is "structural symmetry," e.g., the symmetry between substantive and lexical structures (Chomsky 1981; Abney 1987), between nominal and verbal domains (e.g., Chomsky

1970; Emonds 1970; Ogawa 2001; Megerdoomian 2008), or between syntactic and morphological structures (Baker 1985, 1988). Within the domain of syntax, one can also entertain the notion of "theoretical symmetry." Examples along this line include the symmetry between Merge and Move in the sense that Move is reanalyzed as the combination of Copy and Remerge (Chomsky 1995). Another proposal of symmetry is suggested by Brody (1995, 2000, 2002), who argues that movement (as a derivational notion) and chains (as a representational notion) express the same type of relation. Boeckx (2008) observes a strong affinity between chains and projections. He claims that a chain establishes a formal relation between the launching site, the intermediate site and the landing site (e.g., in the case of successive cyclic movement). This tripartite relation in chains finds a counterpart in projections, i.e., a full-fledged grammatical category (according to the X'-schema) consists of minimal (X^0), intermediate (X') and maximal (XP) projections.

The thesis of symmetry between linguistic modules (i.e., symmetry in a broad sense) underlies one core issue in the domain of biolinguistics (Lenneberg 1967; Hauser, Chomsky, and Fitch 2001; Jenkins 2001). Adopting the original spirit from the influential mathematical biologist D'Arcy Thompson (1917) 1961, Chomsky (2005) stresses that linguists should attempt to describe how the general law of nature helps shape the principles of grammatical structures. He terms this the "third factor," i.e., principles that are not specific to the faculty of language, yet indispensable for the development of the language faculty. Some major components of the third factor include, broadly, the principles or constraints on structural architecture and development of biological objects, and narrowly, the principles of computational efficiency which are superimposed on the core language system. Along this line of research, Vergnaud argues that occurrences as the grammatical formatives can be instantiated in any geometrical dimension and topological medium, which has a profound theoretical consequence to the study of formal recursive systems in general. Indeed, to its extreme, the formalization of occurrences potentially goes beyond Chomsky's third factor if such Chomskyan coinage is restricted to architectural constraints on biological objects. Chapter 3 leads us, as linguists, to a more thorough reexamination of the mathematical ontology of formal systems.

At first glance, the presentation in Vergnaud 2003 appears too abstract, at times metaphysical, to most linguists. To date, this paper remains largely unknown by syntacticians and phonologists. However Vergnaud's conjecture throughout the paper may potentially be a hidden treasure, and it just turns out that hidden treasure takes time to be unearthed. The situation reminds me of another paper which was originally a personal letter sent to Noam Chomsky and Howard Lasnik by a shy young linguist in early 1977. Since it was not the original intention of the author to publish that letter, the letter remains unpublished for three full decades. Until the letter is finally published as Vergnaud (1977) 2008, linguists generally refer to that work as "Vergnaud's famous personal letter." Indeed, Vergnaud's proposal of Case

Filter in that letter has now become a classic, and moreover it has paved the way for the Minimalist Program (Chomsky 1995).

The purpose of this chapter, therefore, is to bring to the fore the central spirit surrounding Vergnaud (2003), which I consider as another hidden treasure that is symmetric to the aforementioned letter. Empirical discussion is kept minimal, but relevant examples are brought up for clarification. The various grammatical structures or types of mental computation proposed in this paper are subject to examination and my discussion is, at times, inconclusive: yet, the purpose is to demonstrate the theoretical relevance between the central tenets of Vergnaud (2003) and other areas of language, and possibly areas outside language. The paper is structured as follows: I will start by summarizing the thesis of symmetry between syntax and phonology in section 2. In section 3, I will revisit the formal notion of occurrence as a computational primitive. Some extension from the discussion of occurrence with respect to the notion of chains and the ontology of syntactic structure will be stated in section 4 and 5. Section 6 concludes the paper with my understanding of Vergnaud's "last message."

2. ARE SYNTAX AND PHONOLOGY SYMMETRIC TO EACH OTHER? IF YES, IN WHAT SENSE?

The term "occurrence" was introduced in Noam Chomsky's (1955) 1975 *Logical Structure of Linguistic Theory*. Chomsky's usage initially adopted from Quine 1940:

(1) Using a device of Quine's [footnote omitted], we can identify an occurrence of a prime X in a string Y as that initial substring of Y that ends in X. (Chomsky [1955] 1975:109)

Adopting the original version (1), the sentence '# New_1 York City is in New_2 York State #' distinguishes two instances of 'New'. The occurrence of 'New_1' is its initial substring, i.e., the initial sentence boundary #, whereas that of 'New_2' is the initial substring 'New_1 *York City is in*'. While the original version of occurrence was based on linearity, its definition has undergone a number of revisions, especially since various versions of phrase structure grammars (Chomsky 1957, 1965), in which it was structure-dependent.[1] One particular case in which occurrence is a syntactic notion is through formalization of movement and chains (see section 4). A movement chain of some displaced element is a list of occurrence(s) of the moved item.[2] In the *wh*-question '*Who did John see?*', the list of occurrences of '*who*' includes the object position of '*see*' and the final landing position Spec-C. We can summarize the list by the set {*see*, Spec-C}.[3] The following definition can be viewed as a useful point of departure (Chomsky 2000:115; emphasis original):

(2) An occurrence of α in context K is the *full context* of α in K.

Chapter 3 goes beyond the commonly assumed definition of occurrence as a syntactic notion. Vergnaud argues that it is a pivotal notion that can be generalized across formal domains. In particular, it is an abstract feature of linguistic objects and moreover, the driving force of linguistic computation (see also Leung 2007). Some caveats are in order while examining chapter 3: occurrence is a formal (i.e., mathematical) feature that assumes various guises subject to domain-specific conditions. This is quite different from saying that syntax and phonology are analogous with respect to the notion of occurrence defined in a classical sense.[4] Indeed, I suspect that Vergnaud's preoccupation is not to question, for instance, whether Spec-T as an occurrence in syntax (e.g., in the case of subject raising) can find a counterpart in the phonological domain (e.g., within syllabic structures), or whether the notion of movement or copies exist in phonology.[5,6] Applying this practice in one fell swoop may run into the risk of reducing one dimension of linguistic knowledge to another, and since such an attempt is very likely to fail, one is forced to offer some ad hoc explanations to apparent irregularities. The spirit of chapter 3 transcends the narrow descriptions of syntax and phonology as two linguistic modules, and treats them as based on domain-general cognitive principles.[7] According to Vergnaud (personal communication, 2006), those cognitive principles should be based on solid mathematical foundation, as any linguistic theories/principles considered as "(virtual) conceptual necessity" (Chomsky 1995) are indeed "mathematical necessity" lest they would have zero value. That is to say, conceptualization in linguistic theorization is largely vacuous without solid mathematical foundation.[8,9] This probably explains why chapter 3 contains discussions of topological space, mathematical transformation and category theory, all of which are related to the ontology of occurrence. On the other hand, whether there exist direct analogies between syntax and phonology turns out to be an empirical issue. Readers who off-handedly skip these parts as nonsignificant would not be able to grasp the true substance of the whole work.

Such an attempt of theoretical mediation at this level of abstraction, while famously labeled as Vergnaud's lifetime achievement, may not be instantly absorbed or acknowledged, though its forthcoming theoretical consequence cannot be overestimated. The mixed reaction is implicitly well known by the linguistic public, given the observation that syntacticians and phonologists are not always keen to communicate with each other,[10] and it is a general consensus that syntactic (and resp. phonological) theory does not have much significant bearing on phonological (and resp. syntactic) theory.[11,12] Such partial mutual ignorance would be regarded as extremely weird from other scientific practices. A simple story from mathematics can illustrate this. Even long before the advent of analytic geometry by François Viète, Pierre de Fermat and René Descartes, ancient Greek mathematicians (circa 400 BC) already discovered the relation between algebra and geometry, arguably two independent mathematical systems, in the sense that algebraic equations can be solved by geometrical representations. The two fields become too intertwined in the sense that advances in one field always stem from another. It should be pointed out that, however, the modern practice of algebraic geometry is not to reduce geometry (and resp. algebra) to algebra (and resp. geometry) any more than biology to chemistry or chemistry to physics,[13] but instead to constitute a combined study whose foundation rests completely upon each individual field. Algebraic geometry has been playing such a central role in modern mathematics because of its exceeding complexity among other fields of mathematics, and since their foundation and methods stem from each individual part, their theoretical consequence can well extend to many other fields of mathematics. This explains why such a field keeps attracting the most brilliant mathematicians (Dieudonné 1972). Indeed, it is almost impossible for mathematicians to make significant progress in modern geometry without the state-of-the-art knowledge of abstract algebra, whereas on the other hand, any advance in the study of topological space stems primarily from discoveries in abstract algebra.

The preceding story apparently does not exert a strong force on linguistics, and postulating "syntactic phonology" or "phonological syntax" as an independent field of study does not seem to impress most modern linguists to date.[14] Most clear-minded linguists who witnessed the theoretical divorce between syntax and phonology since 1980s can easily list two main reasons, which are somewhat related. The first one is theory-internal. Chomsky's theory of universal grammar, to the eyes of many a linguist, appears to be conceptually biased toward syntax, in which core linguistic computation leans toward derivation of syntactic structure, and leaves the issue of phonology as tangential. Any phonological operation that possibly occurs is argued to be external to the core computation. Practitioners who adopt Chomsky's inverted T-model of syntax are also expected to abide by such theoretical imbalance between syntax and phonology. Paragraphs that illustrate such an idea abound, which are too many to list. For important quotations, see Chomsky 1995:8, 221, 229; 2004:107, 208, 136.

This theoretical drive partly initiates the advent of Optimality Theory (OT) (Prince and Smolensky 2004, first published 1993) which starts off as a theory of phonological well-formedness, markedness, and constraint ranking. There was a time when the minimalist framework and OT were on the verge of cross-fertilization. Legendre (2001:3) noticed that OT can function as a metatheory into which various substantive syntactic theories are couched.[15] However such a theoretical merger has not gained much currency, given the apparent incongruence between derivational syntax and OT as a representational theory. At best, what working OT-syntacticians do is to "prevent that a rise in explanatory adequacy goes at the expense of the descriptive adequacy of the system" (Broekhuis and Dekkers 2000:386) by placing the ranking algorithm of OT at the PF wing of the grammar (i.e., output of the core computation), a realistic yet disappointing choice.[16]

The second reason for the lack of interest in the study of parallels between syntax and phonology stems from more rudimentary and foundational issues, e.g., what syntax and phonology are, to what extent Plato's problem or the Poverty of Stimulus arises in syntax/phonology, how much syntactic/phonological knowledge is innate, to what extent syntactic/phonological modules are arbitrary and not constrained by external functions (e.g., perception), and so on (Bermúdez-Otero and Honeybone 2006:545). As a matter of fact, the list of papers presented in the Ninth Manchester Phonology Meeting's Special Session "Phonology and Syntax—the same or different?" (a good few years after both the Minimalist Program and OT had become full-fledged and dominant), some of which were published in the special issue in *Lingua* (Bermúdez-Otero and Honeybone 2006), took various angles toward the syntax–phonology parallelism. In this regard, one can immediately understand that the theoretical merger between algebra and geometry cannot apply blindly to that between syntax and phonology. The emergence of algebraic geometry as a well-defined field of mathematics stems from the fact that one can clearly identify a "conceptual bridge" between the two independent fields (Tabak 2004:103). For example, the use of coordinates can function as this bridge.[17,18] A straight line formed by linking the ordered pairs of coordinates $(0, 0)$, $(1, 1)$, $(2, 2)$, etc., can be translated into the algebraic equation $y = x$. Alternatively, until linguists agree upon a conceptual bridge between syntax and phonology, the debate of syntax–phonology parallelism would be inconclusive, whereas any empirical issue can be tangential here.[19] The central inquiry in chapter 3 is therefore the following conjecture: to what extent can we reconstruct/reduce the two modules to operations of abstract domain-general features? And what is the possible source of distinct properties in the two modules? The pursuit of domain-general descriptions in language was long argued by Vergnaud and his working colleagues, through the formulation of metrical phonology (Halle and Vergnaud 1987a, 1987b) and, in its extreme form, Government Phonology (Kaye, Lowenstamm, and Vergnaud 1980, 1985, 1990).[20] The following paragraph summarizes the spirit:[21]

(3) One sometimes hears that phonology bears no closer relationship to the rest of grammar than it does to non-linguistic systems such as, say, vision. No such point is ever made about LF by proponents of the above model [i.e., inverted T-model], a rather selective interpretation of the autonomy hypothesis. It should be kept in mind that such statements express personal opinions and carry just that weight. Indeed, they hardly rest on principled objectives, and even less on arguments of an empirical nature. (Kaye, Lowenstamm, and Vergnaud 1990:194)

Vergnaud's overall idea in chapter 3 is guided by the notion of mathematical symmetry and moreover mathematical beauty, a guiding principle for research of renowned scientists such as Paul Dirac, Hermann Weyl and Werner Heisenberg.[22] Even in the domain of syntax, Brody (2000, 2006) claims that symmetry is the norm, whereas the departures from symmetry are in need of explanation. Bearing this spirit in our mind, in the following sections, we shall revisit Vergnaud's (2003) notion of occurrences, followed by possible empirical extensions.

3.   GENERALIZING THE NOTION OF OCCURRENCE
IN GRAMMATICAL SYSTEMS

That chapter 3 focuses on the clock and the natural number system is to indicate the ubiquity of occurrences in formal systems. The one-hand clock is a self-contained formal system which abstracts away from other complexities in metrical grids and hierarchical structures, for instance the issue of leveling (see Section 4). Its elements, i.e., the integers that appear on the clock, receive two interpretations.[23] Call them *conceptual* (*cep*) and *contextual* (*tex*) respectively.[24] Vergnaud's clock model contains three elements, i.e., 0, 1, and 2, whereas at the most primitive level of complexity, each *cep* of an integer pairs with its corresponding *tex* of the same element. We can analogize them as the two sides of a coin, starting from the following set of pairings:

(4) $\{(cep_0, tex_0), (cep_1, tex_1), (cep_2, tex_2)\}$

A "bi-*cep*" or "bi-*tex*" clock that contains only "0" and "1" (i.e., $\{(cep_0, tex_0), (cep_1, tex_1)\}$), or other nonnumerical notations that possess the aforementioned dual components, can be used without losing any descriptive power, whereas on the other hand, the use of "0","1" and "2" in the absence of the pairing stated in (4) does not warrant a full-fledged clock system. When I say that *cep* and *tex* constitute the two components/interpretations of an element, I mean that (i) both are theoretically indispensable in defining an element, and (ii) one can possibly identify properties of *cep* by its corresponding *tex* (via (4)), and vice versa. This mirrors our understanding of a coin. To identify a U.S. coin (e.g., one cent) is to identify the mapping between Abraham Lincoln (i.e., *cep*) and Lincoln Memorial (i.e., *tex*), or between George Washington and the Bald Eagle in the case of a quarter. One can immediately identify a cent by either side, under the assumption that the mapping is uniform. Yet this does not entail that we can reduce one component to another, since the two components represent two different facets that define/constitute a coin. Abstractizing further, Vergnaud suggests that *cep* and *tex* represent two "occurrences" of an element. Read the following description in chapter 3 (p. 75 of this volume):[25]

> (5)   By definition, a one-one mapping from the set Σ = {A, B, C} onto itself is a particular subset of the cartesian product $\Sigma \times \Sigma$ which, in particular, includes two "occurrences" of each symbol A, B, C. An occurrence of a symbol is identified as a position of that symbol in the set-theoretic definition of the mapping.

While *cep* and *tex* represent two independent aspects (or algebraic components) of an element, Vergnaud adopts the term "occurrence" to unify them in the following sense: it provides an "index" for concepts (i.e., *cep*) and computational positions (i.e., *tex*).[26] In conceptual semantics, one always differentiates between a concept and an instance of the concept, a type and a token, a sense and a reference, and so on.[27] Thus one can understand *cep* (and resp. *tex*) as a categorial type, and cep_i (and resp. tex_i) a categorial index/token. Since occurrence is now a unifying notion, we expect that mental computation is nothing more than the mapping between occurrences, defined independently in the domain of concepts and the domain of contexts. We are led to the following claims:

(6) a. Mental computation consists of formalization of the mapping relations between occurrences in the domain of concepts and the domain of contexts, i.e., (OCC_{cep}, OCC_{tex}).[28]

b. The complexity of mapping relations corresponds to complexity of the grammatical system (see section 4).

As a result, the functions of occurrence are *indexical* and *computational*. In the formal definition suggested by Vergnaud (chapter 3, his (27)), *I* is the set of indices (i.e., occurrences) for computation.

(7) "Let *O* be some class of objects and let ω be an element of *O*. An occurrence of ω is an element of the Cartesian product *I×O*, where *I* is a set of features that naturally combine with each object in *O*."

An occurrence (in the domain *cep* or of the range *tex*) as a member of the set *I* can be computed by mathematical transformation that takes one element as an input and returns another element, hence a Cartesian product. In its simplest form, each element *n* can map onto its own *dual* (i.e., identity mapping) in forming the pair (cep_n, tex_n), which is already a result of transformation (i.e., 6a). Transformation can also be understood as the clockwise movement of the clock's hand which relates more than one element, and as a result, the following set of transformation can be generated: $\{(cep_0, tex_1), (cep_1, tex_2), (cep_2, tex_0)\}$ (i.e., 6b):

(8)

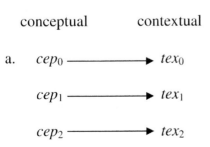

conceptual   contextual

a. $cep_0 \longrightarrow tex_0$

     $cep_1 \longrightarrow tex_1$

     $cep_2 \longrightarrow tex_2$

conceptual   contextual

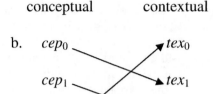

b. cep_0 tex_0

cep_1 tex_1

cep_2 tex_2

In the scenario of cyclic transformation (8b), Vergnaud defines the pair (x, y) as follows:

(9) $(x, y) =_{def}$ "any *occurrence* of x precedes an *occurrence* of y"

The particular transformation relation (x, y), especially the precedence relation between x's and y's occurrence, corresponds closely to the particular setting of the clock(-wise) system.[29] In metrical phonology, we can understand this as analogous to unidirectional parsing of metrical feet, e.g., left-to-right binary parsing feet. Example (10a) is a set of the mapping relations, whereas (10b) shows the corresponding binary metrical grid:[30]

(10) a. {(0, 1), (1, 2), (2, 0)}
     b. (σσ)
       ('σσ) σ
       ('σσ)(ˌσσ)
       ('σσ)(ˌσσ) σ
       ('σσ)(ˌσσ)(ˌσσ)

Alternatively, the following set of anticlockwise mapping relations (11a), along with the corresponding right-to-left parsing grids (11b), are equally well defined:[31]

(11) a. {(0, 2), (2, 1), (1, 0)}
     b. ('σσ)
       σ ('σσ)
       (σσ)('σσ)
       σ (σσ)(σσ)
       (σσ)(σσ)('σσ)

On the other hand, a mixture of clockwise (e.g., (0, 1), (1, 2)) and anticlockwise (e.g., (0, 2)) mapping relations cannot be defined within a single clock system:

(12) *{(0, 2), (0, 1), (1, 2)}

One immediate implication in metrical grids is that a mixture of right-to-left and left-to-right parsing at the same metrical level should be banned.[32] Such a mixture of parsing is indeed attested. Example (13) and (14) represent two cases of mixed metrical structures, contrary to expectations:[33]

(13) ('σσ)

    ('σσ) σ

    ('σσ) (͵σσ)

    ('σσ) σ (͵σσ)

    ('σσ) (͵σσ) (͵σσ)

    ('σσ) σ (͵σσ) (͵σσ)

(14) ('σσ)

    σ ('σσ)

    (͵σσ)('σσ)

    (͵σσ) σ ('σσ)

    (͵σσ)(͵σσ)('σσ)

    (͵σσ)(͵σσ) σ ('σσ)

However, further examination reveals that the "offending" parsing foot in (13) and (14) is uniform in the sense that it always aligns with the opposite edge position. In the case of (13) such as Garawa, the left edge of the first syllable always aligns with a left parenthesis (i.e., #(x), whereas Piro (i.e., (14)) is the mirror language in which the offending right parenthesis always aligns with the right edge of the last syllable (i.e., x)#). This offending parsing foot can be described by positing an edge-marking parameter (Halle and Idsardi 1995:408), and moreover it is not as iterative as normal parsing. Halle and Idsardi suggested that rule ordering exists between the edge-marking parameter/rule and the iterative rule.[34]

The mapping relation of the clock system is moreover restricted in the sense that it is *bijective*, i.e., for any n number of elements, exactly one instance of *texn* must appear in the domain (i.e., the left component) and the range (i.e., the right component). This immediately rules out the following set of mapping relations, and many others:

(15) a. {(0, 1), (2, 1), (2, 0)}

    b. {(0, 1), (1, 0), (2, 1)}

      , etc.

Translating into metrical grids, the following parsing which spans across constituents would be banned:

(16) * ($\times$ [$\times$ $\times$) $\times$]

It stands to reason that the number of possible mapping relations increases depending on the number of elements within the system. Imagine a clock with four symbols. Any of the following mapping relations will be legitimate ("$x{\rightarrow}y$" represents the mapping (x, y)):

(17) a. $0 \rightarrow 1 \rightarrow 2 \rightarrow 3 \rightarrow 0$

  b. $0 \rightarrow 1 \rightarrow 3 \rightarrow 2 \rightarrow 0$

  c. $0 \rightarrow 3 \rightarrow 2 \rightarrow 1 \rightarrow 0$

  d. $0 \rightarrow 3 \rightarrow 1 \rightarrow 2 \rightarrow 0$

  e. $0 \rightarrow 2 \rightarrow 1 \rightarrow 3 \rightarrow 0$

  f. $0 \rightarrow 2 \rightarrow 3 \rightarrow 1 \rightarrow 0$

Note that the two instances of "0" in (17) do not imply any special formal status as far as the mapping relation is concerned. To illustrate one example, (17a) can be set-theoretically represented by {(0, 1), (1, 2), (2, 3), (3, 0)}. This set is equivalent to (18b), which in turn represents the mapping relation (18a):

(18) a. $1 \rightarrow 2 \rightarrow 3 \rightarrow 0 \rightarrow 1$

  b. {(1, 2), (2, 3), (3, 0), (0, 1)}

The recursive system will be well defined, provided that the following conditions are minimally met:

(19) i. Each element $(n{>}1)$ represents a mapping between *cep* and *tex*, i.e., (*cep*, *tex*).

  ii. For $i \neq j$, each cep_i maps with exactly one tex_j, i.e., (cep_i, tex_j).

  iii. The mapping relation is *bijective*.

As a result, we can understand that a clock instantiates the mapping relation between items and contexts. Another way to instantiate this notion of occurrence is through graph theory. One can understand the notion of mapping between occurrences as forming a directed graph (or digraph). A graph consists of a set of edges E and vertices V such that each edge is a pair of vertices. A digraph in graph theory is that an edge is represented by an ordered pair of vertices (v_i, v_j), which can also be represented by a single-headed arrow. All the following graphs in (20) are digraphs which conform to conditions stated in (19) in the sense that each vertex has exactly one outgoing and one incoming edge (cf. 17):

(20)

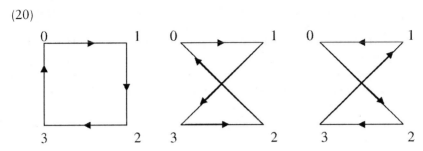

The interdependent relation between *cep* and *tex* with respect to this generalized notion of occurrence can also be shown by the natural number system (Leung 2010). Accordingly, identifying the concepts (not the numerical expressions) of numbers is tantamount to identifying the contextual relations involved. The famous Peano's axioms (PAs) that set up the list of axioms for natural numbers in (21) clearly define the successor function S that is *de facto* a contextual relation:

(21) i. *0* is a natural number.

   ii. Every natural number n has a unique successor $S(n)$ that is a natural number.

   iii. *0* is not the successor of any natural number.

   iv. No two distinct nature numbers have the same successor.

   v. Induction axiom: if *0* has a property Q and if n has Q then $s(n)$ has Q, then every natural number has Q.

As a result, we can establish a mapping relation between various natural numbers *ad infinitum*, starting from "0" which is axiomatically required:

(22) $0 \rightarrow S(0) \rightarrow S(S(0)) \rightarrow S(S(S(0)))$. . .

The axiomatic number theory becomes computable once the set of natural numbers forms a digraph by incorporating the notion of occurrence. For instance, "0" can be assigned different occurrences depending on the mapping relation. Thus "0_0" denotes the first natural number in the PAs, whereas "0_1" denotes something else depending on how the system is defined. This provides the foundation of *positional notations* in decimal systems, i.e., the integer "0" in "101" (= $1_2 0_1 1_0$) and "110" (= $1_2 1_1 0_0$) receives different interpretations based on the occurrence. S is later augmented by the rule of addition and multiplication which are indeed the extension (or short-head representations) of the contextual relation between natural numbers. Note that Classical PAs only define (21) without reference to how the system can further be used, and in this regard integers such as 1 (= $S(0)$) or 2 (= $S(S(0))$), or even the addition operator + do not belong to the original statements of PAs. Leung (2010:227) calls the incorporation of the latter properties the "Functional PAs," i.e., an extended version of natural number theory for the purpose of counting, ordering, and calculation. This numerical (and therefore contextual) relation is argued to be acquired by infants through a list of psychological experiments, in which an infant can conceptualize the arithmetic equation $1+1 = 2$ (Wynn 1992, as quoted in Dehaene 2011:41–43). More interestingly, such arithmetic competence of infants is highly abstract in the sense that numbers and objects are independently processed.[35]

4. CHAINS

Formalizing the notion of occurrence as a category for transformation immediately leads to some serious reconsideration of the notion of chains. Since Government and Binding (GB) theory, it became a consensus that the notion of chains is to capture the displacement property of language, or more specifically, the relation between the moved element and its trace. In other words, movement "forms" a chain (Chomsky 1995:251):[36]

(23) The operation Move forms the chain CH = $(\alpha, t(\alpha))$, $t(\alpha)$ the trace of α.

Indeed, whether there exists any conceptual priority between Move and chains is theory-dependent. Chains would be epiphenomenal if they are nothing but representations of the derivational history of the moved item (e.g., Chametzky 2000). Alternatively, chains can be understood as the formal way of expressing the mapping relation between elements and contexts, following the spirit in chapter 3. This option should not be left out offhandedly since even Chomsky notes that chain links are *de facto* positions (i.e., a set of occurrences), and as a result the notion of head or tail of chains can be theoretically dispensed with, by postulating CH = $<POS_1, POS_2>$ (Chomsky 1995:251–252):

(24) A set of occurrences of ω is a *chain*. (chapter 3, his (28))

Recall (6b) that the degree of *cep-tex* mapping corresponds to the degree of computational/grammatical complexity. This can be illustrated by listing various types of chains. The following list of simplified schemas exhausts the *cep-tex* mapping relations:

(25) conceptual   contextual

a.  $\{(cep_n, tex_n)\}$ for $n = 0, 1, 2$

b. 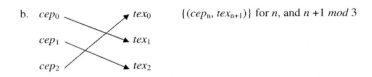 $\{(cep_n, tex_{n+1})\}$ for n, and $n + 1$ *mod* 3

c. 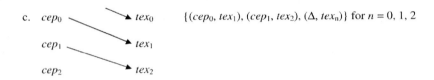 $\{(cep_0, tex_1), (cep_1, tex_2), (\Delta, tex_n)\}$ for $n = 0, 1, 2$

d. 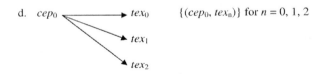 $\{(cep_0, tex_n)\}$ for $n = 0, 1, 2$

e. 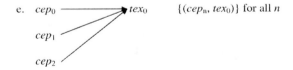 $\{(cep_n, tex_0)\}$ for all n

Chapter 3 (his (84a)) terms (25a) as "chains." For the purpose of clarity, we call this "self-chains" in the sense that they involve a mapping relation between *cep* and *tex* of the same element. Adopting Vergnaud's original notation, one can understand the pair <U, ID> as *cep*, and <U, OCC> as *tex*. Thus a self-chain is formalized as follows:

(26) {<U, ID>, <U, OCC>}, U = A, B, C (chapter 3, his (84))

Abstractizing (26) by algebraic notations, the two facets/components of an element constituent a dual pair in category theory, i.e., S and S^* (dual object):

(27) $X = \{<X, S^*>, <X, S>\}$, $X \in \Sigma$ (chapter 3, his (57))

The schema in (25b) can be called a "cyclic chain" in the sense that each *cep* maps with one and only one *tex* and the mapping is bijective. (25b) differs from (25a) in that the former is recursive, i.e., in the set of mapping relations $\{(cep_0, tex_1), (cep_1, tex_2), (cep_2, tex_0)\}$, computation starts and ends at the same element (in this case "0"). Indeed we suspect (25b) is where linguistic computation originates, with subsequent "adjustments" based on the external factors (e.g., the design features of PF and LF). This adjustment is probably only minor in the physical sense, whereas in topology or mental computation, it could be considered as a quantum leap. One outcome of this adjustment is shown in (25c), in which the cyclic chain is torn (hence a topological change) due to the design features of PF (i.e., precedence relation).[37] Vergnaud calls (25c) a "co-chain," which is based on the following list of mappings (chapter 3, his (85)):

(28) {<A, OCC>, <B, ID>}, {<B, OCC>, <C, ID>}, {<C, OCC>}

One ensuing question in (25c) is what (if any) maps onto tex_0 (i.e., <A, OCC>) so that computation remains intact given the topological change. Imagine a system that only defines precedence relation, and as a result, in the linear string *abc*, the precedence relations *a<b* and *b<c* are well-defined. However such a formal system does not define all elements in the sense that nothing precedes *a*, and *c* does not precede anything. One needs to designate a "start" symbol and an "end" symbol, to *a* and *c*, respectively. According to Vergnaud, something should map onto the peripheral string, yet this thing does not belong to the formal system in the traditional sense. He calls it "joker" Δ, which is reminiscent of Chomsky's (1955) 1975 original use of Δ as the placeholder for generalized transformation. The symbol Δ is functional and maps onto the peripheral tex_0. Since it does not bear any *cep* component, it is not really a formal element in any meaningful sense:

(29) The joker Δ whose function is to map onto the contextual feature of the peripheral element is not an element of Σ.

The "quantum leap" mentioned in the previous paragraph can be geometrically represented by the transformation from (30a) (which demonstrates the mapping relation in (25b)) to (30b) (which demonstrates the mapping relation in (25c) (cf. chapter 3, Vergnaud's (41)):

(30)

a.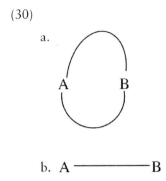

b. A —————————— B

Assume that *A*, *B* represent two points in (30a). Figure (30a) forms a cycle in the sense that one can map *A* onto *B*, then *B* onto *A*. On the other hand, (30b) (cf. 25c) is different in the sense that the mapping relation between *A* and *B* in (30b) cannot be cyclic, i.e., the line can be adequately expressed by the mapping (*A*, *B*) or (*B*, *A*), but not (*A*, *B*, *A*). In Topology, (30a) and (30b) are distinct in the sense that one cannot stretch a cycle to form a line, or extend a line to form a circle. One can only relate them by means of cutting the circle or gluing two ends of a line, which suggests that their topological properties must be different. This "cutting/gluing" operation significantly alters the mapping relations between vertices in the two figures. As a result of the transformation by means of "cutting" (in a metaphoric sense), *A* and *B* in (30b) represent two ends of a string, schematized by (31). This is, we assume, where and when the two jokers Δ emerge. On the other hand, since *A* and *B* form a cycle in (30a), the issue of postulating jokers becomes nonexistent:[38]

(31) Δ_S A————————BΔ_E (Δ_S: the start joker; Δ_E: the end joker)

This algebraic and topological nature of occurrence can be extended to syntax. That is to say, the emergence of Δ at both ends in (31) should find some relevance in syntactic structure. Assume Chomsky's version of Merge which takes two elements as the input. Consider the following (simplified) phrase structure rule (the expression of bar levels is immaterial):

(32) VP → V NP

What creates an NP? Is it the outcome of an instance of Merge? If the answer is yes, then the phrase structure rule (33a) which does not contain binary branching should be ruled out. The alternative rule (33b), while string equivalent to (33a), is theoretically more motivated:

(33)

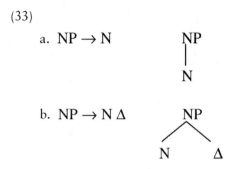

a. NP → N

b. NP → N Δ

On the other hand, if an NP may not be the product of Merge and therefore (33a) is allowed, the mechanism of Merge must be questioned. The following reply (34) by Chomsky (2008:139) shows that he has considered this forthcoming problem as a potential "crisis" to syntactic theory.[39] Yet (34) should be read with great caution, if it is not immediately ruled out as logically flawed:[40]

(34)   Suppose that a language has the simplest possible lexicon: just one LI, call it "one." Application of Merge to the LI yields{one} [*sic*], call it "two[.]" Application of Merge to{one}yields{one, {one}}, call it "three."

Schema (25d) typically describes movement chains as a list of occurrences of the moved item. Notice that this multiple mapping between *cep* and *tex* is intended to be domain general (i.e., not restricted to syntax) depending on the how the conceptual/contextual space is defined in various cognitive domains. Read Vergnaud's description in chapter 3 (p. 84 of this volume):

(35)   "In fact, mental computations in general manipulate structures in which symbols may be connected to multiplicities of adjacent symbols."

In the domain of phonology, the notion of context is mostly (though not only) linearly defined, i.e., $tex_0 > tex_1 > tex_2$ (>: linear precedence), whereas in syntax, $tex_0 > tex_1 > tex_2$ (>: c-command). Under the assumption that multiply mapped components are adjacent, it entails that the relation of linear precedence and c-command should be locally defined.[41] It should be pointed out, however, that the mapping in (25c) does not always correspond to successive cyclic movement in syntax. There exists a possibility in which a single element maps with more than one contextual feature without movement in the traditional sense. One notable example is the analysis of headless free relatives, e.g., English '*John ate whatever Mary bought*', in which the conceptual component of '*whatever*' maps onto the contextual feature of '*ate*' (as its object) and C (as its subject) simultaneously, i.e., {*ate*, C}.[42] One distinctive property of headless free relatives is the matching condition, in which the categorical feature of the *wh*-word (e.g., '*whatever*') matches with the subcategorization feature of the matrix predicate (i.e., '*ate*').[43] An imminent question is the postulation of syntactic analysis that can preserve the dual grammatical category assumed by the free relative *wh*-phrase (i.e., as a *wh*- and a nominal category).[44] Another example, currently under a lot of debate, is control structure. The issue of whether control is movement remains inconclusive, yet it is clear that the two structures share something in common at the mental computational level with respect to the complexity of mapping. In this regard, the control-as-movement debate is an indication of one's theoretical assumption. Advocates of the control-as-movement proposal attempt to understand (if not reduce) mental computation as nothing but syntactic computation, according to which any cognitive affinity between control and movement should be narrowly defined within the syntactic module. On the other hand, one can locate the affinity between movement and control within mental/conceptual computation as a separate generative system.[45]

In reverse, one can invert the mapping direction between *cep* and *tex*, shown in (25d). Is there any case in which various distinct conceptual components match with a single computational context? At first glance it looks implausible given the nature of PF/LF. However since *cep-tex* mappings are mental computations that are independent of the external conditions, what is needed to verify (25d) is having two (or more) elements that are parallel to each other with respect to their individual mapping with the contextual feature of another element. Coordination seems to be one viable candidate for serious consideration. In the sentence '*John and Mary went to the party*', both '*John*' and '*Mary*' (in addition to the conjunction '*John and Mary*') are the mental/conceptual subjects, while other factors will intervene and distinguish the two parallel elements. At the level of PF, the linear relation '*John>Mary*' is established, and such an asymmetry gives rise to other asymmetries. In some languages, the asymmetry is morphosyntactic, e.g., agreement asymmetry between the first and the second conjunct which is attested cross-linguistically. On the syntactic side, the usual assumption is that the first conjunct is somehow higher than the second conjunct, shown by various binding conditions (e.g., '*John_i and his_i mother*', *'*He_i and John_i's mother*'), which leads some linguists to suggest that the two conjuncts stand in a Specifier-Complement relation (Zhang 2009). Indeed, the parallel structure posited for coordination is not a novel idea, yet the central inquiry is at which computational level such a parallel structure should be defined.[46] The *cep-tex* mapping relation suggests that it should be couched in generalized mental computations.

5.   DIMENSIONS OF MAPPING RELATIONS AND CHAINS

Now we consider (again) the following full-fledged clock:

(36)

The movement of the three clock hands represents three transformation relations which constitute three formal systems. While all hands are projected on the same topological medium (i.e., a 2-D plane), they are distinguishable by two crucial aspects, e.g., angular speed (i.e., the longest hand moves the fastest) and the interpretation of the integers on the clock face. Moreover the three systems are built cumulatively in the sense that the angular speed of the second hand determines that of the minute hand, which in turns determines that of the hour hand. A single mapping relation at the level of hours (e.g., (0, 1)) entails a set of 60 mapping relations at the level of minutes (i.e., {(0, 1), (1, 2). . ., (59, 0)}), and moreover 3600 mapping relations at the level of seconds. This contributes to the basic desiderata of a recursive hierarchical system. Indeed, that the three formal systems can be couched in a single topological medium is based on the guiding principle that while they share the same clock signs, the clock signs receive distinct interpretations depending on the level of mapping. As a result, the integer 3 on the clock maps with the set $\{3_h, 15_m, 15_s\}$, 5 maps with $\{5_h, 25_m, 25_s\}$, and so on. This is analogous to the positional notation (mentioned earlier) that the sign '*1*' requires a contextual interpretation, and therefore their two instances in the expression '*11*' are interpreted differently. Recall (24) that a chain is a list of occurrences, i.e., a set of mapping relations between *cep* and *tex,* and as a result, twelve clock signs represent twelve independent hierarchical chains. In this regard, the clock and the decimal system are completely parallel to each other, whereas the former involves more complicated mapping relations than the latter.

Metrical and syntactic structures are further perturbations of hierarchical chains. The various levels of the metrical/syntactic structure represent distinct formal systems based on the notion of mapping that we discussed. Moreover their mutual intersection is reminiscent of Fourier analysis, in which various formal systems superimpose on each other, with the highest level being the most salient. In metrical phonology, the highest metrical grid determines the primary stress which is the most perceptually salient, whereas in syntactic structure, illocution is the most salient interpretation of CP that embeds other substructures. Since metrical/syntactic structure can receive a Fourier-type analysis, various levels of prominence can still be singled out, and various types of meaning can be forced (e.g., focus).

The various levels of mapping relations interface interestingly with chains. Under the assumption that various occurrences of "the same element" (in this case *cep*) form a chain, chapter 3 suggests that in metrical grids the various beats of the same column would form a chain. Vergnaud attributed this conjecture to Morris Halle (chapter 3, his (59)):

(37) *Halle's conjecture* (C_H)

>   Given a metrical grid *M* and some position *i* in *M*, the asterisks in the column above *i* form a chain.

As a result, the following grid contains three chains, including self-chains (indicated by a loop):

(38)

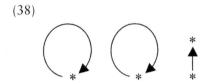

What is potentially more surprising is the syntactic notion of chains. We mentioned that a syntactic chain is a list of occurrences of the displaced item. However since various occurrences of the *same* element would form a chain (i.e., self-chains), it leads to the bold claim that (i) individual syntactic categories form a self-chain, and (ii) the category along with its projection form a chain (i.e., co-chains).[47] Note that the interface condition restricts that the projection is at most a phrasal category. In the following tree diagrams, while the nontraditional "comb" (39b) is not informatively richer than the traditional (39a), readers can easily spot out a better comparison with the metrical grids:

(39)

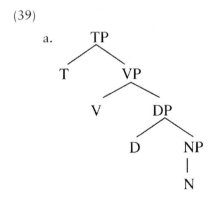

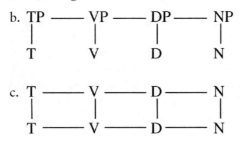

The comb (39b) can be further adjusted to the "ladder" (39c), adopting Chomsky's (1995) Bare Phrase Structure in which the label of a phrase is categorically identical to its head.[48] All connections (shown by the line) between categories can be understood as an instantiation of chains. The two layers of ordered pairs (T, V, D, N) in (39c) represent chains of two dimensions (cf. the minute and the hour hand), whereas the set {(T, T), (V, V), (D, D), (N, N)} represents the same element that maps with different contexts, i.e., self-chains (cf. positional notation).

The theoretical shift from syntactic to mental computation in chapter 3 implies the hidden claim that syntactic constituents in current theory somehow understate the conceptual relation between elements. That is to say, while it is natural to conclude that syntactic constituents (e.g., NP) represents a mental grouping, elements that are standing in mental–computational relation (i.e., *cep-tex* mapping) are not transparently expressed in syntactic structure. Vergnaud's implication is that syntactic structure is superficial, and a deeper level of computation should be pursued. In the last section of chapter 3, Vergnaud goes further and suggests that syntactic structure can be understood by a list of matching relations between the nominal and the verbal domain, which are argued to be formed by the same set of formal features. A list of co-chains is formed between the two domains. For instance cep_V maps onto tex_N, giving rise to the mental grouping (V, N), or cep_N maps onto tex_T and forms another grouping (N, T). Current syntactic theory does not fully accommodate these types of groupings, but instead maintains that VP consists of a V followed by an NP/DP (instead of an N), and NP/DP combines with T′ to form a TP. Vergnaud's suggestion is that the head–complement and spec–head relation as generally construed is poorly understood. While tree diagrams may describe the hierarchical relation between categories, they significantly understate the mental groupings between the atomic units, i.e., the conceptual and contextual components of elements.[49] This line of thought, if tenable, would have some theoretical consequences to our understanding of formal relation between categories. The basic idea is that while the subject DP (which contains a noun) is the specifier of TP (which contains a verb), the mental grouping (N, V) exist side by side (indicated by the double-headed arrow):

(40)

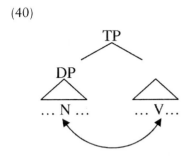

While this long-distance relation between N and V is not properly defined in current syntactic theory, such an extra-dimensional *cep-tex* mapping relation between N and V should be considered. One possible way is to supplement the relatively flat (i.e., 2-D) syntactic structure with an extra dimension that captures the N–V relation. Chapter 5 provides the full illustrations of the parallel domain between V and N, whereas Chapter 7 discusses how the 3-D grammatical structure describes DP-structures.

6. *THE* MESSAGE

The key idea in chapter 3 is that the notion of occurrence is a mental construct that abstractly defines computation at various levels of cognition. What Vergnaud attempts is to abstract from Chomsky's definition of occurrence as a syntactic position (e.g., Spec-T or Spec-C) or even a formal feature (e.g., EPP-, occurrence or edge feature), and to return to Chomsky (1955) 1975 original mention of occurrence and context in the *Logical Structure of Linguistic Theory* (which dates back to Quine's foundations of logic), i.e., occurrence is a mental/mathematical construct of contextuality and locality. The stroke between "mental" and "mathematical" should not be overestimated, since more than once Vergnaud commented that "(virtual) conceptual necessity" as a desideratum of linguistic theory (Chomsky 1995) is semantically vacuous unless it demonstrates "mathematical necessity." While it was (and will be) considered as extremely abstract and probably incomprehensible to many others, it is important (or even imperative) that chapter 3 be recirculated with more serious examination lest it would become as reclusive as its author. Chapter 3 conveys a clear message that one should not be satisfied by merely speculating on the superficial analogy/affinity between syntax and phonology, but instead unearth mental constructs that potentially assume different (sometimes distinct) guises subject to domain-specific conditions. While Vergnaud never underestimates the empirical justification of linguistic theory into which majority linguists have been delving, he understands clearly that linguistic theory eventually needs to couple with mental theory and, ultimately, a mathematical model.[50,51] As long as syntax/phonology can be couched in a theory of mental computation, sometimes conjectures and intuitions are indispensable. Maria Luisa Zubizarreta's comment captures the essence of Vergnaud's mental flow in research: "Vergnaud's thinking spanned from syntax to phonology and from phonology to syntax."[52] It is also my intense feeling that if Jean-Roger Vergnaud had been given more time, not only could he have seen the way in which abstract mathematics plants the seed for linguistic theory, but how the mental theory of language could have supplemented abstract mathematics such as graphs, groups and categories. This level of speculation would be easily considered as bold, premature or even impossible by the field at the present status. But let us briefly recap the history of this person, whose raising analysis of relative clauses is still prevalent in the field after four decades, who wrote a letter that would become a famous anecdote in the history of Syntax, whose abstract case theory which paves the way for the Minimalist Program, and who helped create the field of Charm and Government Phonology which is still an active research program. The list may well continue, but Vergnaud's message in chapter 3 is pretty clear, i.e., it is destined to be an imperfect way to make any conclusion about syntax/phonology parallelism as long as one labels himself/herself as a syntactician or a phonologist. Instead we need to jump into the two (or more) fields and get our hands dirty for detailed analyses, then withdraw ourselves to capture a bird's eye and occasionally intuitionist view. It is through the mutual feeding between microscopic and macroscopic analyses, followed by some conjectures, so that linguistic theory can thrive. Yes, this is easier said than done. But in the history of Science, a few people did seriously exercise this practice and their names marked an era. Once in a while there appeared polymaths who excelled in various fields, and their discoveries were bound to be revolutionary. As Science has evolved into its current form, it becomes more difficult to find universalists (and that's why we call them "Renaissance men"). In the field of mathematics, the famous French mathematician Henri Poincaré was probably the last mathematical universalist widely recognized. In the chapter titled "The Future of Mathematics" of *Science and Method*, we find two thought-provoking paragraphs by Poincaré (1914):

(41)   The isolated fact attracts the attention of all, of the layman as well as the scientist. But what the *true scientist* alone can see is the link that unites several facts which have a *deep but hidden analogy*. (27; emphasis added)

Of the various elements at our disposal we can form millions of different combinations, but any one of these combinations, so long as it is isolated, is absolutely without value; . . . It will be quite different as soon as this combination takes its place in a class of analogous combinations whose analogy we have recognized; we shall then be no longer in presence of a fact, but of a law. And then the *true discoverer* will not be the workman who has patiently built up some of these combinations, but the man who has brought out their relation. The former has only seen the bare fact, the latter alone has detected *the soul of the fact.* (28; emphasis added)

Jean-Roger Vergnaud may not be as prolific, popular or universalist as Henri Poincaré. It may also take generations before Vergnaud will be considered as a "universalist linguist." Only time will tell. However it is an established truth that the two figures share something in common: Both are French; both studied their first degree in the esteemed École Polytechnique; both conceptualize the meaning of analogy at a higher level of abstraction; both set an unprecedented height for scientific standard.

And more importantly, both are true discoverers, and could have made much more discoveries if they had been given more time on this imperfect planet.

NOTES

1. This is also true in phonology. The structural discussion of phonology probably started from Clements's ([1976] 1980) notion of nonlinear phonology. Halle and Vergnaud (1980) and Vergnaud (1980) further illustrated the structural aspects of phonological representations.
2. See Chomsky 1981:45, 1982, 1995:250–252, 2000:114–116, 2001:39–40, 2004:15 for discussion.
3. Other variants of occurrence have been proposed in various versions, e.g., EPP-feature (Chomsky 1995), OCC-feature (Chomsky 2004), and edge feature (Chomsky 2008). To the best of my knowledge, all of these suggestions are widely considered as purely syntactic features.
4. See Hjelmslev's ([1948] 1971) "analogie du principe structurel," and also Anderson's (2006) structural analogy.
5. Vergnaud (2003) "conjectures" the symmetry between movement and nuclear stress rule, i.e., Movement and Nuclear Stress apply in opposite directions. Readers should also be cautious about Vergnaud's passing comment that locality in syntax and obligatory contour principle in phonology stand in equivalent relation.
6. This is true even from the biolinguistic/evolutionary perspective: "The evolutionary scenario being explored here leads us to expect a close match not between syllable structure and *modern* syntax, but rather between syllable structure and the kind of syntax that developed at that stage in language evolution when vocal-tract changes and synonymy-avoidance principles jointly created a need for a syntax of some sort" (Carstairs-McCarthy 1999:151; emphasis original).
7. Cf. van Riemsdijk 2008:227: "General principles of design may very well be active in syntax and phonology in similar ways. Jean-Roger Vergnaud has always been one of the few who have insisted on the importance of exploring the formal connections between the two components of grammar." Indeed there are linguists who strive for a purely computational theory of phonology in the wake of the 'functional' Optimality Theory. Among many others, Hale and Reiss (2000a, 2000b, 2008) argue that a theory of phonological representation and computation should be driven "substance-free," i.e., without any resort to feature bundles that are phonetically or functionally

driven. The view of chapter 3 is compatible with such a view of phonology. See also Kaye 1989 and, later on, Samuels 2009 for more discussion along the same lines.

8. Vergnaud's intuition is probably based on his understanding of the development of mathematics which stays way ahead of human perception of quantity, space, structure and pattern.

9. The debate as to whether mathematical or logical foundation should form the axioms of linguistic theorization is not intended in this paper. What is at issue is whether mathematics is a branch of logic, or the other way round, or neither of them. It is however clear that Vergnaud would take a mathematical stand which is largely independent of logic and moreover that "there are notable differences between mathematicians and logicians" (personal communication, 2005).

10. One piece of evidence to show this is the paucity of conferences and workshops focusing on the issue of syntax–phonology parallelism. Probably the most notable one is the Ninth Manchester Phonology Meeting (May 2001), in which a special session is titled "Phonology and Syntax—the Same or Different?" Some outstanding papers that represent views of both sides were published in Bermúdez-Otero and Honeybone (2006).

11. It should be noted that pre-twentieth-century structuralism did not consider syntax and phonology as ontologically distinct with each other: "During the structuralist period, the relationship between phonology and syntax was largely one-sided, with phonology exerting a direct influence upon syntax" (Bermúdez-Otero and Honeybone 2006:546).

12. Indeed, the term "syntax–phonology interface," found in a great number of literatures, strongly alludes to the independent theoretical status of the two modules.

13. For instance, Scerri (1998) claims that various chemical facts within the periodic table can be adequately described by quantum physics.

14. Certainly this does not entail that there is no interaction between syntax and phonology. Since Chomsky and Halle 1968, it is well known that phonological rules may need to make reference to syntactic structure, e.g., the Nuclear Stress Rule in English. Moreover it is generally agreed upon that focus as a syntactic category usually affects intonation. Certainly phonological intonation is not exclusively entailed from syntactic structure. For discussions about the syntax–phonology interface, see Truckenbrodt 2007.

15. E.g., Government and Binding Theory (Grimshaw 1997), the Minimalist Program (e.g., Broekhuis and Dekkers 2000; Müller 2001), and Lexical-Functional Grammar (Bresnan 2000).

16. Note that not all phonologists agree with this comment. See Rennison 2000 for his blatant rejection of OT as a theory or formalism.

17. As a result, if the axioms of coordinates or analytic geometry are not preserved as such, the field of algebraic geometry will change. For instance non-Euclidean geometry rests upon different sets of axioms, yet assumes great influence on the modern theory of physics. This gave rise to algebraic topology and homology theory, which concern the transformational relation between geometry.

18. This observation also fits into Vergnaud's idea that conceptual necessity stems primarily from mathematical necessity.

19. See also Bromberger and Halle's (1989) influential remarks: "Whether the theories are or are not similar is a contingent matter to be settled in the light of the evidence, and the evidence, as far as we can tell, indicates that they are not formally similar and that the structure of phonology is best thought of as that of a deductive system" (52). "To construct phonology so that it mimics

syntax is to miss a major result of the work of the last twenty years, namely, that syntax and phonology are essentially different" (69).

20. See also Halle and Vergnaud 1987a:chapters 1 and 5 for similar conceptualization.

21. This does not entail that all the particular mechanisms of Government Phonology were strictly adopted by Vergnaud in chapter 3 (esp. given that the notion of government in syntax is dispensed with). It is also difficult to conjecture Vergnaud's latest thought on the actual instantiation of Government Phonology given the demise of Government and Binding Theory.

22. Mathematician Ian Stewart also suggests that mathematical beauty should be considered as a diagnostic of the good theory of mathematics. This is summarized by the last sentence of "Why Beauty is Truth" (Stewart 2007:208; emphasis original): "In mathematics, beauty *must* be true—because anything false is ugly."

23. Under this theoretical setting, digital clocks are analogous to analogue clocks. This also suggests that the clock hand itself may not possess any formal status in the clock system, contrary to general intuitions. Alternatively one can invent another clock system (e.g. a clock without numbers on it) in which the hand functions as a pointer of numbers.

24. Cf. chapter 3, his (48) and (57):

$X = \{<X, S^*>, <X, S>\}, X \in \Sigma$, whereas:

    a. $<X, S>$ = $_{def}$ the symbol X viewed as a member of the domain, i.e., as the left factor in a pairing $(X, \ldots)$
    b. $<X, S^*>$ = $_{def}$ the symbol X viewed as a member of the image (co-domain), i.e., as the right factor in a pairing $(\ldots, X)$

Vergnaud's use of the "left factor" and the "right factor" borrows the insights from the *bra-ket* notation in quantum mechanics. In Leung (2007: 65), I adopt a distinct dual analysis of syntactic derivation in which the conceptual component of lexical items does not play a big role. Instead each syntactic object in the course of derivation functions simultaneously as a context-provider and a context-matcher. In its simplest term, one can re-understand syntactic derivation as a list of context-providing and context-matching relations.

25. This may cause confusion among syntacticians since occurrence is understood contextually as well as conceptually. Later, in chapter 3, Vergnaud's expression of a grammatical element X as formed by the set $\{<X, ID>, <X, OCC>\}$, in which OCC represents the contextual aspect of X, would lead to misunderstanding.

26. Readers who are familiar with abstract mathematics can infer occurrence as an object of categories in Category Theory (Mac Lane 1998), in which the mapping function is structure-preserving (i.e., morphism). Indeed, the clock system, the natural number system and graphs are themselves instantiations of categories.

27. Cf. Jackendoff 1983, 1997, 2002; Langacker 2008.

28. This idea is adopted in Leung 2001:223 with respect to the property of formal systems in general: "Local relations as defined by the computations between elements and contexts adequately define the formal grammar of natural language, and moreover any formal system."

29. Mental computation of higher complexity can define (x, y) in other ways. In the domain of syntax, occurrence can be defined as the various syntactic positions that an element occupies, i.e., A- and A'-positions. See section 4 for details.

30. E.g., Pintupi (Hansen and Hansen 1969, as quoted in Kager 2007).

31. E.g., Warao (Osburn 1966, as quoted in Kager 2007:202).

32. Halle and Vergnaud (1987a:112) noted that such a mixed parsing grid can be generated by a "flip-flop" algorithm in the following order: (i) construct a constituent at the left end, (ii) construct a constituent at the right end, (iii) construct a constituent to the right of the constituent defined at (i), (iv) construct a constituent to the left of the constituent defined at (ii). They noted that such complex iterative algorithms are not found in grammars.

33. E.g., Garawa (Furby 1974, as quoted in Kager 2007) and Piro (Matteson 1965, as quoted in Kager 2007).

34. The spirit of the independence between the two rules is well preserved in the OT constraint ranking algorithm. See Kager 2007 for illustrations.

35. An infant does not show any sign of surprise if one object is changed to another, as long as no objects vanish or are created during the process (Deheane 2011:44). Note that there is a limit to the infant's arithmetic capacity, and one should not be surprised to find out that infants cannot tell the difference between "2+2=3", "2+2=4" or "2+2=5" by experimental settings.

36. The assumption that syntactic chains are the result of movement operations is too widespread in the literature. See, among others, Chomsky 1981, 1982, 1995, 2008; Cheng and Corver 2006; Hornstein 1998, 2008; Nunes 2004; Rizzi 2006

37. Carnie (2008:37–45) has a succinct discussion of precedence and its relation with hierarchical trees.

38. One can also understand the emergence of jokers as a reaction to the interface condition, i.e., a sentence has a beginning and an end at PF. I stress the term "PF" because the abstract syntactic structure as generally understood may be defined independently of linear relations. This is especially true if we consider the formation of a sentence as consisting of set-merge (Chomsky 2001), i.e., members of sets are unordered.

39. This reminds us of the famous *Grundlagenkrise der Mathematik* in the history of foundations of mathematics which appeared in the early twentieth century.

40. Moreover, Chomsky strongly argues that Merge has both formal and evolutionary status. This can be the boldest claim I have ever heard from any scientific theory proposed by any scientist, i.e., the statement of scientific theory suggests itself an evolutionary fable. Since this paper is not a critic of the biolinguistic thesis of Chomsky, I will leave this issue to future work.

41. Locality also fits into Chomsky's third factor as adjacent mapping is more computationally efficient.

42. For detailed discussions, see Leung 2007.

43. See the original discussion of the matching condition by Bresnan and Grimshaw (1978) and Groos and van Riemsdijk (1981).

44. For various proposals, see Citko 2000, 2005; Donati 2006; Chomsky 2008; Ott 2011.

45. See Hornstein 1999, 2001, 2008; Boeckx and Hornstein 2004, 2006 and Boeckx, Hornstein, and Nunes 2010 for the control-as-movement proposal and Landau 1999, 2000, 2003, Culicover and Jackendoff 2001 and Jackendoff and Culicover 2003 for counterarguments. Interestingly, the spirit of unifying control and movement was proposed in other nonmovement theory of grammar, e.g., Langacker 2008.

46. What is of great importance is the theoretical relation between coordination and subordination/dependency relation, which possibly dictates the syntactic treatment. For important discussions of this issue, see Dik 1968; Goodall 1987; Culicover and Jackendoff 1997.

47. This reminds us of Chomsky's (1995) Bare Phrase Structure, in which the label of a phrase is categorically identical to its head, i.e., Merge $(a, b) = \{a, \{a, b\}\}$, a is the label of projection.

48. Of some relevance is Brody's (2000) Mirror Principle.
49. Collins 2002 can be treated as one attempt to formalize such a mapping relation in the absence of labels and phrasal categories.
50. The tension between generality and empirical details extends equally to Science in general: "If abstractness and generality have obvious advantages of the kind indicated, it is also true that they sometimes have serious drawbacks for those who must be interested in details" (Bell 1965:528).
51. Jenkins (2001:3n5) notes that "abstract computations are evidence on a par with any other kind of biological evidence."
52. http://dornsife.usc.edu/news/stories/876/in-memoriam-jean-roger-vergnaud-65.

REFERENCES

Abney, S. 1987. The English noun phrase in its sentential aspect. Doctoral dissertation, MIT.

Anderson, S. 2006. Structural analogy and universal grammar. *Lingua* 116:601–633.

Baker, M. C. 1985. The mirror principle and morphosyntactic explanation. *Linguistic Inquiry* 16:373–416.

———. 1988. *Incorporation: A Theory of Grammatical Function Changing.* Chicago: University of Chicago Press.

Bell, E. T. 1965. The last universalist. In *Men of Mathematics.* New York: Simon and Schuster.

Bermúdez-Otero, R., and P. Honeybone. 2006. Phonology and syntax: A shifting relationship. *Lingua* 116:543–561.

Boeckx, C. 2003. *Islands and Chains.* Amsterdam: John Benjamins.

———. 2008. *Bare Syntax.* Oxford: Oxford University Press.

———, and N. Hornstein. 2004. Movement under control. *Linguistic Inquiry* 35:431–452.

———, and N. Hornstein. 2006. The virtues of control as movement. *Syntax* 9:118–130.

———, N. Hornstein, and J. Nunes. 2010. *Control as Movement.* Cambridge: Cambridge University Press.

Bresnan, J. 2000. Optimal syntax. In *Optimality Theory: Phonology, Syntax, and Acquisition,* ed. by J. Dekkers, F. van der Leeuw, and J. van de Weijer. Oxford: Oxford University Press.

———, and J. Grimshaw. 1978. The syntax of free relatives in English. *Linguistic Inquiry* 9:331–391.

Brody, M. 1995. *Lexico-Logical Form: A Radically Minimalist Theory.* Cambridge, MA: MIT Press.

———. 2000. Mirror theory: Syntactic representation in perfect syntax. *Linguistic Inquiry* 31:29–56.

———. 2002. On the status of derivations and representations. In *Derivation and Explanation in the Minimalist Program,* ed. by S. Epstein and D. Seely. Blackwell: Oxford.

———. 2006. Syntax and symmetry. Ms., ling.auf.net/lingbuzz/000260.

Broekhuis, H., and J. Dekkers. 2000. The minimalist program and optimality theory: Derivations and evaluations. In *Optimality Theory: Phonology, Syntax, and Acquisition,* ed. by J. Dekkers, F. van der Leeuw, and J. van de Weijer. Oxford: Oxford University Press.

Bromberger, S., and M. Halle. 1989. Why phonology is different. *Linguistic Inquiry* 20:51–70.

Carnie, A. 2008. *Constituent Structure*. Oxford: Oxford University Press.

Carstairs-McCarthy, A. 1999. *The Origins of Complex Language*. Oxford: Oxford University Press.

Chametzky, R. A. 2000. *Phrase Structure: From GB to Minimalism*. Oxford: Blackwell.

Cheng, L., and N. Corver, eds. 2006. *Wh-Movement on the Move*. Cambridge, MA: MIT Press.

Chomsky, N. (1955) 1975. *The Logical Structure of Linguistic Theory*. New York: Plenum.

———. 1957. *Syntactic Structures*. The Hague: Mouton.

———. 1965. *Aspects of the Theory of Syntax*. Cambridge, MA: MIT Press.

———. 1970. Remarks on nominalization. In *Readings in English Transformational Grammar*, ed. by R. Jacobs and P. Rosenbaum. Waltham, MA: Blaisdell.

———. 1981. *Lectures on Government and Binding*. Dordrecht, Netherlands: Foris.

———. 1982. *Some Concepts and Consequences of the Theory of Government and Binding*. Cambridge, MA: MIT Press.

———. 1995. *The Minimalist Program*. Cambridge, MA: MIT Press.

———. 2000. Minimalist inquiries: The framework. In *Step by Step*, ed. by R. Martin, D. Michaels, and J. Uriagereka. Cambridge, MA: MIT Press.

———. 2001. Derivation by phase. In *Ken Hale: A Life in Language*, ed. by M. Kenstowicz. Cambridge, MA: MIT Press.

———. 2004. Beyond explanatory adequacy. In *Structures and Beyond*, ed. by A. Belletti. Oxford: Oxford University Press.

———. 2005. Three factors in the language design. *Linguistic Inquiry* 36:1–22.

———. 2008. On phases. In *Foundational Issues in Linguistic Theory*, ed. by R. Freidin, C. P. Otero, and M. L. Zubizarreta. Cambridge, MA: MIT Press.

———, and M. Halle. 1968. *The Sound Pattern of English*. New York: Harper and Row.

Citko, B. 2000. *Parallel Merge and the Syntax of Free Relatives*. Doctoral dissertation, State University of New York, Stony Brook.

———. 2005. On the nature of merge: External merge, internal merge, and parallel merge. *Linguistic Inquiry* 36:475–496.

Clements, G. N. (1976) 1980. *Vowel Harmony in Nonlinear Generative Phonology: An Autosegmental Model*. Bloomington, IN: Reproduced by the Indiana University Linguistics Club.

Collins, C. 2002. Eliminating labels. In *Derivation and Explanation in the Minimalist Program*, ed. by S. D. Epstein and T. D. Seely. Oxford: Blackwell.

Culicover, P. W., and R. Jackendoff. 1997. Semantic subordination despite syntactic coordination. *Linguistic Inquiry* 28:195–217.

———. 2001. Control is not movement. *Linguistic Inquiry* 32:493–512.

Dehaene, S. 1999. *The Number Sense*. Oxford: Oxford University Press.

Dieudonné, J. 1972. The historical development of algebraic geometry. *The American Mathematical Monthly* 79:827–866.

Dik, S. C. 1968. *Coordination: Its Implications for the Theory of General Linguistics*. Amsterdam: North-Holland.

Donati, C. 2006. On wh-head-movement. In *Wh-Movement on the Move*, ed. by L. Cheng and N. Corver. Cambridge, MA: MIT Press.

Emonds, J. 1970. Root and structure preserving transformations. Doctoral dissertation, MIT.

Géraldine, L., J. Grimshaw, and S. Vikner. 2001. *Optimality-Theoretic Syntax*. Cambridge, MA: MIT Press.

Goodall, G. 1987. *Parallel Structures in Syntax*. Cambridge: Cambridge University Press.

Grimshaw, J. 1997. Projection, heads, and optimality. *Linguistic Inquiry* 28:373–422.

Groos, A., and H. van Riemsdijk. 1981. The matching effects in free relatives: A parameter of core grammar. In *Theory of Markedness in Generative Grammar*, ed. by A. Belletti, L. Brandi, and L. Rizzi. Pisa, Italy: Scuola Normal Superiore.

Hale, M., and C. Reiss. 2000a. Phonology as cognition. In *Phonological Knowledge: Conceptual and Empirical Issues*, ed. by N. Burton-Roberts, P. Carr, and G. Docherty. Oxford: Oxford University Press.

———. 2000b. Substance abuse and dysfunctionalism: Current trends in phonology. *Linguistic Inquiry* 31:157–169.

———. 2008. *The Phonological Enterprise*. Oxford: Oxford University Press.

Halle, M., and W. Idsardi. 1995. General properties of stress and metrical structure. In *A Handbook of Phonological Theory*, ed. by J. Goldsmith. Oxford: Basil Blackwell.

Halle, M., and J.-R. Vergnaud. 1980. Three-dimensional phonology. *Journal of Linguistic Research* 1:83–105.

———. 1982. On the framework of autosegmental phonology. In *The Structure of Phonological Representations*, vol. 1, ed. by H. van der Hulst and N. Smith. Dordrecht, Netherlands: Foris.

———. 1987a. *An Essay on Stress*. Cambridge, MA: MIT Press.

———. 1987b. Stress and the cycle. *Linguistic Inquiry* 18:45–84.

Hauser, M., N. Chomsky, and W. Fitch. 2001. The faculty of language: What is it, who has it, and how did it evolve? *Science* 298:1569–1579.

Hayes, B. 1995. *Metrical Stress Theory: Principles and Case Studies*. Chicago: University of Chicago Press.

Hjelmslev, L. (1948) 1971. Le verbe et la phrase nominale. In *Mélanges de Philologie, de Littérature et d'Histoire Anciennes Offerts*, ed. by J. Marouzeau. Repr. in L. T. Hjelmslev, *Essais linguistiques*. Paris: Editions de Minuit.

Hornstein, N. 1999. Movement and control. *Linguistic Inquiry* 30:69–96.

———. 2001. *Move! A Minimalist Theory of Construal*. Oxford: Blackwell.

———. 2008. *A Theory of Syntax*. Cambridge: Cambridge University Press.

Jackendoff, R. 1983. *Semantics and Cognition*. Cambridge, MA: MIT Press.

———. 1997. *The Architecture of the Language Faculty*. Cambridge, MA: MIT Press.

———. 2002. *Foundations of Language*. Oxford: Oxford University Press.

———, and P. Culicover. 2003. The semantic basis of control in English. *Language* 79:517–556.

Jenkins, L. 2001. *Biolinguistics*. Cambridge: Cambridge University Press.

Kager, R. 2007. Feet and metrical stress. In *Cambridge Handbook of Phonology*, ed. by P. de Lacy. Cambridge: Cambridge University Press.

Kaye, J. 1989. *Phonology: A Cognitive View*. Hove: Lawrence Erlbaum Associates.

———, J. Lowenstamm, and J.-R. Vergnaud. 1985. The internal structure of phonological representations: A theory of Charm and Government. *Phonology Yearbook* 2:305–328.

———, J. Lowenstamm, and J.-R.Vergnaud. 1990. Constituent structure and government in phonology. *Phonology Yearbook* 7:193–231.

Landau, I. 1999. Elements of control. Doctoral dissertation, MIT.

———. 2000. *Elements of Control: Structure and Meaning in Infinitival Constructions*. Dordrecht, Netherlands: Kluwer.

———. 2003. Movement out of control. *Linguistic Inquiry* 34:471–498.

Langacker, R. 2008. *Cognitive Grammar*. Oxford: Oxford University Press.

Legendre, G. 2001. Introduction to Optimality Theory in syntax. In *Optimality-Theoretic Syntax*, ed. by G. Legendre, J. Grimshaw, and S. Vikner. Cambridge, MA: MIT Press. 1–27.

Lenneberg, E. H. 1967. *Biological Foundations of Language*. Oxford: John Wiley.

Leung, T. 2007. Syntactic derivation and the theory of matching contextual features. Doctoral dissertation, University of Southern California.

——. 2010. On the mathematical foundations of crash-proof syntax. In *Exploring Crash-Proof Grammar*, ed. by M. T. Putnam. Amsterdam: John Benjamins.

Liberman, M. 1975. The intonational system of English. Doctoral dissertation, MIT.

——, and A. Prince. 1977. On stress and linguistic rhythm. *Linguistic Inquiry* 8:249–336.

Mac Lane, S. 1998. *Categories for the Working Mathematician*. 2nd ed. New York: Springer.

Megerdoomian, K. 2008. Parallel nominal and verbal projections. In *Foundational Issues in Linguistic Theory*, ed. by R. Freidin, C. P. Otero, and M. L. Zubizarreta. Cambridge, MA: MIT Press.

Müller, G. 2001. Order preservation, parallel movement, and the emergence of the unmarked. In *Optimality-Theoretic Syntax*, ed. by G. Legendre, J. Grimshaw, and S. Vikner. Cambridge, MA: MIT Press.

Nunes, J. 2004. *Linearization of Chains and Sideward Movement*. Cambridge, MA: MIT Press.

Ogawa, Y. 2001. *A Unified Theory of Verbal and Nominal Projections*. Oxford: Oxford University Press.

Ott, D. 2011. A note on free relative clauses in the theory of phases. *Linguistic Inquiry* 42:183–192.

Poincaré, H. 1914. *Science and Method*. Trans. by Francis Maitland. London: Thomas Nelson.

Prince, A, and P. Smolensky. 2004. *Optimality Theory: Constraint Interaction in Generative Grammar*. Oxford: Basil Blackwell. [First published as Technical Report TR-2, Rutgers Center for Cognitive Science, Rutgers University, New Brunswick, NJ, 1993.]

Quine, W. V. O. 1940. *Mathematical Logic*. Boston: Harvard University Press.

Rennison, J. 2000. OT and TO—on the status of OT as a theory and formalism. *The Linguistic Review* 17:135–141.

Riemsdijk, H. C. van. 2008. Identity avoidance: OCP effects in Swiss relatives. In *Foundational Issues in Linguistic Theory*, ed. by R. Freidin, C. P. Otero, and M. L. Zubizarreta. Cambridge, MA: MIT Press.

Rizzi, L. 2006. On the form of chains: Criterial positions and ECP effects. In *Wh-Movement on the Move*, ed. by L. Cheng and N. Corver. Cambridge, MA: MIT Press.

Samuels, B. 2009. The third factor in phonology. *Biolinguistics* 3:355–382.

Scerri, E. R. 1998. How good is the quantum mechanical explanation of the periodic table? *Journal of Chemical Education* 75:1384–1385.

Stewart, I. 2007. *Why Beauty Is Truth*. New York: Basic Books.

Tabak, J. 2004. *Mathematics and the Laws of Nature*. New York: Facts on File.

Thompson, D. (1917) 1961. *On Growth and Form*. Cambridge: Cambridge University Press.

Truckenbrodt, H. 2007. The syntax–phonology interface. In *Cambridge Handbook of Phonology*, ed. by P. de Lacy. Cambridge: Cambridge University Press.

Vergnaud, J.-R. (1977) 2008. Letter to Noam Chomsky and Howard Lasnik on "Filters and Control," April 17, 1977. In *Foundational Issues in Linguistic Theory*, ed. by R. Freidin, C. P. Otero, and M. L. Zubizarreta. Cambridge, MA: MIT Press.

——. 1980. A formal theory of vowel harmony. In *Issues in Vowel Harmony*, ed. by R. M. Vago. Amsterdam: John Benjamins.

——. 2003. On a certain notion of "occurrence": The source of metrical structure, and of much more. In *Living on the Edge: 28 Papers in Honour of Jonathan Kaye*, ed. by S. Ploch. Berlin: Mouton de Gruyter.

Zhang, N. N. 2009. *Coordination in Syntax*. Cambridge: Cambridge University Press.

5   Some Explanatory Avatars of Conceptual Necessity
Elements of UG*+

Jean-Roger Vergnaud

1.   INTRODUCTION

Consider the following forms in German:[1]

(1) a. Peter hat **oft dieses Buch** gelesen.
    b. Peter hat **dieses Buch oft** gelesen.

(2) a. Peter hat **oft ein Buch** gelesen.
    b. Peter hat **ein Buch oft** gelesen.

(3) a. *Peter hat **gut dieses Buch** gelesen.
    b. Peter hat **dieses Buch gut** gelesen.

(4) a. *Peter hat **gut ein Buch** gelesen.
    b. Peter hat **ein Buch gut** gelesen.

With respect to the distribution of noun phrases in German, it has been shown that:

(5) (i) while the form *dieses Buch* is a DP, the form *ein Buch* should be analyzed as a bare NP (one without any determiner);

    (ii) the adverbs *oft* and *gut* in (1)–(4) are adjoined at different "heights" within the verb phrase.

(see Prinzhorn 1996; Cinque 1999; Diesing 1992). We assume that "event oriented" adverbs such as *gut* or *oft*, as opposed to subject oriented or speaker oriented adverbs (see Jackendoff 1972), are adjoined within the extended projection of V. The hypothesis in (5ii) can then be schematized as in (6), where φ_0 and φ_1 are two functional categories in the extended projection of V:

(6)

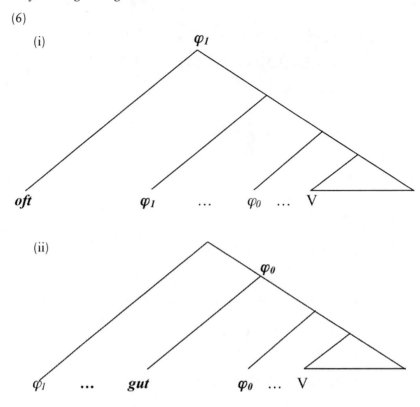

Under the hypotheses above, the most natural interpretation of the paradigm in (1) is that the structural size of a specifier is correlated with that of its X-bar sister. More precisely, (1) suggests the law in (7) (see Prinzhorn 1996):

(7)   Let $X^{\omega} = \{X^1, \ldots, X^n\}$ be a set of (strict or extended) projections of the lexical item X^0, where X^{i+1} immediately dominates X^i, $1 \leq i \leq n$. A specifier of X^i is structurally smaller (in the same sense as in "small clause") than a specifier of X^{i+k}, $k>1$.

This essay stems from a conjecture proposed by M. Prinzhorn in a seminar in Vienna in 1996 in order to derive the distributional law in (7). The conjecture reads as a grammatical version of Archimedes' Principle:

(8)   In the structure $[_X\ Y\ X']$, X the head of X', X' and Y must be of equal structural size.

By (8), for example, a constituent whose specifier is a bare NP must be smaller than one whose specifier is a DP, which is the paradigm (1). The conjecture in (8) is conceptually related to Williams's notion of small clauses, proposed in Williams 1971 and revived in Williams 2003. The theory presented in this essay, however, significantly differs from Williams'. It is founded on Chomsky's hypothesis that a constituent may be explicitly designated as the occurrence of some other constituents by means of an "edge feature" (see Chomsky 1998, 1999, 2001, 2004). In Chomsky 2004, edge features are intended as triggers of A'-movement:

> (9) "It may be that phase heads have an edge feature, sometimes called an "EPP-feature" (by extension of the notion EPP), or an "occurrence feature" OCC because the object formed is an occurrence of the moved element in the technical sense. This edge feature permits raising to the phase edge without feature matching." (p. 15)

Call this the *Items and Contexts Architecture* (ICA). It will be argued that ICA governs A-movement as well. In essence, an *uninterpretable feature* Φ^* will be defined as the "edge version" of some corresponding interpretable feature *F*:

> (10) $\Phi^* = [-F]$, for some interpretable *F*

Following these lines, A-movement (*passive, raising,* certain types of *scrambling, QR,* etc.) is ultimately identified with the distributional law in (7), a refinement and a generalization of Kuroda's original proposal concerning the structure of VP (Kuroda 1988):

> (11) Let $(_U X U)$ be some constituent, *X* the specifier of *U*. *A-movement of X* is the transformation in (i), where *Y, W* are lexical items and $[_\alpha \alpha, \beta]$ is the labeled constituent generated by *Merge(α, β)*:
>
> (i) a. **Input:**
>
> $(_U X U)$
>
>   b. Operations:
>
>   Merge(*Y, X*)
>
>   Merge(*W, U*)
>
>   Merge($[_W W, U]$, $[_Y Y, X]$)

The transformation in (i) is schematized in (ii):

> (ii) $(_U X U) \rightarrow (_W (_Y Y X) (_W W U))$

The transformation in (i) preserves the *specifier-of* relation in the following sense:

> (iii) The extension of the specifier of *U* is the specifier of the extension of *U*.

Informally:

> (12) A-movement is the "parallel growth" of two sister constituents, one the specifier of the other. At each stage, the merging of a head with one constituent is mirrored by the merging of a corresponding head with its sister constituent.

Preliminary formalizations and applications of that idea are found in Megerdoomian 2002 and Vergnaud and Zubizarreta 2001.

Thus, "reconstruction" in A-movement is by necessity partial. This corroborates the conclusions in Chomsky 1995[2] and Lasnik 1999. It would also appear to strengthen the standard unification of A- and A'-movement, since partial reconstruction is the hallmark of *wh*-movement (see Chomsky 1993, 1995; Fox 2000). Nevertheless, we will argue that the two types of movements are distinct, much along the lines of van Riemsdijk and Williams 1981. Indeed, it will be argued that an essential difference between A- and A'-movement is in the nature of the *trace* left by movement: in A'-movement, by contrast with A-movement, the trace is a full copy of the moved constituent, minus the *wh* feature. Another essential difference between the two kinds of movement, related to the first, is that A-movement is strictly phase internal, whereas A'-movement links positions at edges of phases (see sections 11 and 12).[3] This dovetails with the fact that edge properties of phases are typically discourse related. The increased theoretical heterogeneity will be more than offset by the combination of *checking*, the *EPP* and Baker's *Mirror Principle* into a unique structural principle (section 9). Independently, the generalization of ICA to A-movement will indirectly support the theory of argument structure developed in Hale and Keyser 1993, 2002 (in particular, with regard to the possible lexical configurations and to the distribution of specifiers among those).

The general framework is that developed in the course of the past fifty years (see Chomsky [1955] 1975, 1957, 1965, 1995, 1999, 2000, 2004, and references there). This essay follows guiding ideas in these works, as well as in Hornstein and Nunes 2002 and in Lasnik and Uriagereka 2005. It should provide a unification of recent proposals and analyses developed within the Minimalist Program, most notably those referred to earlier and those relating to Kayne's LCA and to the notion of "remnant movement." At a deeper level, central structural principles of syntax will be unified with the theory of PF strings developed in Halle 2008, Halle and Harris 2005, Raimy 1999, 2001, or so we hope.

2. A PRESENTATION OF THE ESSAY: THE CENTRAL HYPOTHESES

The definition in (11) can be viewed as a particular execution of the proposal in Chomsky 1995 concerning A-movement (326–327). An essential observation is that the negation in the sentence in (13) cannot have wide scope over the quantifier *every*:[4]

(13) Everyone seems (not to be there yet).

The structural description of the sentence in (13) must then have the properties in (14) (irrelevant details omitted):

(14) (i) it contains the constituent *(everyone)*

    (ii) it contains the constituent *(everyone seems not to be there yet)*

    (iii) it contains the constituent *(one there yet)*

    (iv) it does **not** contain the constituent *(everyone not to be there yet)*

The property in (14iii) is necessary to account for the thematic relation holding between the NP *one* and the predicate *there*. That property is at the core of the transformational analysis of such forms. A structural description with the properties in (14) includes one or several relations of the form in (11ii).

The same formal structure is found in the case of the raising of a subject from the specifier position of VP to the specifier position of TP. An adequate treatment of that transformation must rely on a conjecture in Lasnik and Uriagereka 2005, which notes that the uniformity of structural organization across categories suggests a symmetry principle. The idea is taken up and developed in section 6, where it is be argued that the extended projection of N and that of V (or v) are constructed from the same primitive formatives arranged in the same hierarchical order (cf. the principle of Categorial Symmetry in (134) in section 6). For concreteness, the ordered sets of components in (15) are postulated for the V and the N systems (see Borer 2004; *R* stands for "Root" in the sense of Marantz 1997, *Asp* stands for "Aspect," and *CL* for "Classifier"):

(15) (i) T, Asp, V, R

    (ii) D, CL, N, R

The abstract system of functional categories should turn out to be richer than assumed previously, but the reduced system in (15) will suffice for our illustration. The combination of a VP with a DP specifier is described as the family of constituent structures in (16):

(16) (i) $(_T T (_{Asp} Asp (_v V R)))$

    (ii) $(_D D (_{CL} CL (_N N R)))$

    (iii) $(_v (_v V R) (_N N R))$

    (iv) $(_{Asp} (_{Asp} Asp (_v V R)) (_{CL} CL (_N N R)))$

    (v) $(_T (_T T (_{Asp} Asp (_v V R))) (_D D (_{CL} CL (_N N R))))$

The collection of structures in (16iii–v) constitutes an instance of A-movement as defined in (11).

This essay provides an account of A-movement based on two hypotheses. The first hypothesis is stated in (17):

(17) The standard *X*-bar schema must be resolved into two formally independent kinds of Merge: *Head-Merge,* which yields *iterated head-complement structures* (IHC) structures, and *EPP-Merge,* which pairs the structures produced by Head-Merge.

This is schematized in (18), where *X, Y, Z, U, V, W* are lexical items:

(18)

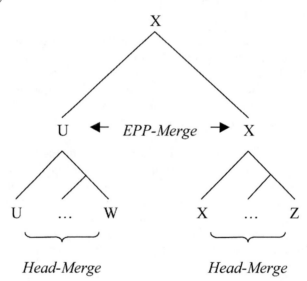

Ultimately, the new *X*-bar architecture in (18) generalizes the analysis in Larson 1988 along the lines in (19) (see section 4):

(19) (i) Every *argument* is analyzed as a *specifier.*

   (ii) The relation *complement-of* is restricted to the formatives that constitute an *extended projection* (in the sense of Grimshaw 1991).

To illustrate, the description in (16) will be analyzed into the two subfamilies in (20):

(20) (a) Constituent structure generated by Head-Merge

   (i) $(_T T (_{Asp} Asp (_V V R)))$

   (ii) $(_D D (_{CL} CL (_N N R)))$

(b) Constituents generated by EPP-Merge

    (i) $(_V$ (V R) (N R))

    (ii) $(_{Asp}$ (Asp V R) (CL N R))

    (iii) $(_T$ (T Asp V R) (D CL N R))

The second fundamental hypothesis underlying the treatment of A-movement in this essay is that the labeling relation in an IHC structure is an *equivalence* in the sense of (21) (see Brody 1997, 2000):

(21) Let Σ be a structural description and let H^* be an IHC arrangement in Σ. Let h^0 and h^1 be a head and its projection, respectively, in H^*. The structural description Σ can be identified with the pair $\{\Sigma[h^0/h^1],$ $h^1\}$, where $\Sigma[h^0/h^1]$ is the structural description obtained from Σ by substituting h^0 for h^1 in Σ:

    (i) $\Sigma \equiv \{\Sigma[h^0/h^1], h^1\}$

Borrowing the term from Brody 1997, 2000, we call *telescoping* the relation in (21i), which is defined here as an equivalence (see also Manzini 1995, 1997, 1998). To illustrate, the IHC structures in (20ai) and (20aii) can be equated with the systems of binary constituents in (22i) and (22ii), respectively:

(22) (i) $(_T$ T Asp), $(_{Asp}$ Asp V), $(_V$V R)

     (ii) $(_D$ D CL), $(_{CL}$ CL N), $(_N$ N R)

Similarly, the three constituents created by EPP-Merge in (20bi), (20bii), and (20biii) can be identified with the three tuplets in (23i), (23ii), and (23iii), respectively, where Y•X denotes the head-complement structure $(_Y$ Y X):

(23) (i) $<(_V$ V N), {V•R}, {N•R}>

     (ii) $<(_{Asp}$ Asp CL), {Asp•V, V•R}, {CL•N, N•R}>

     (iii) $<(_T$ T D), {T•Asp, Asp•V, V•R}, {D•CL, CL•N, N•R}>

Ultimately, every structural description can be reduced by telescoping to a system Ω with the properties in (24):

(24) (i) Ω is a family $\{_{i \in I}\, \omega_i\}$ of arrays of primitive binary combinations (constituents or operations) of the form *(U W)*, where *U* and *W* are lexical items.

     (ii) Each array ω_i in Ω is subdivided into three subarrays $\omega_{i,H1}$, $\omega_{i,H2}$ and $\omega_{i,E}$, where $\omega_{i,H1}$, $\omega_{i,H2}$ are arrays of primitive combinations effected by Head-Merge, and $\omega_{i,E}$ is an array of primitive combinations effected by EPP-Merge.

For example, the array in (23), which represents the structure in (16), is analyzed into the three subarrays in (25):

(25)   (i) {T•Asp, Asp•V, V•R}

     (ii) {D•CL, CL•N, N•R}

     (iii) {($_T$ T D), ($_{Asp}$ Asp CL), ($_V$ V N)}

It appears then that an array ω_i in a reduced structural description $\Omega = \{_{i \in I}\ \omega_i\}$ can be schematized as a $2 \times n$ matrix in which each row represents a maximal "connected" family of applications of Head-Merge and each column represents an application of EPP-Merge. This matrix format is displayed in (26) and interpreted in accordance with the rules in (27) and the notion of structural equivalence in (21):

(26)

H_{1n}	...	$H_{1(j+1)}$	H_{1j}	...	H_{12}	H_{11}
H_{2n}	...	$H_{2(j+1)}$	H_{2j}	...	H_{22}	H_{21}

(27)   (i) Two adjacent lexical items $H_{i(j+1)}$ and H_i in row i such that $H_{i(j+1)}$ precedes H_i are Head-Merged into a constituent labeled by $H_{i(j+1)}$.

     (ii) The two lexical items H_{1j} and H_{2j} in column j are EPP-Merged into a constituent labeled by H_{1j}.

We shall call a matrix such as that in (28) a *Chomsky tableau* or *C-tableau*. To illustrate, the structure in (16) will be represented by the C-tableau (28):

(28)

T	Asp	V	R
D	CL	N	R

Given a family Ω of C-tableaux, structural descriptions equivalent to Ω are obtained by applying the telescoping relation in (21i). For example, combining the jth column with the two rows in the C-tableau in (26) yields the constituent structure in (29):

(29) $\big(_{H1j}$ $(H_{1j}\,(H_{1(j-1)}\,(.\,.\,.(H_{12}\,H_{11})\,.\,.\,.\,)))$ $(H_{2j}\,(H_{2(j-1)}\,(.\,.\,.\,(H_{22}\,H_{21})$ $.\,.\,.\,))))$

One observes that for the class of structures which can be represented by C-tableaux, the notions of "Phrase Marker" and of "Transformation Marker" are isomorphic and may be identified. To illustrate, the first row in the C-tableau in (26) represents the structure in (30), which can be taken as a connected family of primitive constituents or, alternatively, as a connected family of primitive applications of Merge:

(30)

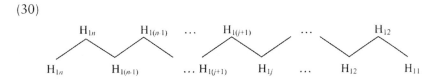

The identification between Phrase Markers and Transformation Markers in the case of structures represented by C-tableaux can be viewed as a generalization of the hypotheses in Epstein 1999. At this point, two fundamental questions arise:

(31) (i) Are C-tableaux primitive objects and, if so, how are they constructed?

    (ii) What is the theoretical status of such combinations of constituents or operations as that in (30)?

In sections 3–4 and in Appendices III–V, we develop an approach to (31ii) whereby every arrangement of items is described as a plurality of constituent structures. For example, a string is a plurality of a certain kind, while a labeled constituent structure is analyzed as a plurality of a different kind. This approach is in the same spirit as that in Hornstein 2005. Ultimately, it provides an account of the labeling relation, and a framework for such interpretive rules as those in (27).

In sections 5–9, we try to develop an answer to (31i) within the framework of ICA (the Items and Contexts Architecture; see section 1). The central hypotheses are stated in (32)–(33):

(32) Let L_M be the grammatical interface level with the mental/brain system M. The primitive objects of L_M are not lexical or grammatical items proper, but rather *roles* played by these items. Every L_M item λ has two roles, that of referring to an object in M, denoted by λ^t, and that of being a context at L_M, denoted by λ^{occ}.

(33) A grammatical structure is primitively defined as a set of mappings between the two types of roles of constituents.

Thus, the functional duality of constituents will be taken to be the basis of grammatical structure (see Vergnaud 2003; chapter 3 in this volume). To illustrate, the *VP* structure in (16i) (= (22i)) will be described as the correspondence υ depicted by the matrix in (34), where $\emptyset$ is a boundary item (see section 5):

(34) $\upsilon(\, H_{1j}) = H_{2j}$, H_{ij} the item in row i and column j in the matrix below

$\emptyset$	T	Asp	V	R
$\emptyset^1$	R^1	V^1	Asp^1	T^1

Within a theory based on (32)–(33), constituency is a property of sets of lexical items derived from the mappings binding the roles of these items in the grammatical structure (see section 8). In particular, the role X^0 is interpreted as the constituent X and the pairing of X^0 with Y^1 in each column in (34) is interpreted as the merging of the items X with Y into the constituent $(_X X\,Y)$ labeled by X ("(W)" means "W is a constituent"):

(35)   (i) $X^0 \Rightarrow (\{X\} = (X))$

   (ii) $(\upsilon(X^0) = Y^1) \Rightarrow (\{X, Y\} = (_X X\, Y))$

With the interpretive rules in (35), the mapping in (34) then yields Head-Merge within the verbal system. An important additional principle is the "duality" hypothesis in (36) (see section 9):

(36)   The role N^0 (resp. CL^0, resp. D^0, etc.) of the nominal category N (resp. CL, resp. D, etc.) is equated with the contextual role V^1 (resp. Asp^1, resp. T^1, etc.) of the corresponding verbal category V (resp. Asp, resp. T, etc.), and reciprocally.

One observes that a lexical item in a structure may be equated with the set of its roles:

(37) $X = \{X^1, X^0\}$

If one assumes that constituency respects such equations between primitive objects as that in (37), duality, combined with the latter equation leads to the equations in (38):

(38)   (i) $(V) = \{(N), (V)\}$

   (ii) $(Asp) = \{(CL), (Asp)\}$

(iii) (T) = {(D), (T)}

etc.

The equations in (38) in turn may be taken to represent particular applications of EPP-Merge, in accordance with the interpretive constituency schema in (39):

(39) $((X) = \{(Y), (X)\}) \Rightarrow (\{X, Y\} = (_X X Y))$

Ultimately, given the rules and principles in (35)–(37) and (39), the mapping in (34) gives rise to the same family of constituent structures as the C-tableau in (28). Baker's Mirror Principle derives from this formal structure (see section 9).

It should be noted here that the mental notion of "context" central to the formal treatment sketched earlier is taken to be an asymmetric notion (see section 5). It will be suggested that that asymmetry is the basis of many features of the mind/brain, such as the focus/background dichotomy. More generally, it relates to the Bayesian architecture of many mental systems and computations: the relation "p in the context of q" reduces to the same abstract concept as the relation "p given q" or "p if q." Independently, the distinction between the two roles λ^0 and λ^1 of the lexical item λ is indirectly related to the distinction between the *terminal* and the *nonterminal* vocabulary in a formal grammar: λ^0 corresponds to a terminal instantiation of λ and λ^1, to a nonterminal instantiation of λ^0.

The above theory immediately accounts for intraclausal A-movement. It can be extended to the standard raising structures such as that in (13) by assuming that a raising "verb" like *seem* corresponds to some stretch of the extended verbal projection (taken to be more complex than the impoverished illustration in (15i)):

(40) A raising verb occupies a connected subpart of the extended projection of the embedded verb.

Even with the clause in (40), though, the preceding theoretical fragment entails that A-movement is bounded. But, clearly, A-movement can be unbounded, as passivized ECM structures show:

(41) Everyone is believed to have been alleged to be likely not to win.

To account for such cases of unbounded exuberance, it will be assumed that some features are *absolutely uninterpretable*, i.e., have no interpretation either as nominal or as verbal features, and that such features can be repeated freely in the extended projection of a category. It is assumed that the feature *[α gender]* and a certain version of the feature *[β singular]* are such absolutely uninterpretable features.

3.   STRINGS, DEPENDENCIES, AND CONSTITUENT STRUCTURE

We first consider the notion of *string* in grammar. A PF sequence of syllables like that in (42) (the PF representation of a Semitic stem) constitutes a string:

(42) [fa-ʕa-la]

The form in (42) may be described as the product of the iterated application of the binary concatenation operator "^" to the set of syllables {*fa, ʕa, la*}, where each syllable *Ca* is actually taken as an unanalyzable entity, as an "atom." The string in (42) is then analyzed as in (43):

(43) fa-ʕa-la ≡ ((fa^ʕa)^la) ≡ (fa^(ʕa^la)) ≡ fa^ʕa^la

This is the view of strings as elements of *free semigroups (monoids)*. A *semigroup (monoid)* is a nonempty set of elements *M* together with a binary operation "·" defined in *M* which is associative and admits a *unit* or *identity* element.[5] A *free* semigroup is one that is generated by a (finite or infinite) set of *atoms* such that no relation holds among these atoms except the trivial ones that hold among any set of elements.[6] We then have the definition in (44):

(44) A string is a concatenation of atomic elements in a noncommutative free monoid.

Unibranching arrangements of lexical items can also be analyzed as strings in the algebraic sense above. A "unibranching" arrangement is a tree in which at most one node is a nonterminal in any set of sister nodes, as in (45):

(45)

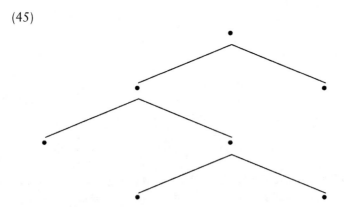

The tree in (45) might typically represent an LF composition of lexical items and their complements (in the sense of X-bar theory), as in (46), where *X, Y, Z* are lexical items:

(46)

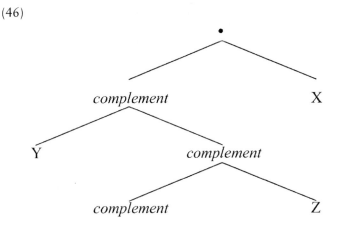

It has often been argued that no independent linear ordering holds at LF, so that a tree like that in (45) should be thought of as a particular planar projection of a "Calder-like" structure (Bobaljik 2002; Bury 2003; Chametzky 1995; Chomsky and Lasnik 1993; Lasnik and Uriagereka 2005; McCawley 1982; Speas 1990; Stowell 1981; Travis 1984).[7] Projecting the abstract constituent structure on a two-dimensional plane breaks the "Calder symmetry." From that standpoint, the tree geometry in (45) is equivalent to any of the other arrangements in (47):

(47) (i) $(•^\wedge(•^\wedge(•^\wedge•)))$

    (ii) $(•^\wedge((•^\wedge•)^\wedge•))$

    (iii) $(((•^\wedge•)^\wedge•)^\wedge•)$

The arrangement in (47i) corresponds to the "right-branching" geometry in (48):

(48)

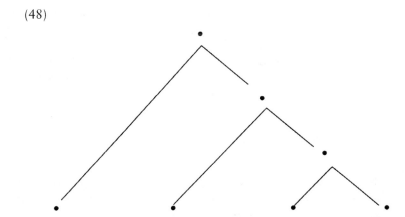

Thus, the structure in (46) is equivalent to that in (49):

(49)

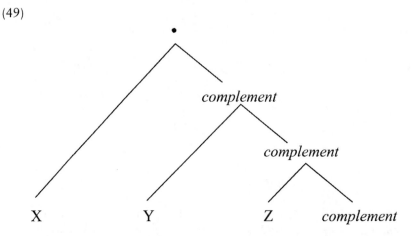

It might seem at first sight that there is a complementary relation between the commutativity and associativity properties of the concatenation operator "^". At the PF level illustrated in (42), this operator is taken to be *associative* and *noncommutative,* reflecting the linear organization of the time axis (cf., e.g., Chomsky and Miller 1963). By contrast, at the LF level, the concatenation operator must be defined as *nonassociative* and *commutative* to represent both the nesting of constituents and its "Calder-like" character. In fact, some authors have identified this alleged algebraic complementarity between LF and PF as the root of the "bracketing paradoxes" in grammar (see, e.g., Marantz 1992). But the complementarity turns out to be illusory once the LF relation of *head-of* is taken into account. The simplest instance of that relation is found when two lexical items are merged into a *compound,* as in the English structure in (50):

(50) $(_N (_A \text{ black}) (_N \text{ board}))$

The labels in (50) indicate the grammatical categories to which the lexical items belong: *black* is an adjective (*A*), *board,* a noun (*N*) and the whole compound, a noun. The compound in (50) *inherits* not only its category, but more generally its distributional properties from the nominal constituent *board.* That constituent is called the *head of* the structure. Intuitively, the notion of "head" can be defined as in (51):

(51) Given a constituent *K* in the context Φ—Ψ, the head of *K* is the element in *K* that carries all the relevant properties of *K* as it relates to its context Φ—Ψ

The "head-of" relation is a general feature of grammatical structure: when two lexical items *X, Y* are merged, the resulting structure has the same broad distributional properties as one of the two constituents *X* or *Y* (see Chomsky [1955] 1975, 1957, 1965, 1967, 1994; Chomsky and Halle 1968). For example, when a verb merges with a complement in the derivation of a sentence, the resulting structure is a verbal constituent, a *Verb Phrase* (*VP*). The converse of the *head-of* relation is called *projection-of*:

(52) (Z is the *head* of $(X\ Y)$) $\Leftrightarrow$ ($(X\ Y)$ is a *projection* of Z), $Z = X$ or Y

One way of accounting for the *head-of* relation in such a structure as (50) is to take that structure to have the two "simultaneous analyses" (descriptions) in (53):

(53) (i) ($_N$ ($_A$ black) ($_N$ board))

(ii) ($_N$ board)

More generally, the structure in (54) has the simultaneous analyses in (55), where X, Y are lexical items:

(54)

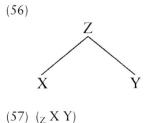

(55) $(X\ Y) \approx Z$, $Z = X$ or Y

A set of simultaneous analyses of the form in (55) is standardly represented by using the head as a *label* for the fuller structures, as shown in (56) or (57), where Z is either X or Y:

(56)

(57) ($_Z$ X Y)

To illustrate, the verbal constituent formed by the verb and its "direct object" in the sentence *[he hit it]* is described as in (58):

(58)

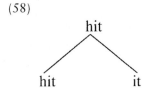

The combination in (58) is an instance of the *head-complement* structure, which plays a central role in the analysis of sentences. The tree in (49) is a multiple *iteration* of that structure, as shown in (59), where X, Y, Z are the same lexical items as in (49) and W is the lexical item that is the complement of Z:

(59)

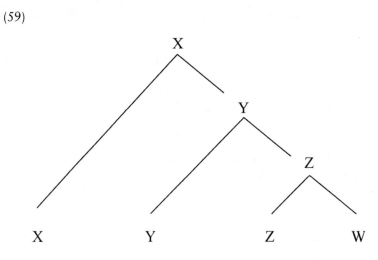

The simplest and most natural hypothesis is that the equivalence between heads and projections stated in (51) and formalized in (55) is relevant to all grammatical relations. When applied to *immediate domination,* it yields an equivalence relation among syntactic trees. For example, the tree in (59) is equivalent to that in (60) modulo head projection ("P→Q" is the relation "Q immediately dominates P"):

(60)

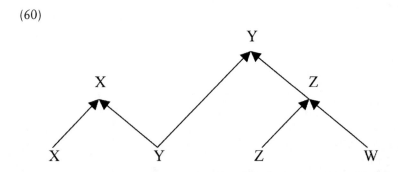

In the tree in (60), it is the head Y that is immediately dominated by X, not its maximal projection as in the tree in (59). What constitutes an equivalence class obviously depends on the particular definition of "tree" adopted.[8] The bracketing depicted by the tree in (60) is improper. To the extent that such structures are admissible, the equivalence class of the tree in (59) also includes the trees in (61)–(62), in addition to those in (59)–(60) ("P→Q" has the same meaning as in (60)):

(61)

(62)

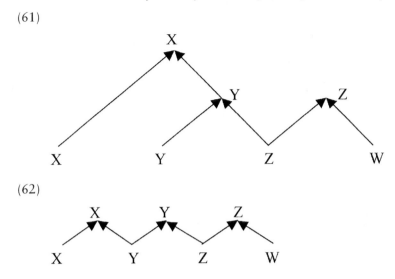

Other notions of "tree" may be considered for grammatical purposes, giving rise to different equivalence classes. The cornerstone of all such equivalence relations is the abstract structure in (63):

(63) Denote by τ the equivalence between a head and its projections. Let K be some constituent structure. The structure K/τ is defined as the set of equivalences classes in K with the domination relation in (i):

(i) A immediately dominates B in K/τ just in case some element of A immediately dominates some element of B in K.

For example, if K is the structure in (59), K/τ is that in (64), where "P $\rightarrow$ Q" has the same meaning as in (60)–(62) and where P/τ is the class of P:

(64)

$$W/\tau \longrightarrow Z/\tau \longrightarrow Y/\tau \longrightarrow X/\tau$$

The correspondence between K and K/τ is the *telescoping relation* of Brody 1997, 2000.[9] Thus, the structure in (64) is the telescoped version of that in (59). The equivalence among the structures in (59)–(62) can now be defined as in (65):

(65) Two trees J and J' are equivalent iff $J/\tau = J'/\tau$

If the notion of "tree" is broadened along the graph-theoretic lines of Appendix III, the equivalence class of the tree in (59) will also include such structures as those in (66)–(68):[10]

(66)

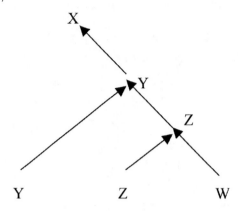

(67)

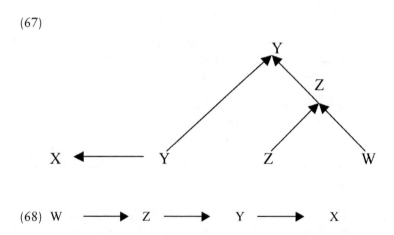

(68) W ⟶ Z ⟶ Y ⟶ X

By definition, a telescoped structure does not distinguish between a constituent and its head or projections, so that, if P/τ dominates Q/τ within the telescoped structure K/τ, $P \neq Q$, any member of P/τ may be deemed to dominate any member of Q/τ. The telescoped structure can then be identified as a dependency relation among lexical items, to wit that obtained by equating each class P/τ with P. For example, the structure in (64) defines the dependency relation in (70) among the lexical items X, Y, Z, W:

(69) W ⟶ Z ⟶ Y ⟶ X

The dependency system in (70) is of course isomorphic with the minimal structure in the equivalence class (shown in (68)), and can be equated with it. It is natural to identify the relation "$P \to Q$" in (70) with *government* in the sense of Chomsky 1981, 1986b. A labeled tree such as that in (59) can

then be analyzed into two components, the government structure in (70) and
the unlabeled constituent structure in (70):

(70)

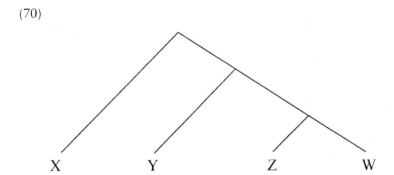

A given unlabeled constituent structure is in general compatible with more
than one government structure. For example, the constituent structure in
(70), which can naturally combine with the linear government structure in
(70), can combine with the government structure in (71) as well:

(71)

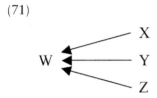

The government system in (71) yields 6 distinct labelings of the constituent
structure in (70). One of these labelings is displayed in (72):

(72)

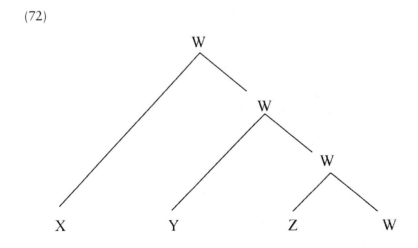

In the above structure, Z is the direct complement of W, while X and Y might be analyzed as specifiers. Other labelings correspond to different arrangements of X, Y, and Z. A central empirical question is whether nonlinear government structures such as that in (71) actually exist. If constituents are binary (see Kayne 1984), a head governs at most one complement. And the specifier-of relation may not fall under government at all. These and other issues relating to the mapping between constituent and government structures define an important part of syntactic investigation (see Chomsky 1970, 1986b).

From the preceding standpoint, an *iterated head-complement* (*IHC*) structure such as that in (59) is characterized as in (73):

(73) A constituent structure is an IHC structure just in case it ultimately telescopes into a *linear government structure*.

Linear government structures in turn can be described as strings in the algebraic sense in (44), as a concatenation of atomic elements in a noncommutative free monoid. To that effect, the elementary dependency $(P \rightarrow Q)$ is equated with the directed graph which has $\{P, Q\}$ as a set of nodes and $\{<P, Q>\}$ as a (singleton) set of edges (see Appendix III):

(74) $(P \rightarrow Q) \approx \{\{P, Q\}, \{<P, Q>\}\}$

The graph in (74) is denoted by $G_{P,Q}$ (it is the "master graph" for the constituent $(_Q P Q)$ in the sense of Appendix III). By definition, an edge in a directed graph such as $G_{P,Q}$ is an *ordered pair*: $<P, Q>$ is distinct from $<Q, P>$. Given the absence of cycle (see Appendix II and Appendix III), the directionality of the edges gives rise to an *ordering* among nodes. The structure in (70) is then identified with the *linear directed graph* in (75):

(75) $\{\{X, Y, Z\}, \{<W, Z>, <Z, Y>, <Y, X>\}\}$

One can define a *concatenation operation* between linear graphs as in (76):

(76) Let G (resp. G') be a linear graph. Let N (resp. N') be the set of nodes in G (resp. G') and E (resp. E'), the set of edges in G (resp. G'). Let U be the maximal node in G and W, the minimal node in G'. The concatenation of G and G' in this order is the graph defined as follows:

(i) $G^{\wedge}G' =_{\text{def}} \{N \cup N', E \cup E' \cup \{<U, W>\}$

That is, the concatenation of G and G' in this order is the graph obtained by joining the nodes and the edges of G and G' and by adding the edge $<U, W>$, which connects the maximal element in G to the minimal element in G'. In particular, the elementary graph $G_{P,Q}$ is the concatenation of the "degenerate" graphs (graphs reduced to one node) $\{\{P\}\}$ and $\{\{Q\}\}$:

(77) $\{\{P, Q\}, \{<P, Q>\}\} = \{\{P\}\}^\wedge\{\{Q\}\}$

Identifying the degenerate graph $\{\{X\}\}$ with X, we have the equation in (78):

(78) $\{\{P, Q\}, \{<P, Q>\}\} = P^\wedge Q$

With these definitions, the structure in (70) may now be represented as in (79):

(79) $W^\wedge Z^\wedge Y^\wedge X$

The LF concatenation defined in (76) is associative and noncommutative.[11] It shares these features with the PF operator which generates the string of syllables in (43):

(43) $\text{fa.\textipa{S}a.la} \equiv ((\text{fa}^\wedge\text{\textipa{S}a})^\wedge\text{la}) \equiv (\text{fa}^\wedge(\text{\textipa{S}a}^\wedge\text{la})) \equiv \text{fa}^\wedge\text{\textipa{S}a}^\wedge\text{la}$

Clearly, the correspondence between linear directed graphs and algebraic strings established in (74)–(78) is both an *injective function* and a *homomorphism*. We then have the result in (80):

(80) An IHC structure derived by successive merging of the lexical items $L_1, L_2, \ldots, L_n$ in this order admits a multiplicity of constituent analyses. These analyses form an equivalence class modulo telescoping in the sense of Brody 1997, 2000 (see Appendix III). The minimal analysis in the equivalence class can be identified with the government structure canonically associated with the class and is isomorphic to the string $L_1^\wedge L_2^\wedge \ldots ^\wedge L_n$ by the correspondence defined in (74)–(78).

In a nutshell:

(81) The lexical items in an IHC structure form a string in the sense of (44).

To summarize so far, we have the result in (80)–(81). The notion of string that has been assumed is the standard "algebraic" one in (44), whereby a string is primitively defined as a concatenation of elements in a free noncommutative monoid. From that definition, various properties follow. For example, the definition entails that the elements of a string form a linearly ordered set.[12] But other structural features follow as well which eventually point to an alternative characterization. This is briefly discussed in the following section.

4.   STRINGS AND UNIBRANCHING STRUCTURES AS FAMILIES OF CONSTITUENT ANALYSES

Within the standard algebraic model discussed earlier, a string is clearly much more than the mere linear ordering of its elements. For it is also an ordering of the *substrings* in it. Consider for example the string $P^\wedge Q^\wedge R$, P, Q, R atomic elements. The string structure implies the three orderings in (82):

(82) $P<Q<R, P<Q^\wedge R, P^\wedge Q<R$

Given the string $s = e_1^\wedge \ldots {}^\wedge e_n$, a substring $e_h^\wedge \ldots {}^\wedge e_k$, $1 \le h \le k \le n$, of s is identified with the linearly ordered subset $\{e_h, \ldots e_k\}$ of $\{e_1, \ldots e_n\}$. The inequalities in (82) may then be simplified to (83):

(83) $\{P\}<\{Q\}<\{R\}$, $\{P\}<\{Q, R\}$, $\{P, Q\}<\{R\}$

In general:

(84)   A string $e_1^\wedge \ldots {}^\wedge e_n$ defines an ordering in the power set of $\{e_1, \ldots e_n\}$

Of course, an ordering relation on some finite set E is always extendable into an ordering of the power set $2E$.[13] The point of (84) is that any *natural homomorphism* between the set of elements E in a string and some other set will *immediately* extend to the power set 2^E.[14] Thus, the form $W^\wedge Z^\wedge Y^\wedge X$ in (79) gives rise to the family of linear sequences of substrings shown in (85), where P is identified with $\{P\}$:

(85)   (i)   W-Z-Y-X

(ii)   (W-Z)-Y-X, W-(Z-Y)-X, W-Z-(Y-X), (W-Z)-(Y-X)

(iii)   (W-Z-Y)-X, W-(Z-Y-X)

The set of analyses in (85) may be taken to represent the range of outcomes when adjacent elements are fused into larger units within the linear structure W-Z-Y-X. Such fusions preserve the government relations. For example, the derived constituent Z-Y-X in (85iii) governs W. On the other hand, the government relations in (85) do not respect the head-projection relation. Thus, X, the presumed head of the constituent Z-Y-X in (85iii), does not govern W in the basic sequence W-Z-Y-X.

The class of analyses in (85) may itself be derived from the set of alternative derivations of the string $W^\wedge Z^\wedge Y^\wedge X$, displayed in (86) (where "$\wedge$" is assumed to be a binary operation):

(86) (i) $(((W^\wedge Z)^\wedge Y)^\wedge X)$

   (ii) $((W^\wedge Z)^\wedge (Y^\wedge X))$

   (iii) $((W^\wedge (Z^\wedge Y))^\wedge X)$

   (iv) $(W^\wedge ((Z^\wedge Y)^\wedge X))$

   (v) $(W^\wedge (Z^\wedge (Y^\wedge X)))$

As a whole, the family of derivations in (86) expresses the associative character of the concatenation operation "$\wedge$". Each derivation in (86) can be interpreted as a particular constituent analysis of the string. There is a simple relation between the sets of analyses in (86) and that (85): pruning an analysis in (86) will yield an analysis in (85). For example, the analysis *(W-Z-Y)-X* in (85iii) is produced by pruning the constituent $(Z^\wedge Y)$ from the analysis $((W^\wedge (Z^\wedge Y))^\wedge X)$ in (86iii). If the higher constituent $(W^\wedge (Z^\wedge Y))$ instead is pruned from that analysis, the analysis *W-(Z-Y)-X* in (85ii) obtains. In most of the structures in (86), as in those in (85), government fails to conform to the head-projection relation. There is one exception: the unibranching tree structure in (86i), in which government relations are projected from the basic sequence *W-Z-Y-X*. The structure in (86i) is the same as that in (59).

It appears, then, that "being a string" really is *a property of sets of constituent analyses*. Specifically, a "string" should be defined as the pairing of a set of items with a *certain class* of (parallel) constituent analyses of that set. In the preceding section, we have seen that an IHC structure is canonically associated with an equivalence class of constituent analyses (modulo telescoping). This suggests that "being an IHC structure" also is a property of sets of constituent analyses. The discussion in section 3 naturally leads to the definition in (87):

(87) An IHC structure is the class of constituent analyses of a linear government structure that conform to the head-projection relation.

Concretely, the IHC structure associated with a given linear government structure Γ can be derived from Γ by means of the rules in (88):

(88) a. $(Q \leftarrow P) \Rightarrow \{Q, P\}$ is a constituent

   b. $(Q \leftarrow P), (R \leftarrow Q) \Rightarrow (R \leftarrow \{Q, P\})$

A condition akin to "strict cyclicity" (see Chomsky 1965; Freidin 1978; Kean 1974) must be imposed if the rules in (88) are to generate the correct syntactic structures. Informally:

(89) Each new constituent constructed by (88) at any given stage of a derivation must include at least one element external to the constituent structure already constructed.

The set of rules in (88) in effect extend the government relation between the lexical items in Γ into a more general relation between lexical items and constituents. The extension is consistent with headedness: if R governs Q in Γ, it governs the constituent headed by Q (cf. (88b)). The extension is also complete when applied to linear government structures, in the sense that any derivation yields a tree that encompasses all the lexical items in the structure. This is not the case with more general structures such as that in (71)–(72), though. The extension of government in such structures would require a rule of the form in (90) (or its symmetric counterpart), together with additional disambiguating principles.

(90) $(R \leftarrow P), (R \leftarrow Q) \Rightarrow (\{R, Q\} \leftarrow P)$

Since a different treatment of the notions of "specifier" and of "adjunct" will be proposed in this essay, we will not pursue the matter further.

Eventually, the head-projection relation will itself be defined as a property of sets of constituent analyses. Then, given a set of items *A,* an *IHC structure over A* will be the pairing of *A* with a certain class of (parallel) constituent anlyses, while a *string over A* will be the pairing of *A* with a different, but related, class of analyses. Such an approach is sketched in section 8 and, from a different standpoint, in Appendix V. The difference between an IHC structure and a PF string will then reduce to whether head-projection restricts the underlying family of constituent analyses or not. In these terms, an IHC structure is a "partial string," one pared down by the head-projection relation:

(91) An IHC structure is a string pared down by the head-projection relation.

As shown by the structure in (71)–(72), there is no immediate generalization of this account for structures containing specifiers (in the sense of X-bar theory). If LF constituent structure does include specifiers in the standard X-bar sense, the results in (80)–(81) and (91) may then appear to be of limited value. But it will be argued later that the classical X-bar functions "specifier-of" and "complement-of" must be recast. A new X-bar architecture will be proposed, which generalizes the analysis in Larson 1988 along the following lines:

(92) The *neo*-X-bar theory or "$X^{\#}$-bar theory"

 (i) Every *argument* is analyzed as a *specifier.*

(ii) The relation *complement-of* is restricted to the formatives that constitute an *extended projection* (essentially in the sense of Grimshaw 1991).

Within $X^\#$-bar theory, merging a head and its complement and merging a head and its specifier are different operations: as we shall see, the EPP is crucially involved in the latter, but not in the former. In other words, the standard X-bar schema is resolved into two formally independent kinds of Merge: *Head-Merge*, yielding IHC structures, and *EPP-Merge*, pairing the IHC structures produced by Head-Merge. The recurrent $X^\#$-bar motif is the structure in (93), where *X, Y, Z, U, V, W* are lexical items:

(93)

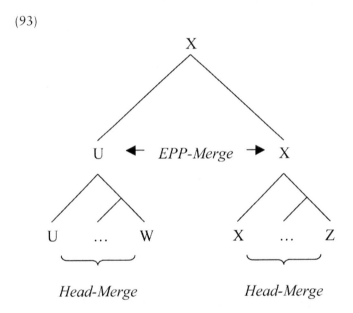

There is a fundamental difference between the $X^\#$-bar motif in (93) and the standard X-bar schema: the latter is recursive, the former is not, as we shall see in sections 6–7. So, within $X^\#$-bar theory, the infinity of syntactic structure must originate in some other component. Indeed, it appears to tie in with the *cyclical nature* of interpretation, in the sense of Uriagereka 1999 and Chomsky 1999 (see also Freidin 1978). Redefining a *phase* as an application of EPP-Merge, recursivity will be shown to ultimately derive from the ability of an IHC structure to partake of several *phases* (see the following discussion).[15] As $X^\#$-bar theory goes, then, the ultimate "building blocks" of syntactic structure are not the standard X-bar schematic arrangements. Rather, they are the IHC arrangements generated by Head-Merge (the *Minimal Computing Units* [*Command Units*—KMB] in Martin and Uriagereka 2000). Variations on this theme have started to inflect the harmony of the syntactic spheres, most notably Brody 1995, 1997, 2000; Chomsky 1994,

1995, 1999; Lasnik and Uriagereka 2005; Manzini 1995, 1997, 1998; Martin and Uriagereka 2000; Rouveret and Nash 2002; Uriagereka 1999; and Williams 2003 (see also Bury 2003; Freidin and Vergnaud 1999; Koizumi 1993; Megerdoomian 2002; Vergnaud and Zubizarreta 2001).

The formal relation between IHC structures and strings discussed above has empirical significance to the extent that it applies to computations at the underlying brain/mental level ($LF_{B/M}$). Brody 1997, 2000, Lasnik and Uriagereka 2005, and Uriagereka 1999 argue that it does. Quite obviously, the correspondence which exists between the two mathematical descriptions does not mean that they are exclusive of each other at $LF_{B/M}$. Constituent structure of the standard kind is a core feature of grammatical architecture, regardless of whether "dependency" strings exist at $LF_{B/M}$ or not.[16] To the extent to which they do, this just means that an adequate mathematical model of $LF_{B/M}$ must associate the two kinds of structures.[17] But the issue may be moot, for the preceding discussion actually brings to light an empirical inadequacy of the standard characterization of strings as objects in a semigroup. Specifically, it has revealed that a string is most appropriately described as a graph and its associated family of constituent structures. We now examine some implications of that fact.

5.   ELEMENTS AND CONTEXTS

The linear government structure in (68), $W \to Z \to Y \to X$, is equated with the directed graph in (75), $\{\{X, Y, Z\}, \{<W, Z>, <Z, Y>, <Y, X>\}\}$, which may be taken to represent the whole equivalence class containing the structures in (59)–(62) and (66)–(68). The central component in such a graph is the *mapping* defined by the set of edges. In the case of (75), this is the mapping in (94):

(94) $<\varnothing, W>, <W, Z>, <Z, Y>, <Y, X>, <X, \varnothing>$

The empty symbol $\varnothing$ in (94) has been added for completeness: it can be identified as a *boundary element*.[18] As has been suggested above (see the discussion below (70)), the mapping in a master graph such as (75) may be identified as the primitive case of the *government* relation:

(95) $<P, Q> \approx (_Q \, P \, Q) \equiv Q$ governs P, P, Q lexical items

Analogously, the string of syllables in (43) is equated with the mapping in (96), where again the empty symbol $\varnothing$ has been introduced for completeness:

(96) $<\varnothing, fa>, <fa, \varsigma a>, <\varsigma a, la>, <la, \varnothing>$

The mapping in (96) in fact is the *precedence relation*:

(97) $<x, y> \equiv x \ precedes \ y \equiv y \ follows \ x$

The critical property of a representation such as that in (94) or in (96) is that every constituent occurs twice in it, with each occurrence corresponding to a distinct function. Following Vergnaud 2003 (chapter 3), we shall argue that:

(98) The functional duality of constituents is the basis of syntactic structure and, more generally, of grammatical structure.

The most general definition of a mapping of the form in (94) or in (96) is in terms of the notion of *context*, as indicated in (99):[19]

(99) $<q, p> =_{def} p$ is in the context of q, p, q constituents

The intuitive notion of context is derived from that of adjacency. This is stated in (101) with the notation in (100):

(100) $p/q =_{def} p$ is in the context of q

(101) p and q are adjacent $\Rightarrow p/q$

That notion of context is symmetrical:

(102) $(p/q) \Leftrightarrow (q/p)$

But for any particular mental/neural system, the symmetry of the relation "in the context of", like that of adjacency, is a fact about the external world. Precisely because the external relation *is* symmetrical in that respect, the mental/neural system can ease its computational burden by considering only one half of the relation, treating it in fact as an asymmetrical construct. This is schematized in (103):

(103)

External world: $(p/q) \Leftrightarrow (q/p)$

Mind/Brain: (p/q)

The reduction in (103) is one of the fundamental insights in the account in Sauzet 1993, 1994, which uses the French term *attenance* to denote the mental concept of context. The syntactic relations of *government* and *head-edness* ultimately derive from the asymmetry of the mental/neural concept. That asymmetry is the basis of many features of the mind, such as the focus/

background dichotomy. More generally, it also relates to the Bayesian architecture of many mental systems and computations: the relation "*p* in the context of *q*" reduces to the same abstract concept as the relation "*p* given *q*." We will not consider these issues here, but just note that the reduction in (103) does not imply that there could be no symmetrical mental notion of "context." It merely implies that such a symmetrical notion could not be a primitive one, but would be a complex one (see section 8).

An arrangement of items (syllables, formatives, etc.) is then ultimately analyzed as a family of mappings $\{_{i \in I} \mu_i\}$, where μ_i, $i \in I$, is a correspondence between an array of atomic constituents and a set of contexts. We will use the following notation:

(104) (i) |u>: the constituent *u*

(ii) <u|: the constituent *u* as a context

The object denoted by <*u*| in (104ii) is the relation in (105), with *x* a dummy variable (a placeholder):

(105) *x* is in the context of |*u*>

That relation can be written *[—|u>]* using the formalism of rewriting rules (see Chomsky 1965). So, we have the notational equivalence in (106):

(106) <u| ≡ [—|u>]

The pairing in (99) will be rewritten as in (107):

(107) <q, p> ≡ <q|p>

With this notation, the class of structures in (59)–(62) and (66)) is reduced to the mapping in (108) (= (94)), equivalently represented as in (109):

(108) {<∅|W>, <W|Z>, <Z|Y>, <Y|X>, <X|∅>}

(109)

$$
\begin{array}{ccc}
|\mathbf{W}> & \leftrightarrow & <\varnothing| \\
|\mathbf{Z}> & \leftrightarrow & <\mathbf{W}| \\
|\mathbf{Y}> & \leftrightarrow & <\mathbf{Z}| \\
|\mathbf{X}> & \leftrightarrow & <\mathbf{Y}| \\
|\varnothing> & \leftrightarrow & <\mathbf{X}|
\end{array}
$$

In the case of the structures considered above, the mapping between atomic constituents and contexts is one-one. Specifically, these structures conform to (110):

(110) (i) Any given atom shows up in only one context.

(ii) Any context is associated with only one atom.

These are not necessary properties of linguistic structures in general, though. Thus, one finds structures in which a constituent may be associated with more than one context. At LF, this is the configuration corresponding to coordination (see section 8). At PF, these are the structures which have undergone reduplication (see Halle 2008, Raimy 1999, 2001). Conversely, one finds structures in which a context may be associated with more than one constituent. At LF, these are the structures which have undergone movement (see below). At PF, this is the configuration for autosegmentality.

The asymmetrical mental/neural notion of "context" gives rise to a corresponding asymmetrical notion of *occurrence*. Thus, the formula in (107) can be used equally to denote the relational pairing of p with q or an occurrence of p in the context of q as shown in (111):

(111) $<q|p> = {}_{def}$ a q-occurrence of p

The notion of "occurrence of an object" is central to any mathematical treatment of linguistic structure. In particular, the standard formalization of syntactic "displacement" is directly or indirectly in terms of this notion (see, e.g., Chomsky 1981: 45, 47, 62; 1995:251–252; 1998, 1999, 2001). Concretely, the outcome of a movement transformation will be described as a *chain* of distinct constituents occurring in the same context (a chain of grammatical functions). For example, the chain for *who* in the structure in (112) will be identified as the set of constituents in the contexts of *who*, of t_2, of t_1, and of t_0 in that structure (where C is the upper complementizer and C′, the lower one):[20]

(112) Mary is [*who* C [she t_2 [wants [t_1 C′ [to t_0 [emulate]]]]]]

This is informally represented as in (113) using the notation introduced in (104):[21]

(113) $<who| \leftrightarrow \{|C>, |wants>, |C′>, |emulate>\}$

Such formalization is particularly apt at representing *reconstruction*.[22] Consider the structure in (114), where the chain for *who* is the set of constituents in the contexts of *who*, of t_2, of t_1, and of t_0, as shown in (115):

(114) [its owner] is [*who* C [every donkey t_2 [wants [t_1 C′ [to t_0 [sentence]]]]]]

(115) <*who*| ↔ {|C>, |wants>, |C'>, |sentence>}

The definite pronoun *its* in the structure in (114) can be construed as bound by the noun phrase *[every donkey]*, even though it is not c-commanded by it at surface structure. The reason for that discrepancy is that the matrix subject in such constructions is equated with the post-copula *wh*-word. A particular effect of that identification is that the chain of the *wh*-word is assigned to the matrix subject. This result is shown in (116) in the case of the structure in (114):

(116) {<*its owner*|, <*who*|} ↔ {|C>, |wants>, |C'>, |sentence>}

Similarly, the chain in (113) is extended as in (117), accounting for the referential disjointness between *she* and *Mary* in (112):

(117) {<*Mary*|, <*who*|} ↔ {|C>, |wants>, |C'>, |emulate>}

The extension of the chain in (115) to that in (116), or of the chain in (113) to that in (117), is in essence the rule proposed in Chomsky 1977 (see also the discussion in Chomsky 1981 and in Barss 1986).[23] The critical question is which of (i) or (ii) in (118) holds:

(118) The assignment of the *wh*-chain to the matrix subject:
     (i)   follows the derivational construction of that chain.
     (ii) is concomitant with the derivational construction of that chain.

Classical reconstruction theory assumes (118i). But it is argued elsewhere that, rather, (118ii) holds and that there is no reconstruction in the standard sense (see Rouveret and Vergnaud, forthcoming).[24]

Apart from the empirical issue in (118), there is the more fundamental result that a natural account of such structures as (112) or (114) is readily available if sentence structure is primitively defined as a *mapping between constituents and contexts,* in the manner of the elementary example in (108)–(109). The problem at this point is to find the proper generalization of the formalism in (108)–(109) that will give rise to such representations as (113) and (115). A subtask is to describe the algorithm that generates chains. We note that there is no interesting semantic definition of the notion "occurrence" despite the fact that that notion is reminiscent of the notion of variable in, e.g., standard predicate calculus. The latter notion is illustrated in (119):

(119) a. (guess) who$_i$ Mary introduced to his$_i$ closest friend?
     b. (guess) for which x, x = someone, Mary introduced x to x's closest friend

Constructing the empirically adequate notion(s) of occurrence is the task of syntactic theory.[25] As has been hinted in (98), the fundamental hypothesis that we want to defend and illustrate is that in (120):

(120) Let L_M be the grammatical interface level with the mental/brain system M. The primitive objects of L_M are not lexical or grammatical items proper, but rather *roles* played by these items. Every L_M item λ has two roles, that of referring to an object in M and that of being a context at L_M. The two roles are denoted by $|\lambda>$ and by $<\lambda|$, respectively. Borrowing Dirac-honored terminology, we call $|\lambda>$ a *ket* and $<\lambda|$ a *bra*.[26]

Some aspects of this hypothesis go back to the suggestion in Rouveret 1987 and the proposal in Manzini 1992 that a syntactic formalization should explicitly dissociate the *content* of an item from its *position*.

The hypothesis in (120) ultimately stems from the proposal in Chomsky (1955) 1975. The latter proposal, itself adapted from Quine's (1951) *Mathematical Logic*,[27] involved taking an occurrence of α in K to be the full context of α in K. This definition surfaces in various guises in subsequent developments, for example in Chomsky 1981:45, 47, 62, in Chomsky 1995:251–252, in Chomsky 1998, in Chomsky 1999, and in Chomsky 2001. Chomsky 1998 suggests the following:

(121) We could, for example, identify this [the full context of α in K-JRV] as K′ = K with the occurrence of α in question replaced by some designated element OCC distinct from anything in K. (45n64)[28]

To illustrate, the context of X in the IHC structure in (59) will be represented as in (122):

(122)

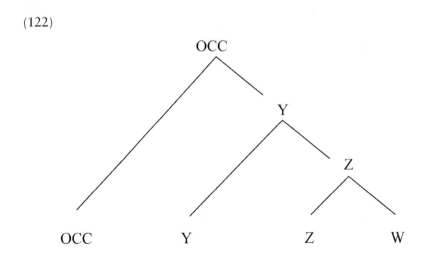

The object in (122) can be represented as in (123):

(123) (OCC Y) ≈ [—Y]

The context "(OCC Y)" is then identified with the bra "<Y|:"

(124) (OCC Y) ≡ <Y|

In Chomsky 1965, the Greek letter "Δ" is used instead of "OCC." The bra "<Y|" may then be equivalently written as ΔY. Indeed, it will be convenient to use a simplified notation for bras and kets. We adopt the notational convention in (125):

(125) (i) |u> ≈ u

  (ii) <u| ≈ Δu

With this notation, the pairing in (107) is written as in (126):

(126) <q|p> ≈ (p, Δq)

Whenever possible, the notation *(p, Δq)* will be further simplified as in (100):

(127) (p, Δq) ≈ p/q

An important part of the program defined by the hypothesis in (120) is to construct a theory of constituent structure consonant with the hypothesis. A governing principle will be that in (128):

(128) Given two mental arrangements (representations or processes) *M* and *M'* such that *M* and *M'* are both (possibly trivial) collections of more elementary mental arrangements, the pair {M, M'} defines a mental arrangement, equal to the union of *M* and *M'*, if and only if the mental coupling in (i) holds:[29]

  (i) (ξ, Δη), with (ξ,η) = (M, M') or (M', M)

Ultimately, every *arrangement* will be defined as a correspondence between constituents and contexts. In the most general case, such mappings may lead to infinite recursion, as in the example in (129):

(129) (i) Set of primitive constituents:

    {A, B, C, D}

  (ii) Mapping:

    {(B, ΔA), (C, ΔB), (D, ΔC), (B, ΔD)}

In the absence of additional principles, the structure in (129) defines the infinite object in (130):

(130) $A \char94 B \char94 C \char94 D \char94 (B \char94 C \char94 D)^\infty$

where $U \char94 V$ denotes the combination of the set $\{U, V\}$ with the pair $(V, \Delta U)$

Indexing the distinct occurrences of B in the mapping in (129) would void the general program, since the theory of such mapping is intended as an account of the notion of "occurrence." There are different ways of barring the monster of uncontrolled recursion. The simplest and most drastic one is simply to require that the correspondence between the set of primitive constituents and the set of contexts be a mapping from the former into the latter.[30] That solution immediately leads to a new, fundamental, difficulty, though. For the question now is how Human Language (HL) attains to (discrete) infinity, one of its design features. Nature's answer, not surprisingly, is identical to Chomsky's. All mental/brain arrangements are organized into *cycles*, such that the content of an embedded cycle is opaque for the cycles that dominate it (the principle of *Strict Cyclicity*; see Chomsky 1965, 1999; Freidin 1978). We explore some implications of this general architecture in the following sections. As a preliminary step, we examine the basic properties of constituent structure in HL.

6. THE SYMMETRY OF CATEGORIES

Generalizing ICA in this fashion will involve adopting a version of the representational system developed in Brody 1997, 2000 and in Manzini 1995, 1997, 1998 (see sections 8–9). A Pollockian geometry (see Pollock 1989) combined with the cyclical principle in Uriagereka 1999 and Chomsky 1999 (see also Freidin 1978) will be critical to the theoretical enterprise (see sections 6–9).

We consider LF constituent structure. The primitive units at LF are *grammatical* and *lexical formatives* (in the sense of Chomsky 1964) denoting objects or properties in the conceptual-intentional systems (*C-I*) (see Chomsky 1995). To illustrate, a verbal form such as *broke* in (131) is analyzed into the set of formatives in (132), where V is the unaccusative verb *break*:

(131) [the donkey broke the rule]

(132) $\{v, V, \text{Asp}_v, \text{Asp}_V, T, \text{Agr}\}$

These formatives are assembled into a unibranching structure, which constitutes the skeleton of the LF representation of the sentence in (131):

(133)

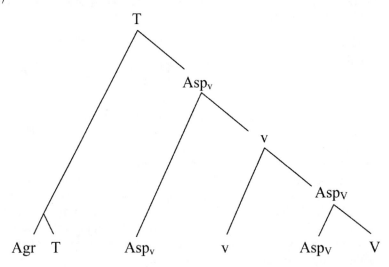

The complete LF representation is obtained by merging the constituents *[the rule]* and *[the donkey]* as specifiers at appropriate stages in the course of the derivation of (133). The verb *break* is analyzed into two formatives, V (the unaccusative *break*) and *v,* following in essence Hale and Keyser 1993, 2002. In Chomsky 1994, this analysis is unified with the proposal in Larson 1988 (see also Brody 1995, Koizumi 1993). The element *v* is a minimal lexical formative, reduced to the categorial feature "[*verb*]." The combination of *v* with V in (133) is an ingredient of the "causative" meaning in the sentence in (131) (see Belvin 1996; Hale and Keyser 1993, 2002; Megerdoomian 2002; Zubizarreta and Oh 2007). The formatives Asp_v and Asp_V are two aspectual elements, associated with *v* and V, respectively. The existence of two kinds of aspect has been argued for in Smith 1997, which distinguishes the *Situation Aspect* from the *Viewpoint Aspect* of a sentence (see also Borer 2004; Zubizarreta and Oh 2007; Wu 2000, 2004). The lower Asp_V in (133) denotes the *Situation Aspect* in the sense of Smith 1997. This is the inherent lexical aspect of the verb, also called "Aktionsart" in the literature, which relates to telicity. The higher Asp_v in (133) denotes the *Viewpoint Aspect* in the sense of Smith 1997 and relates to the perfective/imperfective distinction. In effect, the execution of Smith's theory in (133) combines the *v*-V analysis of unergative verbs with the hypothesis in Travis 1991 and Baker 1996 that an independent aspectual formative intervenes between the lexical verb and the tense formative (*T* in (132)–(133)). The structure in (133) conforms to the revised Pollockian geometry of Baker 1996, whereby the agreement formative *Agr* does adjoin to *T* rather than project a phrase of its own. We come back later to a principled account of that revised geometry.

As argued in Lasnik and Uriagereka 2005, the uniformity of structural organization across categories suggests a symmetry principle. The exact nature of such a principle will depend on the actual form of *X*-bar theory. It has been indicated in section 3 that the standard *X*-bar schema should be replaced by the "$X^{#}$-bar motif" in (93):

(93)

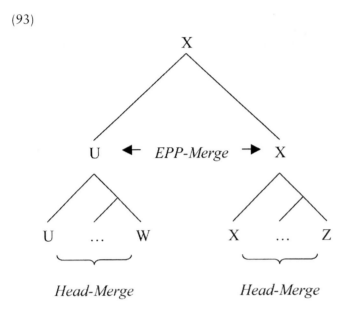

The computational architecture expressed by the $X^{#}$-bar motif is the following: Head-Merge yields IHC structures and EPP-Merge pairs the IHC structures produced by Head-Merge. It was noted earlier that within such a model, the building blocks of syntactic structure are the IHC arrangements, rather than the *X*-bar schematic ones of the standard theory (cf. the discussion of the $X^{#}$-bar motif in (93)). The symmetry principle of Lasnik and Uriagereka 2005 will then apply to the IHC arrangements. The strongest possible form of such a principle is that in (134):

(134) Categorial Symmetry (CS)

> All IHC structures are constructed from the same primitive formatives arranged in the same hierarchical order.

The implications of CS are drastic. It means in particular that a noun phrase and a verb phrase are ultimately made up of the same abstract elements, the categorial distinction between *V* and *N* being contextually determined (see Megerdoomian 2002; Vergnaud and Zubizarreta 2001). The analyses in Borer 1994, 2004, in Krifka 1989, and in Larson 2004 may be taken to anticipate such a principle. We argue in the following that CS is theoretically related to the EPP and that both principles ultimately follow from the syntactic architecture defined in (120).

If CS holds, the representation in (133) is defective, since the extended projections of *v* and of *V* in it are not entirely parallel, the extended projection of *V* lacking a tense formative. We then revise the analysis by providing *V* in (132)–(133) with its own tense formative.

In addition, we shall assume that the lowest component of a phrase is the feature *root* (*R*), in essence a pointer to the "encyclopedic knowledge" associated with the lexical head of the phrase (see Marantz 1997, Borer 2004). Assuming these principles, and registering Baker's dispatch of *Agr* to a parallel universe, the verbal complex in (133) can be reanalyzed as the ordered combination of the two structures obtained from the schema in (135) by successively taking $X = V$ and $X = v$ ("A" stands for "Asp"):

(135) Verb template (v_X)

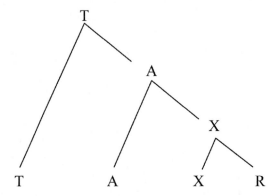

The formative *v* is reduced to the categorial feature "[*verb*]," so the associated root *R* has to be empty. The embedding of v_V in v_v is effected by identifying *T* in v_V as that root, yielding the structure in (136) (modulo the equivalence between head and projection):

(136)

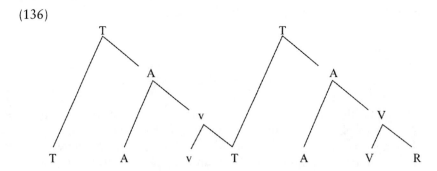

Thus, a clause such as (131) has an "inner tense" and an "outer tense," a generalization of the hypothesis for aspect. The inner tense appears to relate to the distinction between "individual level" and "stage level" predicates (see

Diesing 1990, 1992). The analysis needs to be generalized to structures with "raising verbs." We now consider the hypothesis in (120) in relation to the structures in (135) and (136).

7. PRIMITIVE ASPECTS OF SYNTACTIC STRUCTURE

The constituent structure in (135) is equivalent to the minimal one in (137) (see Appendix III and the discussion of (59)–(62) and (66) in section 3):

(137) The verb template υ_X

$$R \longrightarrow X \longrightarrow A \longrightarrow T$$

The four formatives T, A, X, R in the structure in (137) give rise to the two sets of LF functions in (138) (cf. (120)), with the structure itself identified as the mapping pictured in (139) (= (140)) or, in a different form, in (141) (see (108)–(109) and (126) in section 5):

(138) (i) {T, A, X, R, Ø}

(ii) {ΔT, ΔA, ΔX, ΔR, ΔØ}

(139)

R	↔	ΔØ
X	↔	Δ**R**
A	↔	Δ**X**
T	↔	Δ**A**
Ø	↔	Δ**T**

(140) {(R, ΔØ), (X, ΔR), (A, ΔX), (T, ΔA), (Ø, ΔT)}

(141) {<Ø|R>, <R|X>, <X|A>, <A|T>, <T|Ø>}

As observed in section 5, the relations of government and of headedness manifested in the directed structure in (137) are avatars of the asymmetric nature of the mental/neural notion of "context" (cf. the discussion below

(103) in section 5). Within the *constructivist approach* inherent in the standard generative program, every mental object or structure results from the application of elementary set-theoretic operations to an appropriate array of primitive elements (see Chomsky 1995; Lasnik and Uriagereka 2005). One way to execute that approach in the present case is to define a procedure for assembling the pairs in (139)–(141). A simple procedure would run as follows. First, select pair $<q_1|p_1>$ in the array in (138), then select a pair $<q_2|p_2>$ in the complement of this initial selection, then a pair $<q_3|p_3>$ in the complement of the first two selections, and so on and so forth. The construction is described by the nested structure in (142):

(142) $\{\{\{\{\{<q_1|p_1>\} <q_2|p_2>\} <q_3|p_3>\} <q_4|p_4>\} <q_5|p_5>\}$

The unibranching architecture of the constituent structure in the verb template in (135) would appear to reflect that of the derivation in (142), but the two are actually unrelated. For the five doublets $<q_i|p_i>$, $i = 1, 2, 3, 4, 5$ in (142) can be selected in any order. To illustrate, the constituent structure in (135) can be generated by either of the two derivations in (143):

(143) (i) $\{\{\{\{\{<Ø|R>\} <R|X>\} <X|A>\} <A|T>\} <T|Ø>\}$

     (ii) $\{\{\{\{\{<T|Ø>\} <A|T>\} <X|A>\} <R|X>\} <Ø|R>\}$

The algorithm in (143i) generates the structure in a "bottom-up" fashion, whereas that in (143ii) does it in a "top-down" fashion. In fact, any combination of the two procedures would work, as exemplified in (144):

(144) $\{\{\{\{\{<Ø|R>\} <T|Ø>\} <X|A>\} <R|X>\} <A|T>\}$

The form of the verbal structure in (135) is ultimately defined by the conditions in (145):

(145) (i)   Every ket must be paired with the bra of a distinct formative, and conversely.[31]

     (ii) The mapping is one-one.

The conditions in (145) follow from *Full Interpretation*. The order in which the pairs are selected is irrelevant. What counts is how each pair is formed. In fact, this is true of any version of the standard theory which takes headedness to be a primitive property identified independently of the derivation. Thus, the structure in (135) in section 6 can be derived as in (147), where "Expand" is defined in (146) (see (56)–(57) in section 3 for the notation):

(146) Expand P into $(_P\,Q\,P)$ in $\Sigma =_{\text{def}}$ take the result of merging P and Q with label P and unify it with every occurrence of P in the structure Σ[32]

(147) (i) Expand $\varnothing$ into T (identified with $(_\varnothing\,\varnothing\,T)$)

     (ii) Expand T into $(_T\,A\,T)$ in the structure produced by (i)

     (iii) Expand A into $(_A\,X\,A)$ in the structure produced by (ii)

     (iv) Expand X into $(_X\,R\,X)$ in the structure produced by (iii)

In all these cases, the set-theoretic algorithm plays second fiddle to the fundamental organizing principle, which is *Full Interpretation*. The situation is different with phasal organization, where the set-theoretic construction plays a central role (see below).

There are two possible tacks at this point. One is to take υ_X to be indeed a primitive template, the LF reflection of a structure defined within the external C-I systems. Or, instead, the more general conjecture in (148) can be adopted as a working hypothesis:

(148) IHC arrangements are constructed within grammar subject to boundary conditions defined by systems external to grammar.

As it turns out, the empirically correct approach is the latter. For, besides the form υ_X in (139)–(140), there is another attested LF arrangement of the formatives T, A, X, R, namely that in (149):

(149) $\{<R|\varnothing>, <X|R>, <A|X>, <T|A>, <\varnothing|T>\}$

The tree diagram corresponding to the mapping in (149) is that in (150), the mirror image of υ_X:

(150) Mirror Verb template $(\upsilon_X{}^*)$

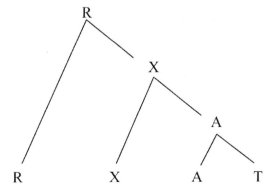

The form $\upsilon_X{}^*$ is the input to morphological interpretation, the *surface structure* of the verbal complex in the sense of Chomsky 1965.[33] The grammatical coexistence of the two forms υ_X and $\upsilon_X{}^*$ is an instance of Baker's *Mirror Principle* (see Baker 1985). By (148), the hierarchical organization displayed by each form reflects a mental/brain architecture external to grammar. The objects denoted by *T, A, X, R* in υ_X and $\upsilon_X{}^*$ are actually *variable formatives*. Each one ranges over a particular set of *values* (e.g., *[+/– Distal]* in the case of *T*) and is *specified* for one of these values in any given structural description (e.g., *[+Distal]*). The most immediate interpretation of the schemas υ_X and $\upsilon_X{}^*$ then runs as follows:

> (151) The form υ_X represents the construction of a mental object, whereby specified formatives are successively incorporated in a preordained order. The symmetric form $\upsilon_X{}^*$ represents the *reading* of an object constructed in accordance with υ_X.

Thus, υ_X depicts iterated applications of *Merge*, albeit in a mental system distinct from the grammatical level LF. And $\upsilon_X{}^*$ depicts the applications of the converse operation *Demerge* (see Fukui and Takano 1998). Elementary IHC structures such as υ_X and $\upsilon_X{}^*$ then relate to the derivational architecture, but indirectly: they are *plans* of derivations taking place at arguably lower mental/brain levels. In that realm, *Merge* and *Demerge* denote the general mechanisms of *synthesis* and of *analysis*, respectively.[34] The question is how Human Language (HL) manages to construct a grammatical representation of this computationally central dichotomy. In other words:

> (152) What is the source of the Mirror Principle?

We try to answer that question in section 9. In the following section, we show how the standard *X*-bar properties of IHC structures emerge from the definition of these structures as correspondences between kets and bras.

8.   CONSTITUENT STRUCTURE FROM KETS AND BRAS

Let us consider the structure υ_X (the verb template) in (135) again. As we have seen in sections 3 and 4, υ_X is just a particular element in an equivalence class of tree structures, which together constitute the syntactic description of the verb template. That equivalence class is defined by the directed graph in (137), now represented as the mapping in (140):

> (140) $\{(\mathbf{R}, \Delta\varnothing), (\mathbf{X}, \Delta\mathbf{R}), (\mathbf{A}, \Delta\mathbf{X}), (\mathbf{T}, \Delta\mathbf{A}), (\varnothing, \Delta\mathbf{T})\}$

From a mathematical point of view, the mapping in (140) is analyzed into three distinct sets of objects: its *domain* (the set of kets in (153i)), its *codomain* (the set of bras in (153ii)), and the correspondence proper between these two sets (the set of pairs in (153iii)).

(153) (i) {|R>, |X>, |A>, |T>,|Ø>} (*domain*)

   (ii) {<R|, <X|, <A|, <T|, <Ø|} (*codomain*)

   (iii) {(<Ø|,|R>), (<R|,|X>), (<X|,|A>), (<A|,|T>), (<T|,|Ø>)} (*correspondence*)

In the simplified notation of (125), the mapping in (140) is analyzed as in (154):

(154) (i) {R, X, A, T,Ø} (*domain, a set of kets*)

   (ii) {ΔR, ΔX, ΔA, ΔT, ΔØ} (*codomain, a set of bras*)

   (iii) {(R, ΔØ), (X, ΔR), (A, ΔX), (T, ΔA), (Ø,ΔT)} (*correspondence*)

A crucial question is how the family of X-bar structures which constitutes the verb template actually emerges from this primitive mapping. In essence, the problem is to link the two central concepts of the theory, that of "bra" and that of "constituent."

A term such as $\Delta\xi$ means "in the context of ξ." An informal notion of "context" has sufficed up to this point. To proceed with the theoretical construction, however, the notion must be codified into some set of syntactic axioms. One of the central principles assumed in this essay is stated in (128) (see section 5):

(128) Given two mental arrangements (representations or processes) *M* and *M'* such that *M* and *M'* are both (possibly trivial) collections of more elementary mental arrangements, the pair {*M, M'*} is a mental arrangement, equal to the union of *M* and *M'*, if and only if the mental coupling in (i) holds:[35]

   (i) (ξ, $\Delta\eta$), with (ξ,η) = (*M, M'*) or (*M', M*)

To the extent that a constituent can be equated with the collection of "terminals" that it ultimately dominates (see Appendix I), the principle in (128) entails the following axioms:

(155) Let *Q* and *P* be two constituents. Then:

   a. (Q, ΔP) $\Rightarrow$ {Q, P} *is a constituent*

   b. {Q, P} *is a constituent* $\Rightarrow$ (Q, ΔP) or (P, ΔQ)

The axiom in (155a) expresses a natural intrinsic relation between the two concepts of "context" and of "constituent." The disjunction in the axiom in (155b) is an *exclusive* one, implying that the two sister constituents *P* and *Q* have asymmetric roles in the mother constituent {*P, Q*}. As has been argued in section 5 (cf. (103)), such an asymmetry is a general feature of the notion of "context" in the mind/brain realm. Consider again the mapping in (154). By the axiom in (155a), that mapping gives rise to the set of constituents in (156):

(156)

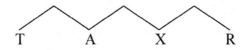

T   A   X   R

By (155b), the preceding set of constituents is the only one that can be derived from the mapping in (154). The system in (155) is then insufficient, since, for example, it cannot generate the complete set of constituents associated with an IHC structure (see section 3, in particular (80)). What is lacking is a formula that links the two notions of "context" and of "constituent" in a recursive manner. Arguably, a natural property of contextuality is the law in (157):

(157) If Q is in the context of P and R is in the context of Q, then R is in the context of the couple *{Q, P}*.

Such a law in effect take the notion of "constituent" to be inherent in that of "context." It provides the missing recursive rule:[36]

(158) $(Q, \Delta P), (R, \Delta Q) \Rightarrow (R, \Delta\{Q, P\})$

The pairing *(R, Δ{Q, P})* in (158) is well defined since the pair *{Q, P}* is a constituent by (155a). The rule in (158) will extend a primitive mapping between atomic units such as that in (154) to a mapping between heads and more complex contexts.

In the rule in (158), the term Q in *(Q, ΔP)* acts as the *boundary* of the constituent *{Q, P}*, its interface with an external structure. This indicates that the pairing *(Q, ΔP)* defines Q as the *label/head of the constituent {Q, P}* at LF:[37]

(159) $(Q, \Delta P) \Rightarrow Q$ is the *label/head* of the constituent *{Q, P}*

Conversely:

(160) A phrase with *label* Q is analyzed as a pair *{{Q, P}, (Q, ΔP)}*.

By (159)–(160), the constituent analysis in (156), assumed to be derived from the mapping in (154), is labeled as shown in (161) ("P→Q" is the relation "Q immediately dominates P"):

(161)

T   A   X

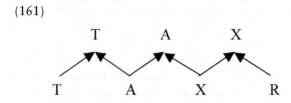

T   A   X   R

The various axioms above relating the two notions of "context" and of "constituent" are incorporated in (162):

(162) Contextuality and Constituency Axioms (CC Axioms)

Let Q and P be two constituents. Then:

a. $(Q, \Delta P) \Rightarrow \{Q, P\}$ *is a constituent*

b. $\{Q, P\}$ *is a constituent* $\Rightarrow (Q, \Delta P)$ or $(P, \Delta Q)$

c. $(Q, \Delta P), (R, \Delta Q) \Rightarrow (R, \Delta\{Q, P\})$

d. $(Q, \Delta P) \Rightarrow Q$ is the *head* of the constituent $\{Q, P\}$

e. A phrase with *label* Q is analyzed as a pair $\{\{Q, P\}, (Q, \Delta P)\}$.

The recursive rule in (162c) (= (158)) extends the set of constituents associated with the primitive mapping in (154). If the two rules in (162a) and (162c) are applied optionally subject to the output constraints in (163) (see Appendix V), the constituent analyses in (164) are derived (where "P→Q" has the same meaning as in (161)):

(163) Given two adjacent formatives F and F' in the domain of the primitive mapping:

a. there exists at least one constituent C such that C dominates both F and F'.

b. if two distinct constituents C and C' dominate both F and F', then either C dominates C' or C' dominates C.

(164)

(i)

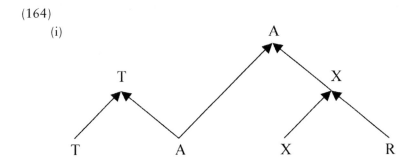

(ii)

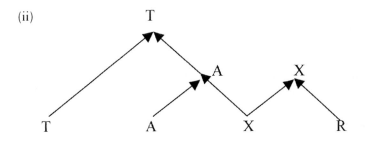

(iii)

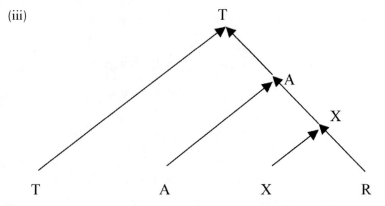

The particular constituent structure in (164iii) is the standard tree description in (135). Other structures shown in section 3 arise from combining parts of the mapping in (154) with constituent analyses derived by (162). For example, the pairing in (166) can be derived by applying (162c) twice, as shown in (165):

(165) (i)   (X, ΔR), (A ΔX) ⇒ (A, Δ{X, R})

      (ii) (A, Δ{X, R}), (T, ΔA) ⇒ (T, Δ{A, {X, R}})

(166) (T, Δ{A, {X, R}})

The pairing in (166) combined with the primitive mapping in (154) can be represented by the diagram in (167), identical to that in (66) in section 3 (here, "P→Q" may represent the relation "Q immediately dominates P" or the relation "Q governs P" depending on the configuration):

(167)

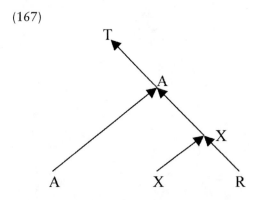

To take another example, the rule in (162a) may apply to the output in (165a), producing the constituent analysis in (168). The latter may in turn be incorporated with the mapping in (154), yielding the structure in (169).

(168) {A, {X, R}}

(169)

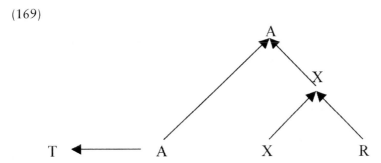

Thus, the system in (162) provides a definition of the notion of "IHC structure" by associating a characteristic class of constituents to a linear dependency structure (such as that in (154), for example); see (73) and (80) in section 3. The head-projection relation reduces to the recursive formula in (162c), more exactly, to the unicity of such a formula within the system. There is a second recursive formula which may relate contexts and constituents, namely the mirror image of (162c) in (170):

(170) $(Q, \Delta P), (R, \Delta Q) \Rightarrow (\{R, Q\}, \Delta P)$

The rule in (170) expresses the natural law for contexts in (171), itself the mirror image of the law in (157):

(171) If Q is in the context of P and R is in the context of Q, then the couple $\{R, Q\}$ is in the context of P.

One could imagine a formal system that includes both recursive formulas in (162c) and in (170). Such a system is presented in (172):

(172) Contextuality and Constituency Axioms (CC Axioms)

Let Q and P be two constituents. Then:

a. $(Q, \Delta P) \Rightarrow \{Q, P\}$ *is a constituent*

b. $\{Q, P\}$ *is a constituent* $\Rightarrow (Q, \Delta P)$ or $(P, \Delta Q)$

c. $(Q, \Delta P), (R, \Delta Q) \Rightarrow (R, \Delta\{Q, P\})$

d. $(Q, \Delta P), (R, \Delta Q) \Rightarrow (\{R, Q\}, \Delta P)$

A symmetrical system such as that in (172) does not give rise to any notion of "head" or "projection." In fact, when applied to a linear dependency structure such as that in (154), the system in (172) will define that dependency as a "string".

The system in (162) describes the fundamental architecture of *bare phrase structure,* with the *label* of a phrase identified by (162d) as its immediate "noncontextual" constituent. The notions of *immediate domination, terminal,* and *nonterminal* are defined as usual. An implicit property of the earlier system is that constituent structure is *binary*. As argued in Freidin and Vergnaud, forthcoming a mapping such as that in (173) is one on which the same grammatical relation holds between Q and P' as between Q and P:

(173) $(Q, \Delta P), (Q, \Delta P')$

The two "contextual" constituents P and P' in the structure defined by (173) must then be conjoined by a logical connector (*and, or, if-then*). Some important consequences follow, but we will not pursue the matter here, referring the reader to chapters 5 and 6.

One issue here is that of the empirical relevance of the notion of constituent just defined. We note that the standard notion of constituent really describes a directly observable property of *phases,* not of IHC structures. However, the current notion is relevant to the abstract LF computations when extended to the EPP-merging of IHC structures, as we argue in section 9.

9.   DERIVING THE MIRROR PRINCIPLE: THE FABRIC OF SYNTAX

The essential step that takes grammatical architecture beyond IHC structures is the fact in (174):

(174) The contextual function of a formative *can itself be a formative.*

For example, the element $<R_X|$ in the mapping in (140) is realized as the morpheme identifying the *conjugation class* when X is a verb. It may be useful at this point to abstract away from the established terminology. Let us denote by O the pivotal category in a clause. The central mapping of clause structure is then that in (175):

(175) $\{<\varnothing|R_O>, <R_O|O>, <O|A_O>, <A_O|T_O>, <T_O|\varnothing>\}$

The contextual formatives are the *uninterpretable formatives* in the sense of Chomsky 1995. A fundamental aspect of the computational system of human language (C_{HL}) is that it uses the contextual formatives of O as the interpretable formatives of a *dual category* O^*:

(176) $<O| = |O^*>, |O> = <O^*|$

More generally:

(177) $<X| = |X^*>, |X> = <X^*|$, for every property X

Within current terminology, $O^* = N$. The interpretable formatives of O^* can in turn give rise to a mapping of the form in (140), as shown in (178):

(178) $\{<\varnothing|R_{O^*}>, <R_{O^*}|O^*>, <O^*|A_{O^*}>, <A_{O^*}|T_{O^*}>, <T_{O^*}|\varnothing>\}$

Structural Case is the signature of the mapping in (178), as distinct from the mere morphological realization of the set of uninterpretable (contextual) formatives of O. The "dual mapping" in (178) is the *specifier of* the mapping in (175). The dual formatives can be viewed as the "glue" of the pivotal category.

It is easy to see that the mapping in (178) gives rise to the inverse of that in (175). The set of pairs in (178) translates into the "dual" set in (180), assuming the identification in (179):

(179) $\varnothing^* = \varnothing$

(180) $\{<R_O|\varnothing>, <O|R_O>, <A_O|O>, <T_O|A_O>, <\varnothing|T_O>\}$

The mapping in (180) corresponds to the constituent structure υ_X^* (the "Mirror Verb template") in (150). Thus, there is a direct link between the EPP, checking and the Mirror Principle. The mirror structure may arise because the contextual (uninterpretable) formatives of O are also realized as the interpretable formatives of the dual O^* category. The required independent realization of O^* (signaled by structural case) is EPP. Why it is required does not follow from any of the previous notions or principles. It could be an effect of Full Interpretation: if a set of elements may give rise to some structure or interpretation, it must do so. So, a ket in some dual category must combine with the other kets in the category to produce a full object.

Of course, the architecture that emerges is quite different from the standard derivational one. We develop some aspects of it in the following. One must note that O and O^* are not completely symmetric. The O^* mapping is not marked by verbal uninterpretable formatives the way the O mapping is (with the person and number features, for example).

10. PHASE CALCULUS AND EXTENSION TO v-V

A phase is the pairing of a category with its dual (specifier). The constituent structure interpretation of a phase is based on the principle in (181):

(181) A ket and its dual form a constituent.

Like all principles, the principle in (181) is governed by the equivalence between heads and projections. In keeping with the spirit of the original definition in (159), the head in a combination $\{x^*, x\}$ is x, because x^* is a *contextual formative*, ultimately a bra with respect to the pivotal category in the phase. The rule in (181) is unordered with respect to the structural interpretive principles of section 8. So, this generates competing constituent structures, as illustrated in (182) (where x stands for $|x>$):

(182) $\{ \{_{n^*} \text{ m}^*, \text{n}^*\}, \{_n \text{ m, n}\}\}$ or $\{ \{\{\text{m, m}^*\}, \text{n}\}, \text{n}^*\}$

The two representations in (182) define the core process in "A-movement."

The connection between V and v is not mirrored by the specifiers (except possibly in the case of the Romance reflexive clitics). In the case of the clausal phases, the "lower" V combines with its specifier (argument). If $<T_V|$ is $|D>$, and if one postulates that a phase must contain the image of every element in it, then the V-phase includes v, as conjectured in Chomsky 1999, 2001.

11.   PHASES AS "SUPERCATEGORIES":
THE COMPUTATIONAL NATURE OF *FOCUS*

In a phase, the pivotal category and its specifier may receive a higher order analysis by which they are described as a "supercategory" whose bras are provided by an external category, the *focus*. There should be one focus per phase, in line with Rizzi's recent proposal, and, more fundamentally with the proposal by Simpson and Wu (2002b).

12.   REMNANT MOVEMENT, COMPLEMENT
CLAUSES, AND *WH*-MOVEMENT

The symmetry produced by the construction of the dual category yields at least one class of remnant movements, those studied in Koopman and Szabolcsi 2000. Another class arises from the notion in section 11.

A complement clause will be analyzed as in Rosenbaum 1967, as independently proposed in Kayne 2003, 2009.

As for *wh*-movement, it relates to focus and to the fact that *wh*-words may partake of the complementizer system (a parameter).

13.   CONCLUSION

Syntax may not relate PF and LF, but rather two more abstract levels, that for *analysis* (AF) and that for *synthesis* (SF) (see (151) and the discussion following (151) in section 6). There is a privileged, but not exclusive, relation between PF and AF on the one hand, and between LF and SF on the other. AF and SF describe computations at other mental levels.

Independently, the generalization of ICA to A-movement will indirectly support the theory of argument structure developed in Hale and Keyser 1993, 2002 (in particular, with regard to the possible lexical configurations and to the distribution of specifiers among those). It will also support the clausal structure brought to light in Rizzi 2004a, 2004b, as well as the general principles for focus established in Simpson and Wu 2002a.

APPENDIX I: ON THE TOPOLOGY OF STRINGS AND OF CONSTITUENT STRUCTURES

Consider the structure in (a):

(a) [Mary Past see John]

A simplified tree description of that structure is given in (b):

(b)

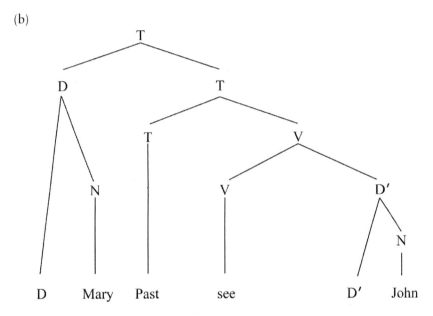

A phrase-marker such as that in (b) combines three kinds of relations among constituents: the *head-projection* relation, the *domination* relation, and *linear ordering*. The head-projection relation is formalized as a *labeling* of the constituent structure (see in particular the discussion of (56)–(58) in chapter 5; see also Appendix V for an alternative formalization of the head-projection relation). The second constitutive relation of phrase-markers, *domination*, defines the hierarchy of constituents. Given two constituents A and B such that A dominates B, the set of lexical items that A dominates includes those that B dominates. If each constituent is equated with the (unordered) set of lexical items it dominates, domination then reduces to *set inclusion*.[38] Conversely, let S be a set of lexical items and let Σ be a family of pairwise disjoint subsets of S partially ordered by inclusion and containing S: Σ represents the hierarchy of constituents in some phrase-marker. For example, the arrangement of constituents in (b) is represented by the partial ordering of sets in (c) when linear ordering is factored out:

(c)

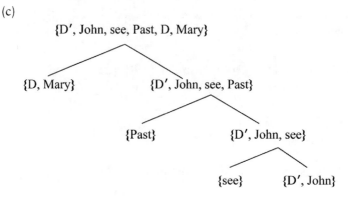

We note that identifying each set in (c) with its grammatical head yields the tree in (d), in effect the *bare phrase structure* version of the original one in (a):

(d)

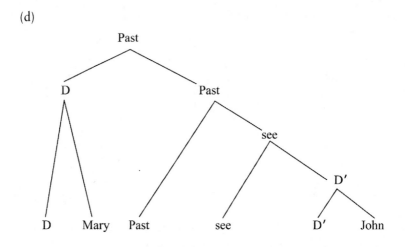

The third constitutive relation of a phrase-marker is the *linear ordering* of its terminals. It has been argued that this ordering is a property of the PF interface, not an intrinsic property of syntactic phrase-markers (Bobaljik 2002; Bury 2003; Chametzky 1995; Chomsky and Lasnik 1993; Lasnik and Uriagereka 2005; McCawley 1982; Speas 1990; Stowell 1981; Travis 1984). In line with this assumption, a constituent structure at LF is frequently visualized as a "Calder mobile," a 3D sculpture shaped as a tree in which sister branches rotate freely around the vertical axis going through the node they stem from. For example, the subtree erected above the items *D', John, see, Past* in (b) can be modeled by the Calder mobile pictured in (e):

(e)

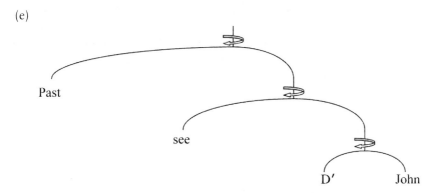

Such mobile sculptures indeed are natural models for structural descriptions that abstract away from the linear PF ordering: with its rotational symmetries, a Calder mobile is a pure representation of domination relations. Specifically, these relations hold among the surfaces described by the branches of the mobile when they rotate around their stems. The domination ordering so defined can be represented as a geometric arrangement of cylinders. Given a Calder mobile K, let s be some stem (node) in K. Denote by σ_s be the surface described by the branches attached to s, and by C_s the narrowest vertical (infinite) cylinder that encloses every surface σ_r such that s dominates r. Clearly, if s dominates r, C_s contains C_r, and conversely. Denote by X_K the set of cylinders canonically associated with K by the preceding construction. The domination ordering within K translates into an inclusion ordering within X_K. A cylinder in X_K is defined by its intersection with some (nonvertical) plane, and so is the whole set X_K. The domination ordering within K then ultimately reduces to the inclusion ordering within a system of planar discs. To illustrate, the domination ordering in the mobile pictured in (e) is represented by the diagram in (f), where the disc delimited by each closed curve represents the set of terminals written within it:

(f)

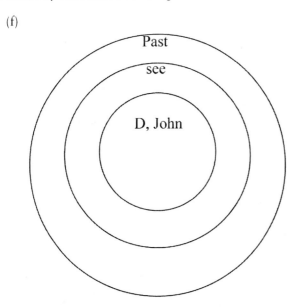

The particular arrangement of discs shown in (f) is characteristic of the uni-branching architecture: a unibranching structure is one whose planar represen-tation is a family of "concentric" closed curves. Planar diagrams such as that in (f) have classically been used to picture inclusion relations among sets. Specifi-cally, the inclusion of the set *B* in the set *A*, denoted by $B \subset A$, is drawn as in (g):

(g)

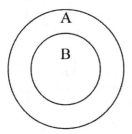

Assuming this convention, the diagram in (f) may be taken to depict the arrangement of sets and terminals in (h), where domination means inclusion and where the items *Past* and *see* are equated with the singleton sets *{Past}* and *{see}*, respectively (see note 34):

(h)

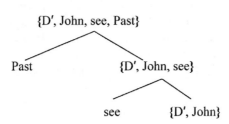

The partial ordering in (h) in turn describes the hierarchy of constituents within the predicate in the phrase-marker in (b); cf. (c). The general result is that the planar diagram which represents the hierarchical structure of a Calder mobile is identical to that obtained when constituents are identified with sets ordered by inclusion. Then:

(i) The smallest topological dimension required to represent the hierar-chy of constituents within a phrase-marker is that of a plane, i.e., 2.

A Calder mobile resides in 3D space, but the constituent structure it defines resides in 2D space.

PF interpretation then requires mapping a 2D structure onto a 1D space (the time axis). The mapping can be visualized as a line running through the planar arrangement of discs that represents the constituent structure. For example, the PF interpretation of the structure represented in (f) (= (h)) can be described as the intersection of the closed curves with a line, as shown in (j):

(j)

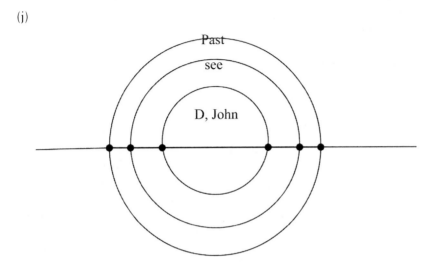

Each closed curve defines two possible positions on the crossing line. The overall structure gives rise to eight possible sequences, from which the PF representation will be ultimately derived. The fundamental difference between a 2D disc and its 1D image is that the former is bounded by one connected line, while the latter is bounded by two disconnected extremities. Correspondingly, the complement of a 2D disc in a plane is a topologically connected area, whereas the complement of a 1D disc (segment) on a line is made up of two disjoint parts. Still, PF interpretation is *topologically continuous* in the following sense:

(k) Two sister constituents are adjacent at PF.

In a planar diagram, sisterhood, or mutual c-command, are defined as follows:

(l) Two objects in a planar diagram are in a sisterhood relation just in case every disc that contains one contains the other.

The property in (k) implies that grammatical constituent structure is binary branching. As argued in Appendix V, adjacency is sufficient to define strings. But the continuity of PF interpretation cannot by itself deliver the complete PF ordering. Additional principles are required. One must distinguish here between the *linear ordering at PF* and the *interpretation of that ordering* as a particular direction on the time axis.[39] As hinted in Kayne 1994, grammatical theory is invariant under time reversal, the time arrow being derived from the production/processing component of the language faculty (see Kayne 1994:37). One may surmise that the principles governing the ordering of morphemes within words are the key, possibly along the lines of Segui and Zubizarreta 1985. The time ordering of constituents within a sentence would then follow from Baker's Mirror Principle. Independently, the linear structure of the PF interpretation will follow from one additional clause and one additional construct. The clause is stated in (o):

(o)   Adjacency is head invariant.

The principle in (o) means that if two objects are adjacent, their heads must be adjacent. Clearly, this principle entails that, of two daughters of an embedded constituent, at most one is branching (if two sisters are both branching, no further merging is possible by (o)). It also implies that the direction of headedness is uniform in a unibranching structure. This still leaves out specifiers and adjuncts. To accommodate the corresponding structures, a *metrics* is introduced on the time axis which allows for a notion of *scale* or *resolution*. Adjacency will then be defined relative to a given scale. Consider a constituent with three daughters, as in (p):

(p)

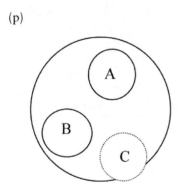

We assume that the resolution required for discs A and B is 1, but that required for disc C is k^{-1}, k some number greater than 1. This means that if PF interpretation operates with resolution 1, disc C is not represented at PF and discs A and B are adjacent. If PF interpretation operates with resolution k^{-1}, disc C is represented, and will be adjacent to both disc A and disc B, i.e., will be located between them. A constituent such as disc C in the diagram in (p) is a specifier or an adjunct. By definition, it gives rise to a dual representation, one with it shown in (q), the other without it shown in (r):

(q)

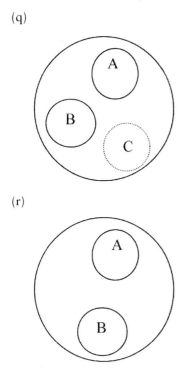

(r)

The dual representations in (q)–(r) reflect the *two-segment* nature of adjunction, extended to specifiers as in Kayne 1994. Additional adjunctions may be defined at ever-finer degrees of resolution. Like the arrow of time, the metrical (in the sense of measurement) nature of the PF representation of specifiers and adjuncts should be expected to fall under the production/processing component of the language faculty. This would imply that the structure would be sensitive to properties like *weight,* which could affect the PF interpretation (see Miller and Chomsky 1963; Hawkins 1994).

APPENDIX II: ELEMENTS OF THE NOTION OF GRAPH

The graphs of interest in the text discussion are the *simple graphs*. A *simple graph* G is a set of *nodes* together with a set of unordered pairs of nodes called *edges*. A *walk* in a graph G is a sequence of nodes $\pi = (w_1, \ldots, w_n)$ such that two consecutive nodes in π form an edge. A *path* is a walk in which all nodes are distinct. A *cycle* is a walk $(w_1, \ldots, w_n)$ in which $w_1 = w_n$ and all other nodes are distinct from w_1 and from each other. Two nodes u and v in G are said to be *connected* if there exists a path $(w_1, \ldots, w_n)$

in G such that $w_1 = u$ and $w_n = v$. A graph G is *connected* just in case any two nodes in it are connected. A *directed graph* or *digraph* is a simple graph in which the edges are *oriented:* given two nodes u and v, (u, v) and (v, u) count as distinct edges and at most one of these two pairs is an edge in G. Given some node u in a digraph G, the *outdegree* (resp. *indegree*) of u is the number of edges in G that have the form (u, v) (resp. (v, u)).

**APPENDIX III: ON THE NOTION OF EQUIVALENCE
                  AMONG CONSTITUENT STRUCTURES**

A graph-theoretic account of syntactic trees and of telescoping might run as follows.[40] First a notion of *PM-graph* is introduced:

(a) A simple graph G is called a *Phrase Marker graph* or *PM-graph* iff. it has the following properties:

   (i) G is connected and contains no cycle.

   (ii)   The nodes in G are labeled by occurrences of lexical items.

   (iii) G is directed.

   (iv)   The nodes in G are of outdegree 0, 1 or 2 and of indegree 1 or 2.

   (v)   There is one and only one node in G whose indegree is 0. This node is called the *root*.

   (vi)   If G contains more than one occurrence of some lexical item L, every occurrence of L in G is adjacent to another occurrence of L.

   (vii) If G contains the edge $<L_j, L_i>$, where L_i and L_j are two occurrences of the same lexical item L, then G also contains an edge $<L'_k, L_j>$, where L'_k is an occurrence of a lexical L' distinct from L.

The various clauses in (a) restrict the class of graphs considered to the type of structures exemplified in (59)–(62) and in (66)–(68) in chapter 5. By (iii), every edge $<W, U>$ is an ordered pair. The ordering is interpreted as *domination:* by definition, U dominates W in G just in case G includes the edge $<W, U>$. Clauses (iv)–(v) state facts about such structures as those in (59)–(62) and in (66)–(68) in chapter 5. In particular, a node may dominate at most two nodes and may itself be dominated by at most two nodes. Clause (vi) states that if the structure contains more than one occurrence of some lexical item L, the occurrences of L label a head and its projections (in the sense of X-bar theory). Clause (vii) states that an occurrence of L may dominate another occurrence of L only when it "branches." To illustrate, the constituent structure in (59) in the text will be represented as the PM-graph in (b):

(b) (i) Lexical items: {W, Z, Y, X}

   (ii) Nodes: {W_0, Z_0, Z_1, Y_0, Y_1, X_0, X_1}

   (iii) Edges: {$<W_0, Z_1>$, $<Z_0, Z_1>$, $<Z_1, Y_1>$, $<Y_0, Y_1>$, $<Y_1, X_1>$, $<X_0, X_1>$}

The constituent structure in (62) will be represented as in (c):

(c) (i) Lexical items: {W, Z, Y, X}

   (ii) Nodes: {W_0, Z_0, Z_1, Y_0, Y_1, X_0, X_1}

   (iii) Edges: {$<W_0, Z_1>$, $<Z_0, Z_1>$, $<Z_0, Y_1>$, $<Y_0, Y_1>$, $<Y_0, X_1>$, $<X_0, X_1>$}

Note that a graph such as that in (d) is excluded by clause (vii) in (a):

(d) (i) Lexical items: {W, Z, Y, X}

   (ii) Nodes: {W_0, Z_0, Z_1, Y_0, Y_1, X_0, X_1}

   (iii) Edges: {$<W_0, Z_0>$, $<Z_0, Z_1>$, $<Z_0, Y_0>$, $<Y_0, Y_1>$, $<Y_0, X_0>$, $<X_0, X_1>$}

In a second step, the notion of *master graph* is introduced:

(e) Given a PM-graph G, the *master graph of G* is the PM-graph derived from G by contracting all edges of the form $<L_i, L_j>$, L some lexical item, where an edge is said to be *contracted* from a graph if it is deleted and its ends are identified (see, e.g., Balakrishnan and Ranganathan 2000).

A master graph is then the structure derived from a PM-graph by "telescoping" all nodes labeled by the same lexical item. The master graph for the structure in (59) in chapter 5 is:

(f) (i) Lexical items: {W, Z, Y, X}

   (ii) Nodes: {W, Z, Y, X}

   (iii) Edges: {$<W, Z>$, $<Z, Y>$, $<Y, X>$}

This is also the master graph for the structures in (60)–(62) and (66)–(68) in chapter 5. In fact, the master graph for this family of structures can be identified with the "minimal structure" in (68) in chapter 5. This leads to the definition of the equivalence relation in (g):

(g) (i) Two PM-graphs are *equivalent* just in case they have the same master graph.

   (ii) Two tree structures are equivalent just in case their associated PM-graphs are equivalent in the sense of (i).

The structures in (59)–(62) and in (66)–(68) in chapter 5 are then equivalent in the sense of (g). Apart from the mathematical significance of this equivalence, there is the question of the empirical content of the representations in (60)–(62) and (66)–(68) in chapter 5. We may take them to describe the possibilities for "head-to-head movement" within the structure.

APPENDIX IV: ON THE LCA

The theory in Kayne 1994 postulates that linear ordering at PF must be derived from antisymmetric c-command at LF. A central construct of the theory is the mapping d defined in (a)–(b):

(a) $d(X)$, X a constituent = $_{def}$ the set of terminals in X (the terminals dominated by X)

(b) $d([X, Y])$, $[X, Y]$ an ordered pair of constituents = $_{def}$ the set of ordered pairs of terminals $[a, b]$ such that a is in $d(X)$ and b, in $d(Y)$

The fundamental principle in the theory is the *Linear Correspondence Axiom (LCA)*:

(c) Linear Correspondence Axiom

$d(A_P)$ is a linear ordering of $d(P)$
where P is some phrase marker and A_P is the maximal set of pairs $[X, Y]$ such that X and Y are constituents of P and X asymmetrically c-commands Y in P.

The LCA has emerged as a principle of great explanatory force (see Kayne 1994, and subsequent work). Paradoxically, it may be inadequate as a law governing the mapping between LF and PF. The LCA assumes that a string reduces to a linear ordering of its constituents. This is stated in (d):

(d) $e_1{}^\wedge \ldots {}^\wedge e_i{}^\wedge \ldots {}^\wedge e_n \approx e_1 < \ldots < e_i < \ldots < e_n$

But, as argued in the text, the ordering immediately defined by $e_1{}^\wedge \ldots {}^\wedge e_n$ is a relation in the *power set* of $\{e_1, \ldots e_n\}$, i.e., is an ordering of the substrings in $e_1{}^\wedge \ldots {}^\wedge e_n$. The problem here is that $d(A_P)$ in (c) does not in general define an ordering of the substrings of terminals. Consider the structure in (e), for example:

(e) $(_K (_L l) (_M (_N n) (_P (_Q q))))$

The phrase marker K in (e) is admissible for the LCA. The set A_K is that in (f):

(f) {[L, N], [L, P], [L, Q], [N, Q]}

The set $d(A_K)$ is that in (g):

(g) {[l, n], [l, q], [n, q]}

The set $d(A_K)$ does define a linear ordering of the set of terminals *{l, n, q}*. But it does not define any ordering among the substrings: there is no pair of nonterminals *[X, Y]* such that *X* dominates *l* (resp. *l^n*) and *Y* dominates *n^q* (resp. *q*) and *X* asymmetrically c-commands *Y*. Thus, the homomorphism defined by the LCA is not a *natural* one in the sense of the text.

Despite this shortcoming, the LCA has led to many elegant and compelling accounts, in particular in terms of the notion of *remnant movement* (see, e.g., Kayne 1998; Koopman and Szabolcsi 2000; for analyses in the same vein, but independent of any "correspondence postulate" such as the LCA, see also Johnson 2001; Lasnik 1999). We argue in the text that remnant movement and other tools that have arisen from the LCA may be recast in slightly different terms, in keeping nevertheless with the spirit of the LCA.

APPENDIX V: GENERALIZED STRINGS AND CONSTITUENT STRUCTURES

The purpose of this appendix is to define a general notion of *structure* under which the notion of *string* in the text will be subsumed. A preliminary step is to introduce a notion of *binary analysis:*

(a) Let *A* be a set of items, called the *carrier set.* A *binary analysis of A,* written *K,* is a *maximal* family of subsets of *A,* called *constituents,* which meets the following condition:

(BA)   For every constituent *C* in *K,* there is a *unique* partition *[D, D']* of *C* such that *D* (resp. *D'*) is either an element of *A* or an element of *K*.[41] The constituent *C* is said to *dominate D and D' in K,* and *D* and *D'* are said to be *adjacent in K.*

Condition (BA) implies that if a constituent in an analysis *K* has three elements or more, then one of its subsets is also in *K*. To illustrate, suppose *A* is the set *{p, q, r, s}*. Each family of subsets in (b) is a binary analysis of *A* in the sense of (a):

(b) 1. {{p, q}, {q, r}, {r, s}}

     2. {{p, q}, {p, q, r}, {r, s}}

     3. {{p, q}, {q, r}, {q, r, s}}

4. {{p, q}, {r, s}, {p, q, r, s}}

5. {{p, q}, {p, q, r}, {p, q, r, s}}

6. {{q, r}, {q, r, s}, {p, q, r, s}}

7. {{q, r}, {p, q, r}, {p, q, r, s}}

8. {{r, s}, {q, r, s}, {p, q, r, s}}

9. {{q, r}, {p, q, r}, {q, r, s}}

10. {{q, r}, {p, q, r}, {r, s}}

11. {{p, q}, {r, s}}

12. {{p, q}, {q, r}, {p, s}, {p, r, s}}

The analysis in (b1) can be identified as a particular type of graph. As we shall see, such graphs, called *chains,* are a central component of the notion of "string" defined in this appendix.[42] The analyses in (b4)–(b8) are particular binary constituent structures (in the standard sense) which may be constructed from the set {*p, q, r, s*}. By contrast, each family of subsets in (c) violates at least one part or the other of the definition in (a):

(c) 1. {{p, q}, {p, q, r}}

2. {{p, q, r, s}}

3. {{p}, {q}, {r}, {s}}

4. {{p}, {q, r, s}}

5. {{p, q}, {q, r, s}}

6. {{p, q}, {q, r}, {p, q, r, s}}

7. {{p, q}, {q, r}, {p, q, r}, {r, s}}

8. {{p, q, r}, {q, r, s}}

The family in (c1) is not maximal, for no constituent in it includes *s.* The constituents in the families in (c2), (c3) or (c4) violate (BA) in (a), for none is binary in the sense of that clause. The constituent {*p, q, r*} in the family in (c7) is ill-formed, for it admits more than one binary partition.

By (BA) in (a), a binary analysis K of A, A some set, must contain at least one subset of the form {*a, b*}, where a, b are elements of A. The collection $E[K]$ of all such pairs in K defines a *graph,* denoted by $G[K]$, with each pair in $E[K]$ identified as an *edge* of $G[K]$. In general, a collection Γ of subsets of A induces a (possibly empty) graph over A:

(d)   Let Γ be a family of subsets of A, A some set. Let $E[\Gamma]$ be the (possibly empty) collection of all the pairs {*a, b*}, a, b elements of A, which belong to Γ. The collection $E[\Gamma]$ defines a graph, which is called the *graph induced by Γ* and is denoted by $G[\Gamma]$. By definition, an edge of $G[\Gamma]$ is an element of $E[\Gamma]$.

Two elements that form a pair in Γ are said to be *adjacent modulo Γ* or *adjacent in $G[\Gamma]$*. An important property of graphs is *connectedness:*

(e) Given a graph G, two nodes a and b of G are *connected in G* just in case there exists a sequence of nodes of G $\{a_1, \ldots, a_n\}$ such that $a_1 = a$, $a_n = b$ and every pair $\{a_i, a_{i+1}\}$, $i = 1, \ldots, n-1$, is an edge of G. Such a connecting sequence is called a *path*.[43]

If the graph G in the above definition is the graph induced by a family Γ of subsets of A, A some set, connectedness in G can be viewed as a property of A relative to Γ:

(f) Given a collection Γ of subsets of A, two elements a and b of A are *connected modulo Γ* just in case they are connected in $G[\Gamma]$.

In other words, two elements of A are connected modulo Γ just in case there exists a sequence of elements of A $\{a_1, \ldots, a_n\}$ such that $a_1 = a$, $a_n = b$ and Γ includes every subset $\{a_i, a_{i+1}\}$, $i = 1, \ldots, n-1$. Such a sequence is called a *path modulo Γ*. For example, p and s in $A = \{p, q, r, s\}$ are connected modulo the analysis in (b1), but not modulo any other analysis in (b). Connectedness modulo Γ, Γ some collection of subsets of A, is an equivalence relation on A. Let $A_1, A_2, \ldots, A_\omega$ be the equivalence classes. Each A_i, $1 \leq i \leq \omega$, is called a *component of A modulo Γ*. If there is only one component ($\omega = 1$), A is said to be *connected modulo Γ*; otherwise, it is *disconnected modulo Γ* with ω components. For example, the analysis in (b1) defines one component, while those in (b2)–(b4) define two components each. In what follows, a set will be said to be simply "connected" or "disconnected" when there is no ambiguity as to the underlying graph structure and to the family of subsets that induces it.

    As just noted, the set $\{p, q, r, s\}$ is connected modulo the binary analysis in (b1). However, removing any pair from that analysis turns $\{p, q, r, s\}$ into a disconnected set (modulo the resulting analysis). The relevant property of the analysis in (b1) is that the graph it induces contains no *cycle*, i.e., no path $\{a_1, \ldots, a_n\}$ such that $a_1 = a_n$. A connected graph that has this property is called a *tree* (see Balakrishnan and Ranganathan 2000:67–72). In a tree, any two distinct nodes are connected by a unique path. Indeed, this is a characteristic property of trees: a graph in which any two distinct nodes are connected by a unique path is a tree. A *structure over A* is now defined as follows:

(h) Let A be a set of items, called the *carrier set*. A *structure over A,* written $\Sigma(A)$, is a *maximal* class of binary analyses of A that meets the following two conditions, where $\Sigma^*(A)$ is the collection of all the constituents in the binary analyses in $\Sigma(A)$:

(S1) The graph $G[\Sigma^*(A)]$ is a tree.

(S2) Given any constituent C in $\Sigma^*(A)$, if C contains a and b, it also contains all the elements in the path connecting a and b modulo $\Sigma^*(A)$.

To illustrate, consider the list of binary analyses in (i):

(i) 1. $\{\{p, q\}, \{p, r\}, \{p, s\}\}$

   2. $\{\{p, q\}, \{p, r\}, \{p, q, s\}\}$

   3. $\{\{p, q\}, \{p, r\}, \{p, r, s\}\}$

   4. $\{\{p, q\}, \{p, q, r\}, \{p, q, s\}\}$

   5. $\{\{p, q\}, \{p, q, r\}, \{p, q, r, s\}\}$

   6. $\{\{p, q\}, \{p, q, s\}, \{p, q, r, s\}\}$

Now, form a new list by effecting a circular permutation of the elements q, r, s in (i). Then, reiterate the process until no new list is generated. Finally, add all the lists so obtained to the original one in (i). The resulting class of binary analyses is a *structure over* $\{p, q, r, s\}$. The graph induced by that structure can be represented by the diagram in (j):

(j)

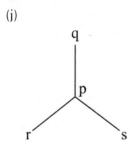

It follows from the maximal character of a structure that its induced tree includes all the elements of the carrier set.[44] Also, two structures that induce the same tree are identical. In a tree, as in any graph, a node may be adjacent to any number of nodes. A tree meeting the condition in (k) is called a *chain:*

(k)   Any node is adjacent to at most two other nodes.

A *string over A* is now defined as follows:

(l)   Let A be a set of items, called the *carrier set*. A *string over A*, written $S(A)$, is a structure over A whose induced tree $G[S^*(A)]$ is a chain.

To illustrate, the list of binary analyses in (m) is a string over $\{p, q, r, s\}$:

(m)   1. {{p, q}, {q, r}, {r, s}}
    2. {{p, q}, {q, r}, {q, r, s}}
    3. {{p, q}, {r, s}, {p, q, r, s}}
    4. {{p, q}, {r, s}, {p, q, r}}
    5. {{p, q}, {r, s}, {q, r, s}}
    6. {{p, q}, {r, s}, {p, q, r, s}}
    7. {{q, r}, {r, s}, {p, q, r}}
    8. {{p, q}, {p, q, r}, {p, q, r, s}}
    9. {{q, r}, {p, q, r}, {q, r, s}}
    10. {{q, r}, {p, q, r}, {p, q, r, s}}
    11. {{q, r}, {q, r, s}, {p, q, r, s}}
    12. {{r, s}, {q, r, s}, {p, q, r, s}}

The graph induced by that structure can be represented by the diagram in (n):

(n)

$$p \text{———} q \text{———} r \text{———} s$$

The above construction provides a *topological* definition of the notions of "string" and of "constituent structure." It has been assumed in the text that this is indeed the relevant characterization for a theory of brain/mental representations and processes. Concretely, the approach advocated replaces the notion of "constituent structure" by a more general notion of *neighborhood* of elements. The latter notion encompasses not only constituents in the standard sense, but also families of constituents within a standard tree structure.[45] It then turns out that the notion of "string" (or of "sequence") can be formalized without reference to ordering. Of course, a chain in the sense defined above can be mapped immediately onto a linear ordering. But, these are two different types of mathematical structures: while, as was just noted, a chain is a *topological* structure, a linear ordering is an *algebraic* one. Within this formalization, an iterated head-complement (IHC) structure will be defined as a particular subpart of a string. The following notions will be useful. A node in a connected graph that is adjacent to only one other node is called a *pendant node*. There are exactly two pendant nodes in a chain. A pair of nodes one of which is a pendant node will be called a *pendant edge*. Given three nodes *a*, *b*, *c* in a chain such that the path connecting *a* to *c* includes *b*, *b* is said to be *closer to c than a*. An IHC structure is now defined as in (o):

(o)   Let *A* be a set of items, called the *carrier set*. An *IHC structure over A*, written *HC(A)*, is a *maximal* subpart of some string *S(A)* over *A* meeting the following two conditions:

(HC1) One of the two pendant edges in the chain induced by *S(A)*, but not the other, is included in all the analyses in *HC(A)*. Let {*a, b*} be that common pendant edge, with a the pendant node in it.

(HC2) If an analysis in *HC(A)* includes the pair {*p, q*}, with *p* closer than *q* to the pendant node *a*, then it also includes a constituent *C* of the form {*D, p*}, with [*D, p*] the partition of *C* mentioned in clause (BA) in (a).

To illustrate, the two lists of analyses in (p) and in (q) are the two IHC structures derived from the string in (m):

(p)   1. {{p, q}, {q, r}, {r, s}}
      2. {{p, q}, {r, s}, {q, r, s}}
      3. {{q, r}, {p, q, r}, {r, s}}
      4. {{r, s}, {q, r, s}, {p, q, r, s}}

(q)   1. {{p, q}, {q, r}, {r, s}}
      2. {{p, q}, {r, s}, {p, q, r}}
      3. {{p, q}, {q, r}, {q, r, s}}
      4. {{p, q}, {p, q, r}, {p, q, r, s}}

Given some string *S(A)*, an IHC structure over *A* is derived from *S(A)* by first selecting one of the two pendant edges in the graph induced by the string and by eliminating all the analyses in *S(A)* that do not contain that pendant edge. In a second step, the resulting class of analyses is further pruned by eliminating all the analyses in it that do not conform to condition (HC2) in (o). It follows from that characterization that every constituent *C* in an IHC structure has the analysis {*D, p*}, where [*D, p*] is the partition mentioned in clause (BA) in (a), and *p* is the element of *C* that is the furthest away from the pendant node in the common pendant edge. This can be summarized by the recursive equation in (r):

(r) $C_i \approx [C_j, p]$

The definition of IHC structures proposed here is different from the one in the text, which starts from the hypothesized equivalence between a head and its projections. No such equivalence is postulated here. On the other hand, it is derived from the equation in (r). Let H be some IHC structure in the above sense. Suppose H includes an analysis containing the constituents in (s):

(s) $C_i \approx [C_j, p]$

$C_k \approx [C_i, q]$

Then, H also includes an analysis containing the pair in (t):

(t) $\{p, q\}$

Thus, p and C_i may be deemed *equivalent modulo H*. In other words, the head-projection relation emerges as a property of the particular class of analyses defined. Thus, the above construction provides an alternative account of the head-projection relation, one that does not rely on any indexing of constituent structure, but rather on a generalized notion of constituent analysis. That generalization takes a constituent structure to be not a single family of constituents, but a multiplicity of such families. It is the particular relations that hold within that multiplicity that define an object as a string or as an IHC structure, or as something else.

APPENDIX VI:[46]   A FORMAT FOR SYNTACTIC ANALYSIS

June 2007

1.   Phrase-Markers and Transformation-Markers

Let E be some expression in some human language. The structural description of E is a *Transformation-Marker (T-Marker)* in the sense of Chomsky (1955) 1975 (*LSLT*); that is, a partially ordered set of *Phrase-Markers (P-Markers)* in Chomsky's sense. The ordering relation is the *subordination relation* between two P-Markers. No empirical content is lost if that relation is restricted to P-Markers which share a constituent:

(183) $[UAW] < [XAY] =_{\text{def}} [UAW]$ is subordinate to $[XAY]$

The subordination relation is best described as a *generalized attachment transformation (GAT)*. The shared constituent A in the formulation of the transformation (cf. (183)) will be called its *pivot*, generalizing a term introduced in Kuroda 1968. Typically, a T-Marker will include "many-to-many" orderings between P-Markers, giving rise to such diagrams as that in (184), where the nodes denote constituents and where a constituent linked to one above it is subordinate to the latter:

(184)

Three questions arise:

(185) (a) What particular forms of GAT are encountered in grammar?

(b) How are the protagonists in GAT labeled?

(c) In what sense do the two occurrences of *A* in the two constituents [XAY] and [UAW] in (183) denote the same constituent? What is the notion of identity involved?

The three questions are linked. There two cases to consider: (i) either the pivot is the head/label of the subordinate P-Marker or (ii) it is not.

2. Phases in a Derivation

A phase—a cyclical domain of computation and interpretation—is a chunk of a constituent. The simplest way to account for the accessibility of specifiers at the margin of a phase is to assume that such constituents are outside the phase. Then, the phase *P(H)* headed by *H* is that part of the immediate projection *H'* of *H* which is not dominated by any other phase within *H'*. Specifically:

(186) Let *P(H)* be a phase with head *H* and let *H'* be the immediate projection of *H*. *P(H)* is the maximal subtree of *H'* made up of the

constituents which are dominated by no other phase within H'. $P(H)$ contains all specifiers and adjuncts attached to the highest phases within H'.

To illustrate, the structure in (187) would be analyzed as in (188) (irrelevant details omitted):

(187) $(_C$ that $(_T$ Past $((she) (_{v\text{-}V}$ see him$))))$

(188) (i) Phase I: $(_{v\text{-}V}$ **see him**)

    (ii) Phase II: $(_C$ that $(_T$ Past $(_{v\text{-}V}$ (she) see$)))$

The description in (188) is in accord with the general definition in (186) to the extent that labeling is construed as an equivalence relation between constituents and their heads, in the spirit of bare phrase structure (Chomsky 1994): if the head of the phase P is identified with P, it is not dominated by P and, by (186), belongs to the next phase above P.

That a constituent K and its head $H(K)$ are treated as equivalent, or nondistinct, by the domination relation in particular means that dominating K is equivalent to dominating $H(K)$. To illustrate, the equivalence in (189) between the lower phase in (188) and its head translates into that in (190) between the higher phase and the whole structure in (187):

(189) $(_{v\text{-}V}$ see$) \leftrightarrow (_{v\text{-}V}$ see him$)$

(190) $(_C$ that $(_T$ Past $((she) (_{v\text{-}V}$ see$)))) \leftrightarrow (_C$ that $(_T$ Past $((she) (_{v\text{-}V}$ **see him**$))))$

Thus, a structural description such as that in (188ii) is ambiguous: on the one hand, it is a representation of the higher phase, with just the head and the specifier of the lower phase included. Call this the *reduced form* of the phase in (188ii). Alternatively, when the head *see* of the lower phase in (188i) is identified with that whole phase, the description in (188ii) is a representation of the complete constituent structure in (187). Call this the *expanded form* of the phase in (188ii). The correspondence between reduced and expanded forms is essentially recursive: a phase substituted for its head in a higher phase may itself be in a reduced or expanded form. That correspondence is the particular instance of GAT in (183) in which A is the head/label of the subordinate constituent *[UAW]*:

(191) The expanded form of a phase P is the result of *substituting* the next lower phases for their respective heads in the reduced form of P.

(192) *H(W)*: the head/label of *W*

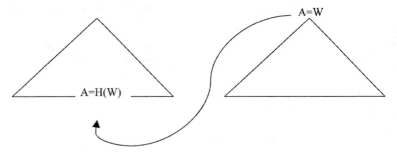

Given this account, the system of phases in (188i–ii) constitutes a *T-Marker*:

(193) The system of phases in (188) is the T-Marker of the structure in (187), with Phase I embedded into Phase II by GAT.

To summarize:

(194) (i)   The equivalence between a phase and its head is realized as a generalized substitution transformation.

(ii) The representation of a simple structure with no movement (such as that in (187)) can be interpreted indifferently as a P-Marker or as a T-Marker, the latter describing a system of phases.

That a representation could be at the same time a P-Marker and a T-Marker is a mere extrapolation of the standard theory, within which a P-Marker represents an equivalence class of derivations (Chomsky (1955) 1975 for example). The difference between the current execution and the standard theory has to do with the form of the rules involved.

3.   Adjuncts as Grafts

The subcase of GAT where the label of the subordinate constituent is distinct from the pivot describes various cases of adjunction. We adopt the analysis of relative clause and other adjunction structures in van Riemsdijk 1998, 2001. To illustrate, the relative clause construction in (195) will be described as in (196), irrelevant details omitted:

(195) [The lawyer that he is] will manage to sell the war.

(196)

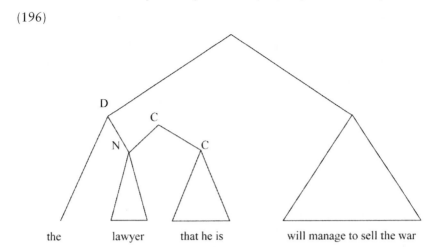

The corresponding GAT analysis is as in (197), where the pivot is italicized:

(197) [*lawyer* that he is] < [the *lawyer*]

The two occurrences of the NP *lawyer* in (197) constitute a chain. One question is whether "chain" is a primitive notion, on a par with "head-projection," for example. A discussion of *wh*-movement should help.

4.   The Nature of *wh*-Movement

The interaction of *wh*-movement and sentential stress discussed in Bresnan 1971 has important implications. As Bresnan 1971 shows, displaced *wh*-phrases in surface forms in English behave as if they were *in situ* for purposes of sentential stress assignment, receiving the sentential stress that would normally be assigned to an element in sentence-final position. For instance, in (198), the raised *wh*-phrase receives sentential stress and there is no sentential stress on the verb although it is final in the surface (pronounced) form of the sentence:

(198) (One knows) [[what BOOKS] Helen has written]

As originally argued in Chomsky and Halle 1968, sentential stress is the PF manifestation of a structural relation. Cinque 1990 proposes the rule in (199):

(199) Sentential stress is assigned to the most deeply embedded maximal projection in the sentential structure.

The rule assigns sentential stress to the complement of the verb *[books]* in the example in (200):

(200) (One knows) [Helen has written [some BOOKS]]

The constituent *[what book]* in (198) must receive sentential stress in the same way as *[some books]* in (200). The simplest and most natural hypothesis is that the complement clause in (198) is reduplicated (copied) at surface structure, and that only complementary parts of the two identical structures are pronounced:

(201) . . . [[~~Helen has written~~ what BOOKS] [Helen has written ~~what BOOKS~~]]

This supposes that *pronunciation* is distinct from *PF interpretation*. In other words, parts of a PF description may be silent, a classical assumption in generative phonology.

A similar analysis by reduplication (copy) can be proposed for a tone sandhi (TS) phenomenon discussed in Simpson and Wu 2002. In Taiwanese, the complementizer *kong*, regularly in clause-initial position, can also be found in clause-final position following its IP complement, as in (202):

(202) A-hui   siong   A-sin   m   lai   **kong**
       A-hui   think   A-sin   NEG   come   KONG
       'A-hui thinks A-sin is not coming'

Clause-final *kong* emphatically reasserts the contents of IP, just as in English forms like (203):

(203) He's gone, I'm telling you!

Thus, the content of the IP in (202) is topic-like and the focus is on the assertion of IP with the use of *kong*. The IP-preposing in *kong*-final sentences can be seen as occurrence of defocusing/topicalization movement, leaving *kong* in prominent S-final position where it is interpreted as the focus.

Where *kong* is S-final as in (202), there are two unexpected tone sandhi patterns (see Section 7.1, this Appendix). First of all the embedded IP-final element *lai* preceding *kong* does *not* undergo TS; if this IP is the leftward complement of *kong* in a final C position, this should mean that the IP and the C and are in the same TS domain and it is expected that this should result in sandhi occurring between the C^0 and the element left-adjacent to it in this TS domain, i.e., the final syllable of the IP, but this does not happen.

The second unusual TS patterning in *kong*-final sentences is that the *sentence-final* element *kong* does in fact undergo TS. This is quite unexpected as no other elements in sentence-final position undergo tone sandhi, simply because the sentence is a self-contained TS domain, as noted. These two facts are recorded in (204):[47]

(204) IP–*kong*: Unexpected complement before head order, unexpected TS changes

    (i) final syllable in IP does not undergo tone sandhi

(ii) *kong* does undergo tone sandhi

Simpson & Wu 2002 suggests that both patterns may have a simple explanation. The unexpected TS patterns in *kong*-final forms is fully parallel to the TS patterns which occur when the complementizer *kong* occurs *before* its complement IP as in (205):

(205) A-hui siong **kong** A-sin m   lai
       A-hui think KONG   A-sin NEG   come

       'A-hui thought that A-sin was not coming.'

Here the overt embedded complement IP triggers TS on the head which precedes it, i.e., *kong* in C^0, and the final syllable in the sentence, *lai,* does not undergo TS, again as expected as it is the final element in its TS domain. This patterning with pre-IP *kong* is noted in (206):

(206) *kong*–IP: Expected complement before head order, expected TS changes

       (i)   final syllable in IP does not undergo tone sandhi

       (ii) *kong* does undergo tone sandhi

In that case, as in the case of *wh*-movement, the simplest and most natural hypothesis is that there is reduplication (copy) of the clause *kong*-IP, with only complementary parts of the two identical structures being pronounced.

To summarize, there is a reduplication (copy) transformation which applies to certain domains. Complementary parts of the two identical domains are pronounced. The process of complementary deletion is formally identical to the LF "reconstruction process" assumed in Chomsky 1993 (sharpened and developed in Fox 2000). The "*wh*-movement" is the outcome of the two processes. In the following, we define a presentation of this transformational system.

5. The Derivational Table

We conjecture that the reduplicative process follows from the presence of a connective, such as *and* or *or,* incorporated with some other formative. *Wh* contains the connective *or* and furthermore is associated with both the margin of a DP and that of a derivational cycle/phase. A derivation is most naturally analyzed along two dimensions, one corresponding to the description of the structure of a phase, and the second, to the succession of phases created by GAT or reduplication. We then have a two-dimensional table such as that in (207).

(207)

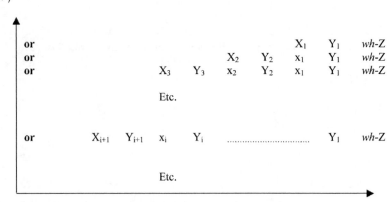

The table must be read as follows. Phase i is schematized as $X_i\ Y_i\ wh\text{-}Z$, where X_i, Y_i, $wh\text{-}Z$ are formatives, X_i, the head. Two consecutive lines depict (i) the reduplication of a phase and (ii) the attachment of its copy to the next higher phase. Only one formative in each column is realized at an interface. The ordering along the two dimensions can be mapped directly onto the time axis. One notes that the two presentations in (208) and (209), where the crossed formatives are those which are not realized, are nondistinct:

(208)

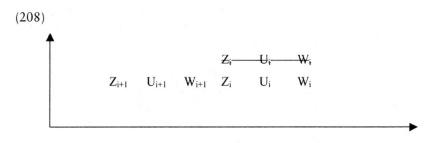

(209)

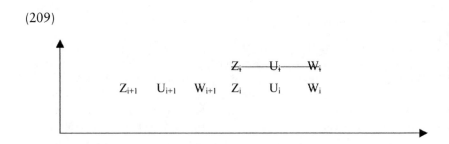

A central question is the following:

(210) Are two copies of the same formatives in a column on a par with the repetition of, e.g., the item *donkey* in a sentence such as *donkeys do not beat donkeys*?

In other words:

(211) Do the two occurrences of *donkeys* in *donkeys do not beat donkeys* form a chain in the same sense as two identical copies in a column of a derivational table do?

The question is all the more critical that anaphora can be argued to involve chains.

6. Anaphora

(212) Mary loves John, and he thinks that Sally does, too.

see Fiengo and May 1994:220.

(213) Mary believes that John is eligible and Sally claims he does, too.

(214) Mary believes John to be eligible and Sally claims he does, too.

(215) $[_{DP}$ *[+def]* φ *NP]*, with φ the agreement features of the nominal expression and *NP* the silent NP component.

The DP constitutes a definite description where the head D is indicated by the feature *[+def]*. At this point whether the agreement features φ are associated with D or N is left open.

(216) [the man who loved her$_2$]$_1$ kissed [his$_1$ wife]$_2$

see Jacobson 1977.

(217) a. [his$_1$ wife]$_2$ = [[[+def] φ_1 man]'s φ_2 wife], with φ_1 and φ_2 the phi-features for *man* and *wife*, respectively

    b. her$_2$ = [[[+def] φ_1 man]'s φ_2 wife]

We assume that:

(218) The feature *[+def]* of the man in such a structure as *the man's wife* is somehow carried to the whole DP.

(219) The structure *[[[+def] φ_1 ~~man~~]'s φ_2 ~~wife~~]* in (217a) is ambiguously realized as *his* or as *her*

(220) In (219), *his* is the PF realization of *[[+def] φ_1]'s* and *her,* of *[[+def] φ_2]]*

An important fact discovered by Jacobson is that *her* in (216) must be analyzed as a copy of the whole antecedent *his wife*, and not merely as a copy of *[+def] wife*. In other words, *her* in (216) must be described as in (217b).

(221) [his$_2$ employer]$_1$ respects [her$_1$ secretary]$_2$

see Brody 1982. The constituents *his employer* and *her secretary* in (221) are described as in (222):

(222) a. [his$_2$ employer]$_1$ = [[[+def] φ_2 ~~secretary~~]'s φ_1 employer]

b. [her$_1$ secretary]$_2$ = [[[+def] φ_1 ~~employer~~]'s φ_2 secretary]

(223) [The employer that was harassing him$_2$]$_1$ fired [the secretary that had denounced her$_1$]$_2$.

(224) a. Le juriste$_i$ sait très bien qu'il$_i$ est en difficulté.
        'The jurist$_i$ knows very well that he$_i$ has a problem'

b. *Il$_i$ sait très bien que le juriste$_i$ est en difficulté.
    'He$_i$ knows very well that the jurist$_i$ has a problem'

c. Il$_i$ sait très bien que le juriste qu'il$_i$ est est en difficulté.
    'He$_i$ knows very well that the jurist that he$_i$ is has a problem'

d. Pierre$_i$ sait très bien que le juriste qu'il$_i$ est est en difficulté.
    'Peter$_i$ knows very well that the jurist that he$_i$ is has a problem'

e. *Il$_i$ sait très bien que le juriste que Pierre$_i$ est est en difficulté.
    'He$_i$ knows very well that the jurist that Peter$_i$ is has a problem'

f. *Le juriste qu'il$_i$ est sait très bien que Pierre$_i$ est en difficulté.
    'The jurist that he$_i$ is knows very well that Peter$_i$ has a problem'

g. Le juriste que Pierre$_i$ est sait très bien qu'il$_i$ est en difficulté.
    'The jurist that Peter$_i$ is knows very well that he$_i$ has a problem'

h. Le juriste qu'il$_i$ a nommé sait très bien que Pierre$_i$ est en difficulté.
    'The jurist that he$_i$ appointed knows very well that Peter$_i$ has a problem'

7. Chains

Chain I: a list of copies.
Chain II: an item with a list of contexts.
The central question is what defines an "occurrence" of a constituent. The original proposal in Chomsky (1955) 1975, adapted from Quine's *Mathematical Logic,* was to take an occurrence of α in K to be the full context of α in K. This proposal surfaces in various guises in subsequent developments, for example in Chomsky 1981:45, in Chomsky 1995:251–252, in Chomsky 1998, in Chomsky 1999, and in Chomsky 2001. Chomsky 1998 suggests the following:

(225) Chomsky's conjecture (C_c)

"We could, for example, identify this [the full context of α in K-JRV] as $K' = K$ with the occurrence of α in question replaced by some designated element OCC distinct from anything in K." (p. 45, note 64)

Chomsky 2001 identifies OCC with the EPP-feature (the feature that requires the presence of a specifier).

7.1. A Note on Taiwanese

Taiwanese is a variety of Chinese which is grammatically similar to Mandarin Chinese. Like Mandarin, Taiwanese is SVO in its basic word order and shows a highly dominant head-initial ordering across its syntactic categories. Taiwanese is also a variety of Chinese with significant tone sandhi phenomena, and the seven tones of Taiwanese are all subject to regular change when they occur in syllables in certain environments. Essentially, the citation/lexical tone of a syllable undergoes change to a fully predictable sandhi tone when a syllable precedes some other tone-bearing syllable in the same tone sandhi domain. For example, in (226) below the third tone of the verb *khi* 'go' changes to a tone 2 when followed by an overt object which itself has a tone. Were the object not to be present (and occur perhaps as a *pro*) or were there to be an overt element following the verb which had "neutral-tone"/no tone as in (227), there would be no change in the citation tone of the verb, i.e., no tone sandhi/TS:

(226) **khi3** pak8kiang1 → **khi2** pak8kiang1
      go   Beijing
      'go to Beijing'

(227) **zau2** a-NT → **zau2** a-NT
      run   already
      'already ran'

TS never occurs in an element/syllable in sentence-final position, as there is no overt S-internal element to trigger TS in the final element in a sentence, and TS is not triggered across sentence boundaries.

Three generalizations can be noted concerning the domains for TS. First of all, as illustrated earlier, an overt complement consistently triggers tone sandhi on the head which selects it, indicating that a head and its complement are in a single TS domain. Secondly, a head does not trigger tone sandhi on the final syllable of its specifier, indicating that the specifier of a head constitutes a TS domain independent of the head. Thirdly, the final syllable of an adjunct does not undergo tone sandhi, so adjuncts may also be considered to be self-contained tone sandhi domains.

NOTES

* Many thanks to Sylvain Bromberger, Noam Chomsky, Morris Halle, Samuel Keyser, Tommi Leung, Rita Manzini, Karine Megerdoomian, Henk van Riemsdijk, Alain Rouveret, Bill Rutherford, and Andrew Simpson. Central ideas in this chapter have been presented at various conferences, workshops, and meetings. In particular, in Firenze 2003, Utrecht 2002 (TILT), USC 2002–2005, and Vienna 2002–2005.

+ This manuscript was a long time in development, and is the fruit of collaborations and projects that have remained unfinished; for this chapter in particular, with Robert Freidin, Martin Prinzhorn, Alain Rouveret, and Vergnaud's students.

1. The data in (1) are missing from the original manuscript, but have been reconstructed by Henk van Riemsdijk, p.c. with the editors. There are some semantic differences, which Jean-Roger does not address in this paper:
   - (2b)/(4b) have a specific/wide-scope reading of *ein Buch*; it is known in German that this interpretation results with scrambling of an indefinite noun phrase.
   - (1b) is the unmarked reading, with the interpretation: 'As for this book, Peter has often read it'. (1a) is a marked event reading: 'Events of Peter reading this book are frequent'.
   - (4a) is grammatical when *gut* has a quantificational reading: 'a little more than'. In this case, *gut* is presumably part of the NP/DP.

2. Chomsky 1995, 326–327. One should note that this analysis forces a reanalysis of quantifier float.

3. This supposes a slight revision of the definition of phases in Chomsky 1999 and in subsequent works.

4. See Lasnik 1999. See also Hornstein 1995 for a different account.

5. The binary operation "·" is associative if the identity in (a) holds for every triplet $\{a, b, c\}$ of elements in M:

   (a) $((a \cdot b) \cdot c) = (a \cdot (b \cdot c))$

   The *unit* element e is defined by the identity in (b), where a is any element in M:

   (b) $a \cdot e = e \cdot a = a$

6. The definition of a free semigroup can be made precise as follows:
   (a) A semigroup F is *free with basis* X, X a subset of F, iff. the following holds: if ϕ is any function from the set X into a semigroup H, then

there exists a unique extension of φ to a homomorphism φ^* from F into H.

The unit element (see note 3) of a free semi-group can be identified with the "empty atom" $\varnothing$.

7. See Appendix I.

8. The notion of "tree" can be primitively defined in graph-theoretic terms: a *tree* is a connected graph without cycles (see, e.g., Appendix II, Appendix V, and Balakrishnan and Ranganathan 2000). The standard grammatical notion can be subsumed under the more general graph-theoretic one; see Appendix II, Appendix III, and Appendix V.

9. See also Manzini 1995, 1997, 1998. The standard graph-theoretic term for "telescoping" is *contraction;* see Appendix III and Balakrishnan and Ranganathan 2000.

10. The equivalence class associated with the structure in (94) in the text contains 18 distinct structures altogether.

11. The noncommutativity ultimately follows from the directed character of the graphs in the domain of the operator.

12. Within a graph-theoretic model such as that in (112) in the text, the non-commutativity of concatenation follows from the directed character of the elementary graphs involved; see note 9.

13. This can be done as follows. Let E be a set ordered by the relation "$<$". Let U and W be two subsets of E such that U has a *least upper bound u* and W has a *greatest lower bound w* (u is the least element in E comparable to, and greater than, every element in U; w is defined in a symmetrical fashion; such bounds may or may not exist; see Birkhoff 1995:6). Then:

(a) $U < W$ iff. $u < w$

The primitive relation $u<v$ can in turn be identified with the relation $\{u\}<\{v\}$.

14. This is relevant to the theory in Kayne 1994; see Appendix IV.

15. As we will see, the phases, as constituents, form a hierarchical structure.

16. Dependency grammar can be described as the result of "telescoping" phrase structure grammar; cf. Brody 1997, 2000. See Abney 1996, Hudson 1984, Robinson 1970 for a comparison of dependency and phrase structure grammar.

17. This correspondence is the "labeling" of standard theory; see Chomsky 1994, for example. An alternative formalization of the head-projection relation is sketched in Appendix V.

18. The empty symbol in the text formula is to be distinguished from the lexical items: it is not an element of the domain or image of the mapping in (94), which thus is not a circular permutation. On the other hand, we suggest elsewhere that strings can advantageously be analyzed as "presentations" of circular permutations (see Vergnaud 2003, republished as chapter 3 of this volume).

19. The choice of q as the contextual element in the pair *(q, p)* is obviously arbitrary. The theory would remain unchanged if p rather than q were taken as the contextual element. See the discussion in section 6.

20. The chain in (112) is that for *who.* It does not include the object position of *emulate.* We are assuming that the lowest position occupied by *who* in the structure is at the margin of the vP headed by *emulate.* The object position of *emulate* is occupied by a strict subconstituent of *who,* to wit *someone* (see section 11; see Appendix "A Format for Syntactic Analysis".

21. Other approaches than the text one are possible. Thus, Freidin and Vergnaud 2004 argues that an A$'$ chain should instead be represented as

a list of phases in the context of the moved constituent. For example, the chain for *who* in (112) in the text would be formalized as in (i) under this proposal:

(i) <who| ↔ {|C she wants>, |want C'>, |C' to>, |to emulate>}

22. A "reconstruction rule" was originally proposed in Chomsky 1977 to account for the interpretation of displaced items. The issue is further discussed in Burzio 1981 and in Chomsky 1981:62, 144–145, 345–346.

23. The same rule will account for the structures in (a) and (b) discussed in Chomsky 1981:145, 346, respectively:

(a) [PRO to be 18 years old] is what everyone wants most
(b) [Pictures of each other] are what they like to see

24. The cited work was part of an ongoing collaboration by Alain Rouveret and Jean-Roger Vergnaud, which was left unfinished.

25. In particular, any theory of meaning presupposes some notion of *occurrence*. For example, QR ("Quantifier Raising") relies on the assignment of a special system of grammatical functions to the affected constituent.

26. This is not taken as implying that the L_M formatives and their duals are like kets and bras in theoretical physics, i.e., describe amplitudes of distributions in some abstract space. However, the L_M objects may be subject to analogous mathematical treatments at some theoretical level.

27. See Quine 1951:chapter 7, §56 (p. 297).

28. Chomsky 2001 identifies OCC with the EPP-feature (the feature that requires the presence of a specifier). Given category K with label OCC, OCC must be checked by external or internal Merge. We come back to that below.

29. The union of two collections A and B is the smallest collection that includes every element in A or in B.

30. We argue elsewhere that that constraint ultimately underlies *OCP* (see Vergnaud 2003, republished as chapter 3 in this volume).

31. Thus, the condition in (145i) ensures that the array is connected, so that a constituent structure may be built which includes all of the items in it.

32. The operation "Expand P into $(_P Q P)$" is the rewriting rule in (i):

(i) $P \rightarrow (_P Q P)$

33. We assume Distributed Morphology (see Halle and Marantz 1993) as the theory of the mapping between surface structure and PF.

34. In the particular case of IHC structures, the relation between synthesis and analysis can be formalized as a *push-down storage automaton* (see Chomsky 1962). Note that the synthesis/analysis dichotomy is separate from the *production/perception* one.

35. The union of two collections A and B is the smallest collection that includes every element in A or in B.

36. The fact that the relevant class of constituent structures is defined by recursive principles does not entail that it is infinite. For these principles are interpretive principles which apply to a finite domain.

37. At PF, the abstract boundary of the constituent will be interpreted as its prosodically prominent part (see Halle and Vergnaud 1987).

38. Technically, the relation that holds between an element and a set containing it is the relation ∈, not the inclusion relation ⊂. By the text definition, then, a constituent does not *dominate* any terminal (although it contains them). The difficulty can be overcome by identifying every terminal x with the singleton set $\{x\}$, a move in accordance with bare phrase structure theory. See also note 35 in chapter 5.

39. One may note that, as formulated, the LCA really implies no correspondence between syntactic structure and PF ordering. It is a constraint on the form of syntactic structure, which must define a linear ordering of its terminals. But, by itself, it does not require that this linear ordering be that at PF. To obviate this, the LCA could be reformulated as in (i) (see (c) in Appendix IV):

   (i) $d(A_P)$ is the PF ordering of $d(P)$

40. See Appendix II for the definitions of the relevant notions.

41. Given some set S, a partition $[C, C']$ of S is a pair $[C, C']$ of collections of elements of S such that every element of S is in C or in C' and no element of S is both C and C'. The term "collection" here is intended as theoretically neutral: a collection needs not be a *set* in the technical sense of set theory. In the same vein, the definitions in the appendix overlook the distinction between the *element a* and the *singleton set {a}* whenever no harm will ensue. This is tantamount to eliminating the notion of *preterminal node* in tree representations (*a* as an element counts as a *terminal*, whereas *{a}* counts as a preterminal node dominating *a*).

42. A chain gives rise to an ordering. The set-theoretic representation of the ordering associated with the chain in (b1) in the text is given in (i):

   (i) $\{\{p\}, \{p, q\}, \{p, q, r\}, \{p, q, r, s\}\}$

43. See Appendix II.

44. Let $\Sigma(A)$ be a structure over A. Suppose that there is some element a of A that is not connected to the induced tree $T[\Sigma(A)]$. By definition, $\Sigma^*(A)$ includes no pair $\{a, x\}$, x an element of A distinct from a. It is possible to extend $T[\Sigma(A)]$ by connecting a to an arbitrary node in $T[\Sigma(A)]$, say b. Let T' be the tree so obtained. Clearly, an analysis including the pair $\{a, b\}$ and meeting condition (S2) in (h) can be added to $\Sigma(A)$. Denote by $\Sigma'(A)$ the resulting class of analyses. $\Sigma'(A)$ meets conditions (S1) and (S2) in (h), with $G[\Sigma'^*(A)] = T'$. But, then, $\Sigma(A)$ is not maximal, which contradicts the hypothesis that $\Sigma(A)$ is a structure.

45. It appears that the particular arrangements thus defined have a natural interpretation in terms of the topological theory of Kuroda 1971.

46. Many thanks to Alain Rouveret for providing the document containing this manuscript.

47. The emphatic-assertive *kong* occurs in complementary distribution with both yes/no question particles and also *wh*-phrases in Taiwanese.

   "This complementary distribution with question particles is expected if *kong* and question particle elements occur as alternative competing instantiations of the same basic C^0 head position, with *kong* and question particles encoding opposite semantic values—declarative assertion vs. interrogative +Q. If *kong* encodes a declarative/non-interrogative value of C^0, it will also naturally fail to license *wh*-phrases which require an interrogative C^0 to be present."
   Simpson & Wu, p.10

REFERENCES

Abney, S. 1986. *A Grammar of Projections*. Ms1. University of Tubingen.

Baker, M. 1985. The Mirror Principle and morphosyntactic explanation. *Linguistic Inquiry* 16:373–415.

———. 1996. On the structural positions of themes and goals. In *Phrase Structure and the Lexicon*, ed. by J. Rooryck and L. Zaring. Dordrecht, Netherlands: Kluwer.

Balakrishnan, R., and K. Ranganathan. 2000. *A Textbook of Graph Theory*. New York: Springer.

Barss, A. 1986. Chains and anaphoric dependence: On reconstruction and its implications. Doctoral dissertation, MIT.

Belvin, R. S. 1996. Inside events: The non-possessive meanings of possession predicates and the semantic conceptualization of events. Doctoral dissertation, University of Southern California.

Birkhoff, G. 1995. *Lattice Theory*. Providence: American Mathematical Society.

Bobaljik, J. 2002. A-chains at the PF-interface: Copies and covert movement. *Natural Language and Linguistic Theory* 20:197–267.

Borer, H. 1994. The projection of arguments. *University of Massachusetts Occasional Papers in Linguistics* 17.

———. 2004. *Structuring Sense: An Exo-Skeletal Trilogy: Book II, The Normal Course of Events*. Oxford: Oxford University Press.

Bresnan, J. 1971. Sentence stress and syntactic transformations. *Language* 47:257–281.

Brody, M. 1982. On circular readings. In *Mutual knowledge*, ed. N. V. Smith, 133–146. New York: Academic Press.

———. 1995. *Lexico-Logical Form: A Radically Minimalist Theory*. Cambridge, MA: MIT Press.

———. 1997. Mirror theory. Ms., University College London.

———. 2000. Mirror theory: Syntactic representation in perfect syntax. *Linguistic Inquiry* 31:29–56.

Bury, D. 2003. Phrase structure and derived heads. Doctoral dissertation, University College London.

Burzio, L. 1981. Intransitive verbs and Italian auxiliaries. Doctoral dissertation, Cambridge, MA: MIT.

Chametzky, R. A. 1995. Dominance, precedence, and parameterization. *Lingua* 96:163–178.

Chomsky, N. (1955) 1975. *The Logical Structure of Linguistic Theory*. New York: Plenum.

———. 1957. *Syntactic Structures*. The Hague: Mouton.

———. 1962. Context-free grammar and pushdown storage. *Quarterly Progress Report* 65:187–194.

———. 1964. Current issues in linguistic theory. In *The Structure of Language*, ed. by J. Fodor and J. Katz. Mahwah, NJ: Prentice Hall.

———. 1965. *Aspects of the Theory of Syntax*. Cambridge, MA: MIT Press.

———. 1967. The formal nature of language. In *Biological Foundations of Language*, ed. by E. Lenneberg. 397–442. New York: John Wiley.

———. 1970. Remarks on nominalization. In *Readings in Transformational Grammar*, ed. by R. Jacobs and P. Rosenbaum. Waltham, MA: Ginn.

———. 1977. On *wh*-movement. In *Formal Syntax*, ed. by P. Culicover et al. New York: Academic Press.

———. 1981. *Lectures on Government and Binding*. Dordrecht, Netherlands: Foris.

———. 1986a. *Knowledge of Language*. New York: Praeger.

———. 1986b. *Barriers*. Cambridge, MA: MIT Press.

———. 1991. Some notes on the economy of derivation and representation. In *Principles and Parameters in Comparative Grammar*, ed. by R. Freidin. Cambridge, MA: MIT Press.

———. 1993. A minimalist program for linguistic theory. In *The View from Building 20: Essays in Linguistics in Honor of Sylvain Bromberger*, ed. by K. Hale and S. J. Keyser. Cambridge, MA: MIT Press.

———. 1995. *The Minimalist Program*. Cambridge, MA: MIT Press.

————. 1998. Minimalist inquiries: The framework. In *Step by Step: Essays on Minimalist Syntax in Honor of Howard Lasnik*, ed. by R. Martin, D. Michaels, and J. Uriagereka. Cambridge, MA: MIT Press.

————. 1999. Derivation by phase. *MIT Occasional Papers in Linguistics* 18.

————. 2000. *New Horizons in the Study of Language and Mind*. New York: Cambridge University Press.

————. 2001. Derivation by phase. In *Ken Hale: A Life in Language*, ed. by M. Kenstowicz. Cambridge, MA: MIT Press.

————. 2004. Beyond explanatory adequacy. In *Structures and Beyond*, ed. by A. Belletti, 104–133. Oxford: Oxford University Press.

————, and M. Halle. 1968. *The Sound Pattern of English*. New York: Harper and Row.

————, and H. Lasnik. 1993. The theory of principles and parameters. In *Syntax: An International Handbook of Contemporary Research*, ed. by J. Jacobs, A. von Stechow, W. Stemefeld, and T. Vennemann. Berlin: Walter de Gruyter.

————, and G. A. Miller. 1963. Introduction to the formal analysis of natural languages. In *Handbook of Mathematical Psychology*, vol. II, ed. by R. Duncan Luce, R. R. Bush, and E. Galanter. New York: John Wiley.

Cinque, G. 1990. *Types of A-bar Dependencies*. Cambridge, MA: MIT Press.

————. 1999. *Adverbs and Functional Heads: A Cross-Linguistic Perspective*. New York: Oxford University Press.

Diesing, M. 1990. The syntactic roots of semantic partition. Doctoral dissertation, University of Massachusetts–Amherst.

————. 1992. Bare plural subjects and the derivation of logical representations. *Linguistic Inquiry* 23:353–380.

Epstein, S. 1999. Un-Principled Syntax: The Derivation of Syntactic Relations. In *Working Minimalism*, ed. by S. Epstein and N. Hornstein, 317–345. Cambridge, MA: MIT Press.

Fiengo, R., and R. May. 1994. *Indices and Identity*. MIT Press, 220.

Fox, D. 2000. *Economy and Semantic Interpretation*. Cambridge, MA: MIT Press.

Freidin, R. 1978. Cyclicity and the theory of grammar. *Linguistic Inquiry* 9:519–549.

————, and J.-R. Vergnaud. 1999. Some central concepts of phrase structure and movement. Ms., University of Southern California and Princeton University.

————, and J.-R. Vergnaud. To appear. The structure of syntax. Ms., University of Southern California and Princeton University.

Fukui, N., and Y. Takano. 1998. Symmetry in syntax: Merge and demerge. *Journal of East Asian Linguistics* 7:27–86.

Grimshaw, J. 1991. Extended projection. Ms., Brandeis University.

Hale, K., and S. J. Keyser. 1993. On argument structure and the lexical expression of syntactic relations. In *The View from Building 20: Essays in Linguistics in Honor of Sylvain Bromberger*, ed. by K. Hale and S. J. Keyser. Cambridge, MA: MIT Press.

————. 2002. *Prolegomenon to a Theory of Argument Structure*. Cambridge, MA: MIT Press.

Halle, M. 2008. Reduplication. In *Foundational Issues in Linguistic Theory*, ed. by R. Freidin, C. P. Otero, and M. L. Zubizarreta. Cambridge, MA: MIT Press.

————, and J. Harris. 2005. Unexpected plural inflections in Spanish: Reduplication and Metathesis. *Linguistic Inquiry* 36.2. 195–222.

————, and A. Marantz. 1993. Distributed morphology and the pieces of inflection. In *The View from Building 20: Linguistics Essays in Honor of Sylvain Bromberger*, ed. by K. Hale and S. J. Keyser, 111-176. Cambridge, MA: MIT Press.

————, and J-R. Vergnaud. 1987. *An Essay on Stress*. Cambridge, MA, MIT Press.

Hawkins, J. A. 1994. *A Performance Theory of Order and Constituency.* Cambridge: Cambridge University Press.

Hornstein, N. 2005. What do labels do? Some thoughts on the endocentric roots of recursion and movement. Ms., University of Maryland.

———. 1995. Putting truth into universal grammar. *Linguistics and Philosophy* 18:381–400.

———, and J. Nunes. 2002. On asymmetries between parasitic gaps and across-the-board constructions. *Syntax* 5:26–54.

Hudson, R.A. 1984. *Word Grammar.* Oxford: Basil Blackwell.

Jackendoff, R. 1972. *Semantic Interpretation in Generative Grammar.* Cambridge, MA: MIT Press.

Jacobson, P. 1977. The syntax of crossing coreference sentences. Doctoral dissertation, University of California, Berkeley.

Johnson, K. 2001. What VP ellipsis can do, what it can't, but not why. In *The Handbook of Contemporary Syntactic Theory,* ed. by M. Baltin and C. Collins. Malden, MA: Blackwell.

Kayne, R. 1984. *Connectedness and Binary Branching.* Dordrecht, Netherlands: Foris.

———. 1994. *The Antisymmetry of Syntax.* Cambridge, MA: MIT Press.

———. 2003. Antisymmetry and Japanese. *English Linguistics* 20:1–40.

———. 2009. Antisymmetry and the lexicon. *Linguistic Variation Yearbook* 8:1–31.

Kean, M.-L. 1974. The strict cycle in phonology. *Linguistic Inquiry* 5:179-203.

Koizumi, M. 1993. Object agreement phases and the split VP hypothesis. *MIT Working Papers in Linguistics* 18.

Koopman, H., and A. Szabolcsi. 2000. *Verbal Complexes.* Cambridge, MA: MIT Press.

Krifka, M. 1989. Nominal reference, temporal constitution and quantification in event semantics. In *Semantics and Contextual Expression,* ed. by R. Bartsch, J. van Benthem, and P. van Emde Boas. Dordrecht, Netherlands: Foris.

Kuroda, Y. 1968. English relativization and certain related problems. *Language* 44:244–266.

———. 1971. Two remarks on pronominalization. *Foundations of Language* 7.2:183–198.

———. 1988. Whether we agree or not. *Lingvisticae Investigationes* 12:1–47.

Larson, R. K. 1988. On the double object construction. *Linguistic Inquiry* 19:335–391.

———. 2004. Sentence-final adverbs and scope. In *Proceedings of NELS 34,* ed. by K. Moulton and M. Wolf. Amherst: University of Massachusetts Graduate Student Linguistic Association.

Lasnik, H. 1999. *Minimalist Analysis.* Malden, MA: Blackwell.

———, and J. Uriagereka. 2005. *A Course in Minimalist Syntax.* Malden, MA: Blackwell.

Manzini, M.-R. 1992. *Locality.* Cambridge, MA: MIT Press.

———. 1995. From merge and move to form dependency. *UCLA Working Papers in Linguistics* 7:323–345.

———. 1997. Adjuncts and the theory of phrase structure. In *Proceedings of the Tilburg Conference on Rightward Movement,* ed. by D. Le Blanc and H. Van Riemsdijk. Amsterdam: John Benjamins.

———. 1998. Dependencies, phrase structure and extractions. In *Specifiers,* ed. by D. Adger et al. Oxford: Clarendon Press.

Marantz, A. 1992. The *way*-construction and the semantics of direct arguments in English: A reply to Jackendoff. In *Syntax and Semantics 26: Syntax and the Lexicon.* New York: Academic Press.

———. 1997. No escape from syntax: Don't try morphological analysis in the privacy of your own lexicon. In *Proceedings of the 21st Penn Linguistics Collo-*

quium, ed. by A. Dimitriadis, L. Siegel, C. Surek-Clark, and A. Williams. Philadelphia: UPenn Working Papers in Linguistics.

Martin, R., and J. Uriagereka. 2000. Some possible foundations of the Minimalist Program. In *Step by Step: Essays on Minimalist Syntax in Honor of Howard Lasnik*, ed. by R. Martin, D. Michaels, and J. Uriagereka. Cambridge, MA: MIT Press.

McCawley, J. 1982. Parentheticals and discontinuous constituent structure. *Linguistic Inquiry* 13:91–106.

Megerdoomian, K. 2002. Beyond words and phrases: A unified theory of predicate composition. Doctoral dissertation, University of Southern California.

Miller, G. A., and N. Chomsky. 1963. Finitary models of language users. In *Handbook of Mathematical Psychology*, eds. R.D. Luce, R. Bush, and E. Galanter, 419–492. New York: John Wiley and Sons, Inc.

Pollock, J.-Y. 1989. Verb movement, universal grammar, and the structure of IP. *Linguistic Inquiry* 20:365–424.

Prinzhorn, M. 1996. Seminar [Title Unknown]. University of Vienna.

Quine, W. V. 1951. *Mathematical Logic*. Cambridge, MA: Harvard University Press.

Raimy, E. 1999. Representing reduplication. Doctoral dissertation, University of Delaware, Newark.

———. 2001. *The Phonology and Morphology of Reduplication*. Berlin: Mouton de Gruyter.

Riemsdijk, H. van 1998. Categorial feature magnetism: The endocentricity and distribution of projections. *Journal of Comparative Germanic Linguistics* 2:1–48.

Riemsdijk, H. van 2001. A far from simple matter: Syntactic reflexes of syntax-pragmatics misalignments. In *Semantics, Pragmatics and Discourse: Perspectives and Connections—a Festschrift for Ferenc Kiefer*, ed. by I. Kenesei and R. M. Harnish. Amsterdam: John Benjamins.

Riemsdijk, H. van, and E. Williams. 1981. NP-structure. *The Linguistic Review* 1:171–217.

Rizzi, L., ed. 2004a. *The Structure of CP and IP: The Cartography of Syntactic Structures*. Vol. 2. New York: Oxford University Press.

———. 2004b. Locality and left periphery. In *Structures and Beyond: The Cartography of Syntactic Structures*, vol. 3, ed. by A. Belletti. New York: Oxford University Press.

Robinson, J. J. 1970. Dependency structures and transformational rules. *Language* 46:259–285.

Rosenbaum, P. 1967. *The Grammar of English Predicate Constructions*. Cambridge, MA: MIT Press.

Rouveret, A. 1987. Syntaxe des Dépendances Lexicales: Identité et Identification dans la Théorie Syntaxique. Thèse d'Etat, Paris-7.

———, and L. Nash. 2002. Cliticization as unselective attract. *Catalan Journal of Linguistics* 1:157–199.

Sauzet, P. 1993. Attenance, gouvernement et mouvement en phonologie. Les constituants dans la phonologie et la morphologie de l'occitan. Doctoral dissertation, Université Paris 8.

———. 1994. Extensions du modèle a-linéaire en phonologie: syllabe, accent, morphologie. Mémoire d'Habilitation à diriger des recherches, Paris VII.

Segui, J., and M. L. Zubizarreta. 1985. Mental representation of morphologically complex words and lexical access. *Linguistics* 23:759–774.

Simpson, A., and Z. Wu. 2002a. IP-raising, tone sandhi and the creation of S-final particles: Evidence for cyclic Spell-Out. *Journal of East Asian Linguistics* 11:167–199.

———. 2002b. Agreement, shells, and focus. *Language* 78:287–313.

Smith, C. 1997. *The Parameter of Aspect*. Dordrecht, Netherlands: Kluwer.

Speas, M. 1990. *Phrase Structure in Natural Language.* Dordrecht, Netherlands: Kluwer Academic.

Stowell, T. 1981. Origins of phrase structure. Doctoral dissertation, MIT.

Travis, L. 1984. Parameters and effects of word order variation. Doctoral dissertation, MIT.

———. 1991. Derived objects, inner aspect and the structure of VP. Paper presented at the North East Linguistics Society (NELS) 22.

Uriagereka, J. 1999. Multiple Spell-out. In *Working Minimalism*, ed. by S. Epstein and N. Hornstein. Cambridge, MA: MIT Press.

Vergnaud, J.-R. 2003. On a certain notion of "occurrence": The source of metrical structure, and of much more. In *Living on the Edge*, ed. by S. Ploch. Berlin: Mouton de Gruyter.

———, and M. L. Zubizarreta. 2001. Derivation and constituent structure. Ms., University of Southern California.

Williams, E. 1971. Small clauses in English. Ms., MIT.

———. 2003. *Representation Theory.* Cambridge, MA: MIT Press.

Wu, Xiu-Zhi Zoe. 2000. *Grammaticalization and the Development of Functional Categories in Chinese.* Doctoral dissertation, USC.

———. 2004. *Grammaticalization and Language Change in Chinese: A Formal View.* London and New York: Routledge Curzon.

Zubizarreta, M. L., and E. Oh. 2007. *On the Syntactic Composition of Manner and Motion.* Cambridge, MA: MIT Press.

6   Grafts and Beyond
Graph-Theoretic Syntax[*]

*Katherine McKinney-Bock and
Jean-Roger Vergnaud*

1.   INTRODUCTION

The generative theory of phrase structure has undergone several major revisions over the years in an attempt to rid itself of posited primitives, which while seemingly empirically motivated, were nevertheless stipulations. For example, binary branching, which was stipulated in X-bar theory, is derived in Minimalism through the operation Merge. We argue that certain mechanisms in current generative syntax that are useful at narrow syntax must also be interpreted at the interfaces, and we argue that this idea runs into difficulties. One example of this is multidominance as it is realized in current theories. Multidominance, the sharing of constituents by two separate maximal Phrase-markers, has been argued to provide an adequate representation of the chains associated with particular cases of displacement (e.g., right node raising, ATB *wh*-movement, headless relative clause formation, cf. McCawley 1982; van Riemsdijk 2001, 2006; Citko 2005; Gracanin-Yuksek 2007; Wilder 2008; de Vries 2009, a.o.). Multidominance is used at narrow syntax to represent movement, but at the interfaces multidominance structures are problematic for linearization algorithms because these types of structures create ordering paradoxes with items that are multiply dominated (see Wilder 2008, de Vries 2009).

A second, more general problem that we sketch the beginnings of a solution to here is that of long-distance grammatical relationships, which require additional grammatical mechanisms like locality constraints, copying and indexing operations, and agreement operations in order to constrain the power introduced by movement or agreement. These operations take place across a larger domain of syntactic structure than an immediate Merge relationship and so require conditions on what levels of structure the relationship can span in order to avoid unbounded dependencies.

At its roots, this new approach to syntax dispenses with a notion of *tree*, and relaxes syntactic representations to allow for simple *graphs*. In doing this, we take narrow syntax to be a more abstract representation from which constituent structure (represented as a tree) is derived and used at the interfaces. This two-tiered system provides a novel resolution to some of the problems discussed previously, while the increased mechanism of a "deeper" narrow syntax than before is motivated by the minimalist idea that narrow syntax shouldn't require conditions relevant only at the interfaces.

Finally, we illustrate this new conceptualization of syntax with an old empirical problem: split-antecedent relative clauses. There is difficulty in representing relative clauses with split antecedents that bind reciprocal anaphors (cf. Perlmutter & Ross 1970, McCawley 1982, Link 1984, Wilder 1994):

(1) Mary met *a man* and John met *a woman* who know *each other* well.

The issue is how to connect a relative clause with a plural relativizer to two antecedent nominals, each in a separate clause.

A solution to the problem of split-antecedent relatives lies in an observation by Wilder 1994 that the structure in (1) has a similar interpretation/agreement as its counterpart in (2), which reverses the relativized and matrix clauses:

(2) *A man* who Mary met and *a woman* who John met know *each other* well.

While Wilder dismisses the possibility that (1) and (2) are structurally derived from the same source, we argue to the contrary that these two structures are essentially from the same source: three independent CPs linked by grafting (see van Riemsdijk 2001, 2006). We treat *[a man]* and *[a woman]* as calluses, or shared constituents, and coordinate the two CPs *[Mary met a man]* and *[John met a woman]*.

However, we depart slightly from the standard analysis of such structures, and posit an asymmetry in the structure that allows for a third context for the DP (as related to [Spec, CP]). Simple reassignment of this asymmetry to one CP or the other will obtain the reversal of (1) and (2). Then, from narrow syntax, we generate a set of classical Phrase-markers which are used at the interfaces.

We show that the split-antecedent relative clause (SARC) structure is not unique to relative clauses. Instead, a general notion of coordinating sets of grammatical formatives allows SARC to be derived from the same syntax as a host of other coordinated structures, rather than requiring additional stipulated syntactic mechanisms. Within *graph-theoretic syntax,* we argue SARC are a natural, predicted phenomenon.

The paper is outlined as follows: first, we illustrate particular issues with multidominance as it currently stands, followed by the theoretical proposal. Then we turn to the empirical discussion at hand, relative clauses, followed by an analysis of coordination. Putting the two together, we show how SARC are naturally derived. Finally, we take a look at the broader picture and some remaining open issues: quantification and the primitives of clause structure.

2. MULTIDOMINANCE IN THE LITERATURE

Multidominance has been discussed under a variety of different guises and formalizations, for example: Parallel Merge (Citko 2005), grafting (van

Riemsdijk 2001, 2006), External Re-Merge (de Vries 2009). Although we recognize that there are theoretical differences that correlate with the different terms and different discussions, we refer to the general idea of merging a single constituent with two different heads that dominate that constituent as *grafting*, following van Riemsdijk 1998, 2001.

Most accounts of grafting converge on the notion that the *source independence* of Merge (Chomsky 2004), which states that Merge does not distinguish where items that are Merged originate, predicts the existence of the type of Merge that creates a graft. The idea governing source independence is that the only way to see the difference between Internal and External Merge is to look at a "bigger picture" of the syntactic structure to see if the item already exists in the derivation, or if it is still in the numeration. With source independence, instances of grafting are not excluded because grafting involves looking at a bigger structure than a simple Merge relationship; it minimally involves two Merge relationships: in (5), the Merging of (α, δ) and (β, δ).

(3)

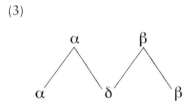

It could be argued even further that distinguishing cases of grafting from cases of Internal Merge involves looking all the way up to the root, to ensure that the two heads that dominate the grafted point do not end up re-Merging at the root (an Internal Merge). The following two trees illustrate this point.

(4)

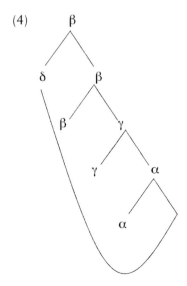

(5)

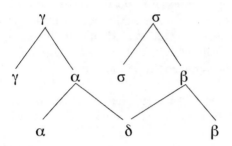

In (4) and (5), the Merge relationships Merge(α, δ) and Merge(β, δ) are present, and so the figure in (3) is present in both (4) and (5). However, in (4), when the entire structure is taken into account, δ appears to be a case of Internal Merge, while (5) appears to be a case of multidominance.[1]

To compare, here are the three cases of Merge discussed in the literature:

(6) External Merge:

(7) Internal Merge:

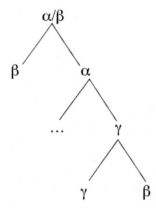

(8) The case of 'grafting' (van Riemsdijk 2001, 2006), or 'External Re-Merge' (de Vries 2009)

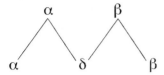

We return to this in section 3, as this description of grafting is a bit fragile in the sense that it is not clear how the structure created by grafting differs from a general X-bar theory; rather, it is one of many possible configurations created by different projections and headedness—another one being the X-bar configuration.

While the literature on multidominance points out that it is predicted by Merge, the utility of multidominance is restricted by these theories to certain constructions involving free relatives (van Riemsdijk), parentheticals (de Vries), or coordinated *wh*-questions (Citko 2005)—and various constraints are proposed to restrict Merge to these phenomena. What is focused on is the linearization problem created by grafted structures such as those in (8). For example, Citko 2005 addresses the issue of linearization with a constraint on multidominance structures that prevents them unless there is an antisymmetric projection that "brings together" the parallel structures and creates an antisymmetric relationship between the parallel projections that is essentially a Spec-Comp c-command relationship. Additionally, Citko's constraint states that movement of some constituent within the projections must occur in order to prevent a derivation crash. Van Riemsdijk 1998, 2001 addresses linearization by allowing for the grafted constituent (in his case, the free relative or transparent free relative) to be inserted into the PF string at the point where the graft occurs.

The criticism we put forth for these accounts of grafting is that limiting the exploration of Merge construction-specific instances and working out complex linearization algorithms for these constructions, rather than exploring the underlying Merge mechanism, takes too lightly the fact that grafting is part of the more general Merge mechanism. We take grafting to be a generalized phenomenon that extends beyond coordinate structures and free relatives or other parentheticals. One of the important milestones in generative grammar is that everything follows from a set of nondiscriminating computational rules instead of construction specific mechanisms. The grafting mechanism is not construction specific, and "grafting Merge" is a predictable consequence of a general Merge mechanism. We take this to account for regular relative clauses, extendable to movement in general. At the root of our account is a more specific notion of *occurrence* of a certain constituent.

In fact, a non-homogenous theory of displacement, with both move-ment (traces or copy/deletion) and sharing, requires rules for both types of structures. We take such a theoretical heterogeneity to be unnecessary, and extend the notion of sharing to all notions of multiple occurrences, includ-ing those of Internal (re-)Merge as well as External (re-)Merge. We take this as a **generalization of grafting**. This generalized mechanism will require a somewhat more refined notion of a chain of occurrences.

2.1.   On the Notion of Occurrence in a Tree

To illustrate what we mean by a chain of occurrences, we restrict to a system that allows only sharing. In the case of (coordinated and regular) relative clauses, sharing involves the head noun. Given the following tree as a repre-sentation of our core sentences:

(9)   Mary met *a man* and John met *a woman* who know each other well.

(10)   *A man* who Mary met and *a woman* who John met know each other well.

(11a)

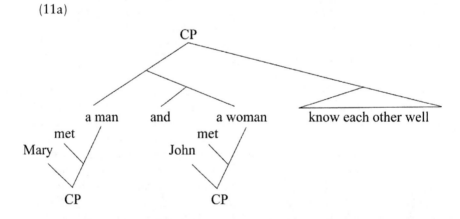

Both (9) and (10) could come from (11a). Crucially, this is because the shared NP occurs in the same argument positions in both (9) and (10). The maxi-mally simple way to treat these structures is to derive them from the same source. However, this tree still remains insufficient to account for which CP is relativized and which is matrix (this is also present in van Riemsdijk's account of grafting). To illustrate, we start with a simple headed relative clause, representing the head noun by a variable, *x*:

(11b)

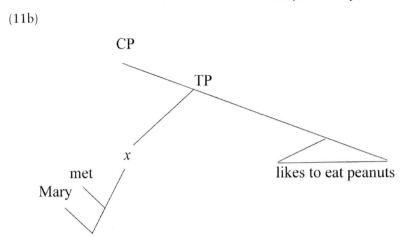

The preceding representation is underspecified for local grammatical relationships for the noun in three contexts: <*x,*—likes to eat peanuts>, <*x*, Mary met—>, <*x,*—C>. Instead, it only represents the noun in two (local) contexts: the argument position of two CPs. However, the pronounced position of the noun will be in a nonargument position the CP domain of the relative clause. If we were to relativize *x likes to eat peanuts,* we could represent *x* in the context of Spec, CP:

(11c)

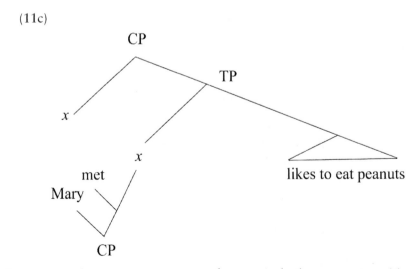

But now, we have two occurrences of *x:* one in both argument positions, shared, and one in [Spec, CP]. We have moved to a heterogeneous system with both copying and sharing. In order to maintain only sharing, we require a diagram like the following:

(11d)

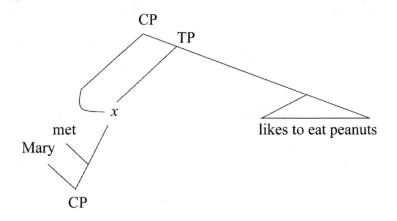

Now, *x* is represented in all three of the observed grammatical contexts expressed in the relative clause. But, if we define our syntactic trees following traditional graph theory, our tree is no longer a tree—we have introduced a cycle.

The purpose of the above illustration is to demonstrate the problems encountered when introducing local grammatical relations between the shared noun and the three contexts to which it belongs. As we move away from the heterogeneous system of both local sharing and long-distance copy-movement/indexing (a concept that gives overly tremendous power to the theory), trees seem to be insufficient representations of grammatical relations, even for a simple headed relative clause. An elegant solution is proposed in Wilder 2008. We will follow a lightly different route. Rather, we *generalize grafting* and represent every grammatical relation as a local relationship between two grammatical formatives. To that effect, we adopt a **graph representation of narrow syntax.** Using generalized grafting (i.e., *graphs*), we define cycles based on entirely local relationships—there are no long-distance grammatical relationships in these structures. This is a more explicit formulation of what it means for one object to "share," or really, to *occur in multiple contexts.*

3. FROM *GRAFTING* TO *GRAPHS*

3.1. On Phrase-markers

A classical Phrase-marker—one without traces—is a derivation in which only External Merge applies (we are assuming the standard approach, cf. Chomsky 1995, 2001, 2005, 2008 and work cited there). Specifically, a new constituent can be formed by merging a pair of maximal constituents drawn from an array of formatives or from the list of antecedently constructed constituents. The important point here is that two applications of External Merge will not share any constituent, yielding the classical Phrase-marker structure without multidominance or movement. If, as has been assumed elsewhere (see chapter 5 of this volume), Merge is restricted to applying to pairs of formatives, with the merging of nonterminals arising from headedness/labeling, then External Merge will have to allow for overlapping applications, e.g., in order to generate the *X*-bar schema or to allow heads to project multiple times in any case (see below).

The following condition adequately describes the standard workings of such derivations:

(12) Given two applications of Merge to two distinct pairs of formatives $\{f_i, f_j\}$ and $\{f_i, f_k\}$ sharing the element f_i, f_i must be the head/label in at least one of the relations Merge(f_i, f_j) and Merge(f_i, f_k).

This translates into the following condition on Phrase-markers:

(13) **Condition on Phrase-markers**
    Let *P* be some classical Phrase-marker and let (f_i, f_j), (f_i, f_k), f_i, f_j, f_k distinct formatives in *P*, be a pair of grammatical relations in *P* which share the formative f_i. At least one of the two relations is labeled/headed by f_i.

A classical Phrase-marker *P* then is a graph with the following two restrictions:

(14) (i) *P* is a tree (in the graph-theoretic sense).[2]

    (ii) *P* obeys the condition in (13).

We note that, due to the head/label relation, a classical Phrase-marker will in general admit more than one representation (see also chapter 5). To illustrate, the unibranching tree in (15), with heads as indicated, could also be drawn as in (16):

(15)

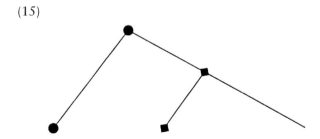

(16)

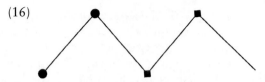

Similarly, the X-bar diagram in (17) could be drawn as in (18):

(17)

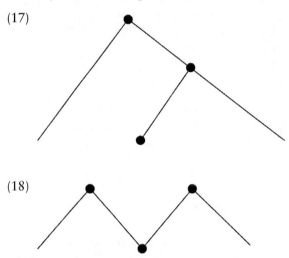

(18)

In what follows, we will only use the more standard drawings in (15) and (17), keeping in mind that there are equivalent drawings.

Representational problems immediately arise when Internal Merge gets involved. More generally, classical Phrase-markers cannot adequately represent nontrivial chains, i.e., lists of grammatical relations which share a formative f_i (see Chomsky 1981, 1995), as only External Merge can be applied and f_i can only be in one context/Merged once. It is possible to draw "augmented" Phrase-markers in which multiple occurrences of a formative are coindexed, as is standardly done in current theory.

(19)

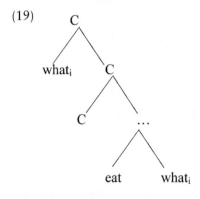

There is a conceptual difficulty, though: such chimeras with indexing or traces are excluded by *Inclusiveness* (Chomsky 1995: 225), as indexes are artificial mechanisms that are externally imposed on the structures.

For a certain number of structures, the difficulty can be overcome by using "intersecting" Phrase-markers, or restricted multidominance in the sense of the literature discussed in section 2. A representation along the lines of (20) would be required.

(20) 'Internal Merge'

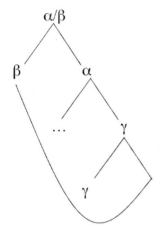

The preceding diagram illustrates the case of internal merge while respecting Inclusiveness: the two occurrences of β are not indexed or "copied" so there is no additional mechanism that would violate Inclusiveness.

Still, the theory cannot be extended to the most general case. In particular, standard *wh*-chains cannot be naturally described in terms of intersecting Phrase-markers, even assuming a derivation by phase. Such a description would require that any two phases along a *wh*-"path" intersect as in (4), violating cyclicity. The problem is this: a single *wh*-word "moves" cyclically, and so has a Merge relationship inside each phase of a clause. With a copying/indexing mechanism, several copies of the *wh*-word end up in the derivation, one of which is pronounced. If there is no copying, then the single *wh*-word is in a Merge relationship with all the positions to which it has been cyclically Merged. This is in violation of the Phase Impenetrability Condition, because the *wh*-word's position in a tree is "visible" in the derivation even after Spell-out of several phases after the *wh*-word was Merged into this position.

However, *setting aside the issue of wh-cyclicity temporarily*, in order to respect Inclusiveness and avoid copying, one needs to admit graphs with cycles, e.g., as in (21):

(21)

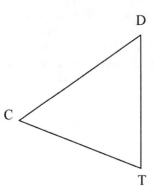

The elementary graph in (21) represents a chain of two occurrences of *D*, with one occurrence in the context of *T* and one, in the context of *C*, say, in the specifier positions of *T* and *C*, respectively. In other words, (21) represents the raising of D from the specifier position of T to that of C (or, alternatively, the lowering of *D* from the specifier position of *C* to that of *T*). So, a proper representation of nontrivial chains then requires that the condition in (14i) in turn be relaxed (repeated below):

(22) (i)   *P* is a tree (in the graph-theoretic sense).

Still, classical Phrase-markers seem to be the right objects to describe interpretive properties of expressions at the interface levels. At least, we shall assume as much. Then, in the spirit of CAT theory (Williams 2002), we propose a two-tiered architecture (as in chapter 5 of this volume). Narrow syntax will be formalized as a graph in the general sense. Phrase-markers will be read from that graph, subject to various conditions, in particular, locality conditions of various types (cyclical restrictions, etc.). To illustrate, the elementary graph in (21) gives rise to the two classical Phrase-markers in (23):

(23)

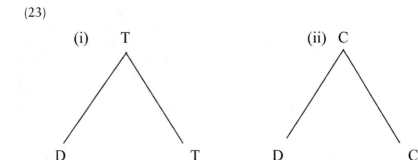

The fact that the two occurrences of *D* across the two classical Phrase-markers in (23) are occurrences of the *same* formative is enshrined in the primordial syntactic graph in (21). Again, the architecture is that of CAT theory, in which constituent structures are read from linear arrangements of categories and transformations apply to such linear arrangements, not to the "emergent" constituent structures. So:

> (24) Grammatical computations do not apply directly to Phrase-markers, but instead to more abstract representations, such as that in (21), from which Phrase-markers are ultimately derived (see chapter 5).

The roots of our approach are at the intersection of several lines of research: (i) recent work within the Minimalist Program (Chomsky 1999, 2001, 2005, and work cited there), (ii) CAT theory (Williams 2002), (iii) graft theory, (iv) antisymmetric syntax (Kayne 1994, 2005, and work cited there), (v) the theory of relators (den Dikken 2006), (vi) work by Schein (2001, 2002, 2007, 2009), (vii) the work in articulatory phonology (Browman & Goldstein 1986, 1992, 2000; Goldstein, Byrd, & Saltzman 2006; Saltzman & Byrd, 2000; Saltzman, Nam, Krivokapic, & Goldstein 2008) and, finally, (viii) work in chapter 5.

4. GRAPH-THEORETIC SYNTAX

We assume the existence of a labeling relation, construed as an ordering relation between the merged items. Assuming labeling, Merge is taken to apply to pairs of *grammatical formatives*, in the sense of Chomsky 1964 (also chapter 5). Merge applied to some α, some β, establishes one of two possible grammatical relationships between α and β. If α is the head, then β is either a Complement of α or a Specifier of α. From this, two varieties of Merge are established: *Selectional-Merge (S-Merge)* and *Checking-Merge (C-Merge)*. S-Merge creates a Head-Complement relation, or *selection* relation (Chomsky 1965), e.g., the pair (C, T) in the upper phase of a clause. C-Merge creates a Head-Specifier relation, or *checking* relation (Chomsky 1993), e.g., the pair (T, D).

A derivation is represented as a graph with labeled edges. The edge $(f_i, f_j)_x$ with end points/vertices f_i and f_j, f_i and f_j formatives, represents the x-merging of f_i and f_j, $x = S$ (*selection*) or C (*checking*):

(25)

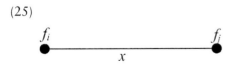

We call a derivational graph an *M-graph* ("*M*" for "Merge"), and the notion of M-graph is akin to that of *T-marker* in the sense of Chomsky 1975.

Assuming labeling, an *M*-graph is a directed graph. For example, the one-edged graph in (25) should be oriented as shown in (26) if f_j is the head of $(f_i, f_j)_x$:

(26)

If *x* in (26) is C (*checking*), f_i is in the relation *Specifier-of* to f_j.

(27)

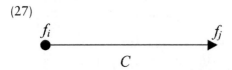

Checking is itself a symmetrical relation. *Specifier-of* is just the relation that arises when two formatives in a checking relation are ordered by labeling/headedness. Arguments are uniformly treated as specifiers (cf. Bowers 1993; Hale & Keyser 1997; Larson 1988; Liao et al. 2009; Liao 2009; Lin 2001; Megerdoomian 2002; Prinzhorn et al. 2004; Zubizarreta et al. 2001).

In our discussion, we will consistently disregard the directed character of the graph, indicating the direction of labeling/headedness only when it cannot be induced from the non-directed configuration.

4.1.   Symmetry

We assume that syntactic configurations are governed by basic *symmetry* principles (cf. Lasnik and Uriagereka 2005, chapters 5 and 7 of this volume). Thus, there is a one-one correspondence between the constituents in the specifier of *X* and the constituents in *X*.

For example, adopting the standard analysis of the lower phase in a clause, one expects the relations in (28) to hold, with labeling implicit:

(28)

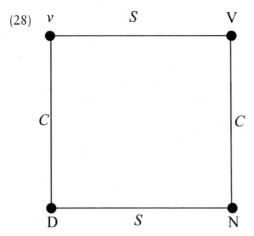

4.2. From Graphs to Phrase-Markers

Phrase-markers can be read from graphs. If one were to construct a tree based on Merge of (X, Y), with head projection/labeling, one could build a Phrase-marker from the graph. In other words, X → Y means that X and Y are Merged and Y projects.

(29)

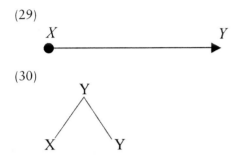

(30)

And so on:

(31)

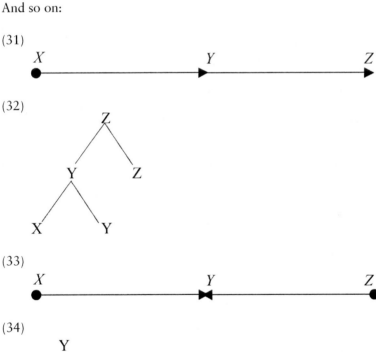

(32)

(33)

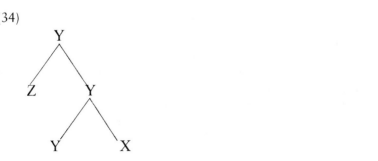

(34)

Essentially, graphs are more abstract representations of a set of possible trees, and our proposed condition on Classical Phrase-markers in (13) serves to produce trees that are interpretable at the interfaces.

5. OBSERVATION ABOUT SYMMETRY: RELATIVE CLAUSES

Returning to the basic observation, structures that contain multiple CPs are "reversible" between matrix and relative clauses without severe interpretational consequences:

(35) Mary met *a man* and John met *a woman* who know *each other* well.

(36) *A man* who Mary met and *a woman* who John met know *each other* well.

The symmetry arises in the fact that *a man* and *a woman* are interpreted as arguments (consequently, specifiers) of both verbs, in both sentences. The natural asymmetry arises with which CP undergoes relativization and receives a restrictive interpretation. The relativization/interpretation results from which C participates in some (D, C) relationship (see section 6). This symmetry/asymmetry arises for regular relative clauses as well:

(37) Mary met *a man* who knows her well.

(38) *A man* who Mary met knows her well.

One difficulty of having a grafting representation in the narrow syntax is the issue of asymmetry. A tree containing one item linked to two positions, without additional notions, represents the multiple occurrences of the shared constituent as symmetrical (van Riemsdijk 2006, his 9a):

(39) I ate what was euphemistically referred to as a steak.

Here, *[a steak]* exists in the following contexts:

[I ate ———]
[something was euphemistically referred to as ———]

The two separate CPs described as sharing the constituent *[a steak]* are on a par. Then, the asymmetry in the construction between the matrix and the relative clause remains unaccounted for.

To account for this asymmetry, we return to the basic notion of M-graph and begin with a similar configuration for the higher (subject) phase (in [37]), given some subject relative clause (40):[3]

(40) A man that knew Mary laughed.

(41)

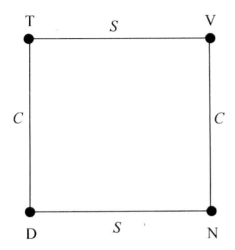

We follow the proposal in Chomsky 2008 that C is the "locus of agreement" for the higher phase, in the nominative domain, and that T only inherits the ability to agree when selected by C, otherwise resulting in a nonfinite ECM structure (Chomsky 2008: 143).

With the incorporation of C into the phase, the M-graph is as follows. The C-relationship between *T* and *D* comes from the *C-T* relationship.

(42)

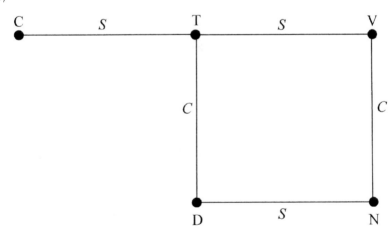

The relative clause is built like the matrix clause, and the {D, N} pair is shared, in the argument position of both verbs:

(43)

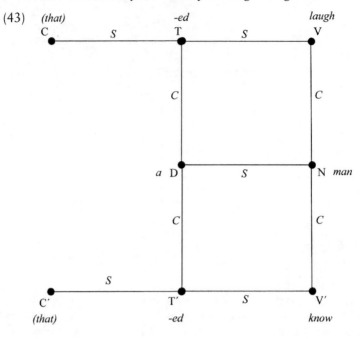

Following the standard raising analysis of relative clauses (cf. Kayne 1994), D is in a relationship with the C′ that is the relative clause. This relationship is a checking relationship between C′ and the nominal domain. C′ is the head/label of the pair {D, C′}:

(44)

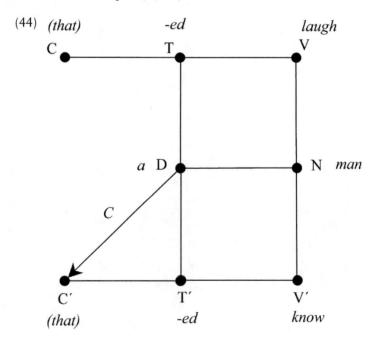

We return to the condition on classical Phrase-markers (in [13]):

(45) Given two applications of Merge to two distinct pairs of formatives {f_i, f_j} and {f_i, f_k} sharing the element f_i, f_i must be the head/label in at least one of the relations Merge(f_i, f_j) and Merge(f_i, f_k).

Under this condition, we rule out Phrase-markers containing the following:

(46) {X, Y}, {Y, Z}

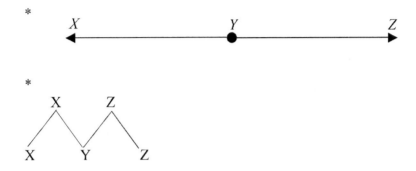

We see that the condition rules out the pairs {D, C} and {D, T′} from the same Phrase-marker:

(47)

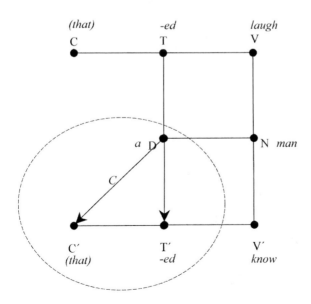

With the condition in place, some relevant maximal Phrase-markers are:

(48)

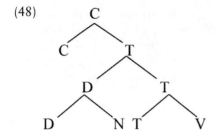

(49)

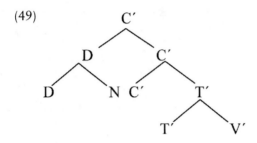

(50)

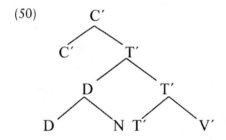

Importantly, we rule out Phrase-markers that contain multiple occurrences of the D-N pair:

(51) *

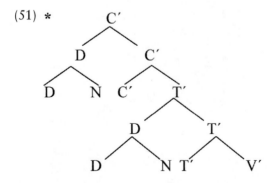

Then, PF interprets a restricted family of Phrase-markers, for example, the set (42)–(44). Leaving the details of linearization across a family of Phrase-markers to future work, we postulate the following: Spell-out to PF of a family of Phrase-markers involves looking at ordering information across multiple trees, which is dependent upon the same object occurring in multiple Phrase-markers.

We now turn to how the observed symmetry in the data is obtained, through the 'reversal' of relativized and matrix clauses. The graph maintains identical argument relations for the head noun *a man* in the above sentences. What reverses is which CP is relativized, and which is matrix. A simple reassignment of the {D, C} checking relationship from one clause to the next will obtain this result.

(52) CP = (A man) laughed
      C'P = (A man) knew Mary

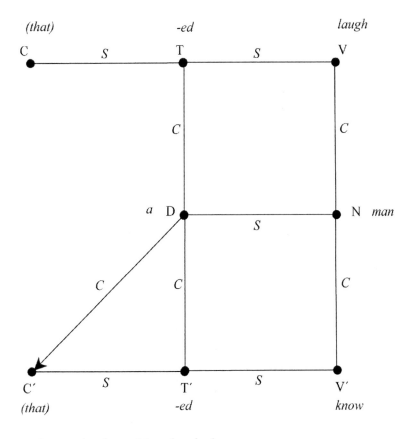

→ *A man that knew Mary laughed.*

(53)

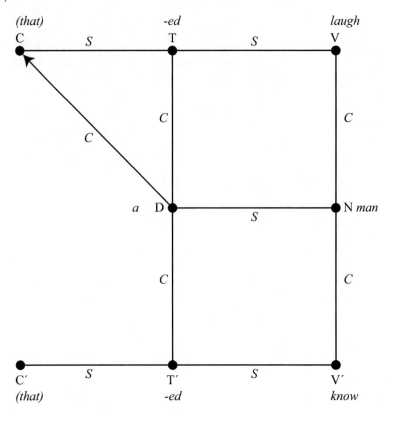

→ *A man who laughed knew Mary.*

6. COORDINATION AND DERIVING SPLIT-ANTECEDENT RELATIVES

With the structure for a relative clause in place, we turn to the cases of coordination and split-antecedent relative clauses, to incorporate a more general notion of coordination for these structures.

In fact, the split-antecedent relative clause structure is not unique; there is no reason to derive split-antecedent relative clauses in a special way that is distinct from simple headed relatives. In fact, there is a family of structures that arise from a general notion of coordinating sets of grammatical formatives, within the structure proposed in Section 5.

Starting with a simple example, we coordinate two clauses containing {John, Mary, sing, dance}. There are two possibilities, at first glance:

(54) The woman sings and the man dances.

(55) The woman and the man sing and dance (respectively).

To coordinate these clauses, we incorporate a notion of *dimension*, such that a *dimension* labels both vertices in some Merge relationship. Using this notion of *dimension*, we introduce a *dimension* for and:

However, we have been discussing the nominal and verbal domains, which are in a close checking relationship within the phase. So, our and dimension is really a *binary dimension {and, and'}* that spans both the nominal and verbal domain. So, the coordinated pair {Mary, sings} and {John, dances} appears as:

(56)

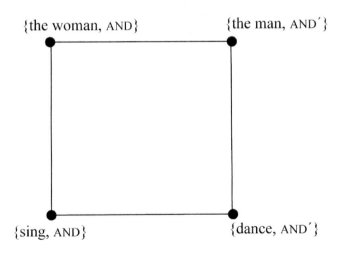

Using the binary dimension for *and,* we achieve a syntactic coordination of simple clauses.

(56) has been simplified, however, across the {T, V} and {D, N} domains. Turning back to our subject phase, we can coordinate the four vertices {T, V, D, N} as earlier, creating a cube:

(57)

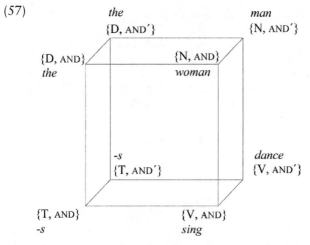

This can be expanded to the M-graph we provide for the regular headed relative clause—but, to either clausal domain (circled in the following). This will result in a coordination of matrix clauses, or a coordination of relative clauses, as we observe in our original examples:

(58) *Mary met a man* and *John met a woman* who know each other well.

(59) *A man who Mary met* and *a woman who John met* know each other well.

(60)

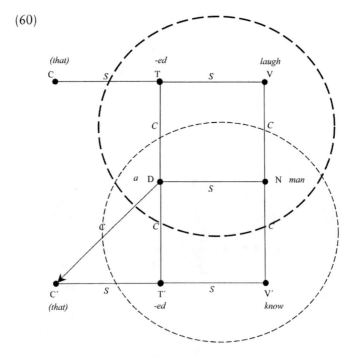

→ *A man that knew Mary laughed.*

Each of the circled clausal domains can be coordinated, resulting in either coordinated CPs which are *matrix clauses:*

(61) Mary met a man and John met a woman who know each other well

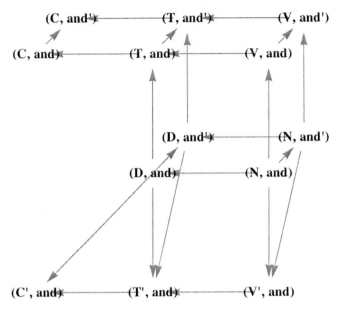

Or, coordinated CPs which are *relative clauses:*

(62) A man that Mary met and a woman that John met know each other well.

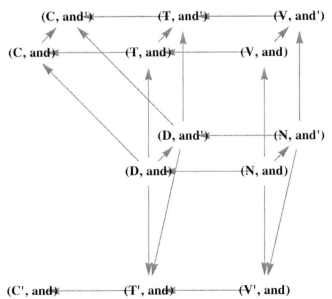

As with regular relative clauses, the two structures are obtained from a simple reversal of the relationship between D and C. In this case, the coordinated sentences have two Cs, so we are dealing with the additional complexity of two relationships between Ds and Cs. Otherwise, the structure is the same as the regular relative clause.

When *and* coordinates seemingly more than just a clause, a family of coordination arises (see McKinney-Bock in prep):

(63) A man who Mary met and a woman who John met danced and sang.

(64) A man and a woman who Mary met and who John met danced and sang.

(65) A man and a woman who Mary met danced and sang.

etc.

A configuration for the collective interpretation of the phrase [*who know each other well*] involves the scope of *and* with respect to the CP(s). We follow the semantics of Schein 2001, 2002, 2007, 2010, and believe that a syntactic representation of Schein's account is natural in the system we have been discussing.

7.   A BRIEF NOTE ON SYNTACTIC COORDINATES

Given the structure for a lower ("object") phase:

(66)

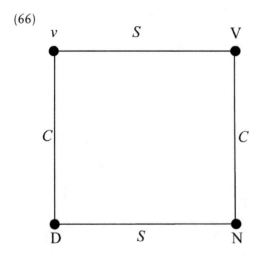

We have left the labeling of edges somewhat simplified throughout, for purposes of our discussion. However, labels are built of more fundamental grammatical formatives which occur in grammatical pairs (see chapters 5

and 7 of this volume; Liao 2011; McKinney-Bock 2013). In the previous section, we introduced an informal idea of *dimension* to support the more complex examples, where a dimension consists of a binary pair of formatives.

More fundamentally, we analyze the labels v, V, D, N as combinations of more elementary categories/features, L = Lexical, F = Functional, V = Verb (category), N = Noun (category). To wit:

(67) $v = (V, F)$
     $V = (V, L)$
     $D = (N, F)$
     $N = (N, L)$

In each binary pair (X, Y) in (67), the first symbol denotes a category type, the second, the range of "values" associated with that type in the pair (X, Y). That particular feature analysis is predicated upon the assumption that the lexical content of a category type in a structure is identified as a particular element in a paradigm, i.e., a particular element in a domain of values for some other type or in the lexicon as a whole. The second "coordinate" Y in a pair (X, Y) should then be equated with either *lexical* or *functional* (i.e., φ) *features*, the nature of these being variable.

Note that the set of coordinates is really the Cartesian product of two binary dimensions, {F, L} and {N, V}.

8. CONCLUSION

This paper has put forth a substantial revision of syntactic theory and relativization, and also provides an empirical contribution within the domain of relative clauses.

Theoretically, we have a graphical representation of the symmetry between headed relative clauses and their "reversed" counterparts. The locus of the asymmetry (which CP is relative/matrix) is a C-Merge relationship between D and one C. A "reassignment" of the D-C relationship will flip which clause is relative and which is matrix.

For split-antecedent relative clauses, we show that split-antecedent relative clauses have the same underlying structure in this system as regular headed relative clauses. A general coordination mechanism builds on top of this and generates a family of coordinated structures with relative and matrix clauses. This coordination will be the same, independent of whether the CP is relativized or not. This accounts for our two core sentences:

(68) A man who Mary met and a woman who John met know each other well.

(69) Mary met a man and John met a woman who know each other well.

Within a broader domain, we *generalize grafting* and represent all grammatical relations as local relationships between two grammatical formatives. To that effect, we adopt a **graph representation of narrow syntax.** This more fundamental representation in narrow syntax, or more abstract representation, gives rise to classical Phrase-markers which play different roles at the interfaces. There are no long-distance grammatical relationships in these structures, which homogenizes the system. Ours is an explicit, generalized formalization of what it means for one object to "share," or, to *occur in multiple contexts.*

NOTES

   *   (Prepared by the first author) Many thanks to Roumyana Pancheva, Tommi Leung, and Roger Wei-Wen Liao for their valuable discussions and insights. Thanks to Maria Luisa Zubizarreta, Barry Schein, Richard Arratia, Audrey Li, Roger Liao, Sarah Ouwayda, Andrew Simpson, Barbara Tomaszewicz, Mary Byram, and Khalil Iskarous and the GLOW 2010 audience for their helpful comments. I am also indebted to my advisor and coauthor, Jean-Roger Vergnaud; without his guidance and collaboration, this research would not have been, or have continued to be, possible.

1. Notice here that we are referring to a representation of a tree, rather than referring to the derivation. However, this is not crucial to the discussion at hand of source independence. Rather, in the case of (4), if the structure in (5) had been Merged first, the *Extension Condition* would have been violated to create (4) when β is Merged with γ. So an additional condition on Merge is required to rule out instances of grafting *when looking at how a derivation might proceed.*

2. A tree is a simple graph without cycles (as in standard graph theory; see, e.g., Balakrishnan and Ranganathan 2000).

3. Here, we have used an unergative verb *laugh* for one of the CPs, and we have used a subject relative clause *that t knew Mary* for the other CP. The structure we draw is simplified for purposes of explanation, containing only the subject phase with the Agent-Verb relationship. The argument structure for both (a) the ergative and (b) the transitive verb is simplified. For (a), we assume that an unergative verb contains only one phase with the Agent DP and T-V. For (b) we refer readers to McKinney-Bock (2013) for a discussion on how the subject and object phases (CP and vP phases) overlap and how more complex argument structure is built.

REFERENCES

Balakrishnan, R., and K. Ranganathan. 2000. *A Textbook of Graph Theory.* New York: Springer.

Bowers, J. 1993. The syntax of predication. *Linguistic Inquiry* 24:591–656.

Browman, C., and L. Goldstein. 1992. Articulatory phonology. *Phonetica* 49:155–180.

———. 2000. Competing constraints on intergestural coordination and self organization of phonological structures. *Les Cahiers de l'ICP, Bulletin de la Communication Parlée* 5:25–34.

———. 1986. Towards an articulatory phonology. *Phonology Yearbook* 3:219–252.

Chomsky, N. 1964. Current issues in linguistic theory. In *The Structure of Language*, ed. by J. Fodor and J. Katz. Mahwah, NJ: Prentice Hall.

———. 1975. *The Logical Structure of Linguistic Theory*. Chicago: University of Chicago Press.

———. 1981. *Lectures on Government and Binding*. Dordrecht, Netherlands: Foris.

———. 1995. *The Minimalist Program*. Cambridge, MA: MIT Press.

———. 2001. Derivation by phase. In *Ken Hale: A Life in Language*, ed. by M. Kenstowicz. Cambridge, MA: MIT Press.

———. 2005. Three factors in the language design. *Linguistic Inquiry* 36:1–22.

———. 2008. On phases. In *Foundational Issues in Linguistic Theory: Essays in Honor of Jean-Roger Vergnaud*, ed. by R. Freidin, C. P. Otero, and M. L. Zubizarreta. Cambridge, MA: MIT Press.

Citko, B. 2005. On the nature of merge: External merge, internal merge, and parallel merge. *Linguistic Inquiry* 36:475–496.

Dikken, M. den 2006. *Relators and Linkers: The Syntax of Predication, Predicate Inversion, and Copulas*. Cambridge, MA: MIT Press.

Goldstein, L., D. Byrd, and E. Saltzman. 2006. The role of vocal tract gestural action units in understanding the evolution of phonology. In *From Action to Language: The Mirror Neuron System*, ed. by M. Arbib. Cambridge: Cambridge University Press.

Gracanin-Yuksek, M. 2007. About sharing. Doctoral dissertation, MIT.

Hale, K., and S. J. Keyser. 1993. On argument structure and the lexical expression of syntactic relations. In *The View from Building 20: Essays in Linguistics in Honor of Sylvain Bromberger*, ed. by K. Hale and S. J. Keyser. Cambridge, MA: MIT Press.

———. 2002. *Prolegomenon to a Theory of Argument Structure*. Cambridge, MA: MIT Press.

Kayne, R. 1994. *The Antisymmetry of Syntax*. Cambridge, MA: MIT Press.

———. 2005. *Movement and Silence*. Cambridge: Cambridge University Press.

Larson, R. 1988. On the double object construction. *Linguistic Inquiry* 19:335–391.

Lasnik, H., and J. Uriagereka. 2005. *A Course in Minimalist Syntax*. Malden, MA: Blackwell.

Liao, W.-w. R. 2009. Indefinites in Chinese and the theory of D-V merge. Paper presented at NELS 40, November 13–15, MIT.

———, and J.-R. Vergnaud. 2009. Of NPs and phases. Ms., University of Southern California.

Lin, T. J. 2001. Light verb syntax and the theory of phrase structure. Doctoral dissertation, University of California, Irvine.

McCawley, J. 1982. Parentheticals and discontinuous constituent structure. *Linguistic Inquiry* 13:91–106.

McKinney-Bock, K. 2013. Building phase structure from items and contexts. Doctoral dissertation, University of Southern California.

Megerdoomian, K. 2002. Beyond words and phrases: A unified theory of predicate composition. Doctoral dissertation, University of Southern California.

Perlmutter, D. M., and J. R. Ross. 1970. Relative clauses with split antecedents. *Linguistic Inquiry* 1:350.

Riemsdijk, H. van 2001. A far from simple matter: Syntactic reflexes of syntax-pragmatics misalignments. In *Semantics, Pragmatics and Discourse: Perspectives and Connections—a Festschrift for Ferenc Kiefer*, ed. by I. Kenesei and R. M. Harnish. Amsterdam: John Benjamins.

———. 2006. Grafts follow from merge. In *Phases of Interpretation*, ed. by M. Frascarelli. Berlin: Mouton de Gruyter.

Saltzman, E., and D. Byrd. 2000. Task-dynamics of gestural timing: Phase windows and multifrequency rhythms. *Human Movement Science* 19:499–526.

————, H. Nam, J. Krivokapic, and L. Goldstein. 2008. A task-dynamic toolkit for modeling the effects of prosodic structure on articulation. In *Proceedings of the Speech Prosody 2008 Conference*, ed. by P. A. Barbosa, S. Madureira, and C. Reis. Campinas, Brazil.

Schein, B. 2001. The semantics of right-node raising and number agreement. Paper presented at the Semantics Workshop, Center for Cognitive Science, Rutgers University.

————. 2002. Number agreement in Lebanese Arabic. Paper presented at the Linguistics Colloquium, MIT.

————. 2007. Simple clauses conjoined. Paper presented at the Symposium on Philosophy and Linguistics, American Philosophical Association, Eastern Division, Baltimore, MD.

————. 2010. Conjunction reduction redux. Ms., University of Southern California.

Vergnaud, J.-R., and M. L. Zubizarreta. 2001. Derivation and constituent structure. Ms., University of Southern California.

Vries, M. de 2009. On multidominance and linearization. *Biolinguistics* 3:344–403.

Wilder, C. 1994. Coordination, ATB and ellipsis. *Groninger Arbeiten zur Germanistischen Linguistik* 37:291–331.

————. 2008. Shared constituents and linearization. In *Topics in Ellipsis*, ed. by K. Johnson. Cambridge: Cambridge University Press.

Williams, E. 2002. *Representation Theory*. Cambridge, MA: MIT Press.

7 On Merge-Markers and Nominal Structures[1]

Wei-wen Roger Liao and Jean-Roger Vergnaud

This chapter presents a novel analysis of nominal structures under the framework of symmetric syntax (originally proposed in chapter 5 of this volume, and later developed in Liao 2011). We begin by reviewing a long-standing dilemma in the analyses of nominal syntax. That is, it always leads to some conceptual problems whether we assume the single-constituent analysis or dual-constituent analysis. With respect to nominal syntax, the classifier constructions in (Mandarin) Chinese will be examined at length, in comparison (and contrast) with the corresponding constructions in English. From the perspectives of locality and selectional restriction, neither the single-constituent analysis nor the dual-constituent analysis makes full explanation for the syntactic properties of the nominal structures. These problems, however, can be accounted for once we adopt the idea that syntactic computations are in fact executed at a more abstract level (which we call Merge-markers), and (surface) phrase structures are actually constructed from these abstract syntactic units by independent mapping mechanisms.

This paper is organized as follows. Section 1 presents a controversy in nominal syntax. We show that neither the single-constituent nor the dual-constituent analysis may fully capture all of the empirical facts in Chinese. Section 2 introduces a similar problem noted by Kayne (2005) regarding the sub-extraction problem. Kayne's proposal is that a partitive construction, such as [lots of money], which appears to be a single-constituent structure, actually involves two separate constituents, connected by a pair of connective (of, OF). We then compare the solution in Kayne (2005) with the Relator-Linker theory in den Dikken 2006. Their accounts are generalized into a theory of parallel (symmetric) syntax. Section 3 provides a brief introduction to the novel syntactic architecture. In section 4, we argue that nominal syntax, with special reference to classifier constructions in Chinese, offers empirical support to our claim. It will be shown that the conceptual paradox met by the standard analyses may find its way out through our novel account, along with many other theoretical issues raised in classifier constructions and nominal syntax in Chinese and English. We conclude our discussion in section 5.

1. A DILEMMA OF NOMINAL STRUCTURES

1.1. Single-Constituent Analysis versus Dual-Constituent Analysis

Since Abney (1987), it is generally assumed that universally a nominal expression should be analyzed as a Determiner Phrase (DP), in which a determiner takes a Noun Phrase (NP) as complement, cf. (1a). Later, an additional functional projection (Number Phrase) is also introduced into the structure by Ritter (1991), as in (1b):[2]

(1)

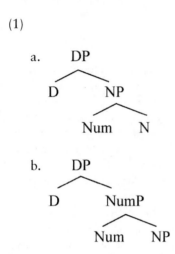

a. DP
   D   NP
         Num   N

b. DP
   D   NumP
         Num   NP

Along this line, it has been an issue of whether an additional functional projection should be added to the structure in languages with overt classifiers. In Chinese, for example, a classifier is obligatory between a numeral and a noun:

(2) a. san   zhi   gou
      three CL   dog
      'three (individual) dogs'

    b. yi   ge   ren
      one   CL   person
      'one (individual) person'

There have been two major competing proposals regarding syntax of classifiers. The first camp proposes that a classifier and a noun head two independent constituents (Fukui and Takano 2000; Huang 1982). This approach suggests that a classifier builds an independent constituent that is adjoined to (or forms a small clause with) NP. The other camp, however, argues that a classifier should be analyzed on a par with Num and D as an extended projection in the nominal structure (Borer 2005; Li 1999; Simpson

2005; Tang 1990, among others). The two competing approaches can be illustrated as follows:[3]

(3)

    a. Dual-constituent analysis

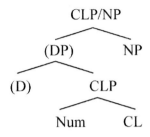

    b. Single-constituent analysis[1]

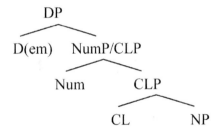

Let us briefly review the advantages and drawbacks of the two competing analyses. The dual-constituent analysis has the advantage of accounting for certain distributional facts. For example, it predicts that Numeral (or Number) and Classifier form a single constituent, excluding the matrix NP. This analysis is plausible since it predicts that N and CL have parallel syntactic statuses. The parallelism between N and CL can be evidenced in Korean, where N and CL are both able to take Case-marking, and hence the dual-constituency analysis is supported:

(4) Case-marking of classifiers in Korean (Park 2008)

    a. ku-nun   [chayk] [sey   kwen-ul]   ilkessta.
        He-Top   book   three   CL-Acc   read
       'He read (the) three books'.

    b. ku-nun   [chayk-ul]   [sey   kwen]   ilkessta.
        He-Top   book-Acc   three   CL   read

c. ku-nun   [chayk-ul]   [sey kwen-ul]   ilkessta.
   He-Top   book-Acc   three CL-Acc   read

Another pattern that cannot be easily accounted for by the single-constituent analysis is when a classifier is assigned a theta role. Consider the following facts in English (van Riemsdijk 1998) and in Chinese:

(5) a. John **ate** a tray of **pastries**.   [head = pastries]

    b. John **carried** a **tray** of pastries.   [head = tray]

    c. John **turned over** a **tray** of **pastries**.   [head = tray or pastries]

(6) a. John **he-le** [san   ping   **shui**].   (theme = water)
      John   drank   three   bottle   water
      'John drank three bottles of water'.

    b. John **da-po** [san   **ping**   shui].   (theme = bottle)
      John   break   three   bottle   water
      'John broke three bottles of water'.

The fact that classifiers, as well as nouns, can be assigned theta-roles again confirms the idea that classifiers and nouns display parallelism. It further indicates that a classifier should be treated as a substantive category (or as a special "semifunctional" category, as suggested in van Riemsdijk's work) because a functional category is very unlikely to be involved in theta structures (Lebeaux 1988).[4]

Despite being conceptually appealing, the dual-constituent analysis has great difficulties capturing a primitive syntactic relation between CL and N, viz. the strong (local) selection found between CL and N (since the analysis predicts that the classifier and the noun belong to two separate constituents). Given the common assumption about head selection (subject to strict locality), N and CL cannot engage in a local selectional relation if the dual-constituent analysis is assumed. The local selection between CL and N, then, provides strong support instead for the single-constituent analysis. Since CL is the immediate extended projection of N, the selection can be easily accounted for within the latter analysis. The classifier constructions hence lead us to a conceptual paradox in the standard theories.

1.2. DP-Internal Remnant Movement: Kayne (2005)

The controversy between the dual-constituent and the single-constituent analyses recalls a proposal made in Kayne (2005) with respect to the notorious subextraction problem:

(7) a. *Money,* John has [$_{DP}$ lots of *t*].

    b. *Who* did you see [$_{DP}$ a picture of *t*]?

The subextraction problem arises when *money* and *who* are extracted from the larger DPs. Unexpectedly, such extractions incur no violations of locality constraints. One attempt, introduced in Chomsky (1977), to solve the subextraction problem is to propose a restructuring rule, which reanalyzes the larger DP into two smaller object phrases: [lots of money] → [lots of]+[money]. The extraposed/restructured DP (*money* or *who*) is thus free to move. In Kayne's proposal, however, the ad hoc restructuring rule can be dispensed with, if we may assume that *of* is generated outside DP (and even outside the matrix VP). Kayne's analysis is outlined in (8), which is reminiscent of the dual-constituent DP analysis:

(8) a. have [$_{SC}$ [money] [lots]]

   b. OF$_{Case}$ [$_{VP}$ have[$_{SC}$ [money] [lots]]]   (Merging *OF*)

   c. [money [OF$_{Case}$ [$_{VP}$ have [$_{SC}$ t$_{money}$ [lots]]]]]   (NP movement to Spec, *OF*P)

   d. of [money [OF$_{Case}$ [$_{VP}$ have [$_{SC}$ t$_{money}$ [lots]]]]]   (Merging *of*)

   e. [$_{VP}$ have [$_{SC}$ t$_{money}$ [lots]]] [of [money] [OF$_{Case}$ t$_{VP}$]]

                                             (remnant movement to Spec, *of*P)

   f.

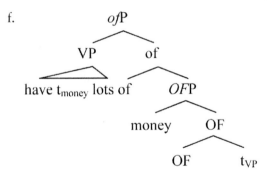

The resulting structure also contains two DP constituents (one headed by *lots* and the other by *money*) that are connected by a pair of connective (of, OF). Two features in Kayne (2005) should be emphasized here: the Small Clause analysis and the pairing of connectives (see Moro 2000 for a discussion of small clauses in the antisymmetric approach). Following Kayne's analysis, it might be possible to solve the tension between the local selection and the dual constituents of CL and N if we assume that CL and N originally form a small clause, and the dual constituents are subsequently derived by remnant movements, as in (9):[5]

(9) a. he   san   ping   (de)   shui
      drink three bottle$_{CL}$ DE   water
    'drink three bottles of water'

b.   drink [$_{SC}$ [water] [three-bottle$_{CL}$]]

c.   DE$_{Case}$ [$_{VP}$ drink[$_{SC}$ [water] [three-bottle$_{CL}$]]]   (Merging *DE*)

d.   [water [DE$_{Case}$ [$_{VP}$ drink [$_{SC}$ t$_{water}$ [three-bottle]]]]]   (NP movement to Spec, *DE*P)

e.   (de) [water [DE$_{Case}$ [$_{VP}$ drink [$_{SC}$ t$_{water}$ [three-bottle]]]]]   (Merging *de*)

f.   [$_{VP}$ drink [$_{SC}$ t$_{water}$ [three-bottle]]] [(de) [water] [DE$_{Case}$ t$_{VP}$]]
(remnant movement to Spec, *de*P)

In this way, the contrast between the single-constituent and the dual-constituent analyses can also be neutralized. However, the question remains even if we adopt the small clause analysis (despite the concern about the ill-defined nature of "small clauses") since many additional stipulations are still needed in order to account for the parallel patterns of theta-role and Case-assignments of CL and N. We shall return to this question in section 2.

1.3.   The Relator-Linker Analysis: Den Dikken (2006)

Kayne's treatment of the linking pair (of, OF) finds its kin in den Dikken's (2006) work, who develops a similar theory on independent grounds. However, for den Dikken, these connective pairs are more widely applied. One element of the connective pairs is a syntactic realization of the joint of predication relation, called Relator. A Relator is always accompanied by a (possibly covert) shadow copy, called a Linker. Den Dikken then success-fully relates the "coupling" effect of relator-linker to the syntax of Predicate Inversion. The structures are illustrated here:

(10)   Predication (a Relator ρP mediates between the argument and predicate)

[$_{ρP}$ Argument [ρ = Relator Predicate]]

(11)   Predicate Inversion (Relator raises to Linker λ and subsequently triggers predicate-raising)

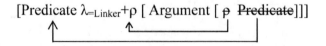

For den Dikken, a grammatical Relator is identified as a functional head that bridges an argument to its predicate. In the transformation of predicate inversion, the Linker (the shadow copy of the Relator) attracts the head-raising of the Relator to the Linker, and in turn licenses raising of the predicate (irrelevant to our purpose here, den Dikken also assumes that a raised predicate always contains some empty element that needs to be licensed). Predicate Inversions can apply in verbal or nominal domains, reflected by different types of Relator-Linker pairs (their phonological realizations are subject to language-specific rules). In English, for example, the verbal linker is realized as the raised auxiliary *is,* as in (12), while *of* is the nominal counterpart, as in (13):

(12) a. [Brian [is($= \rho$) [$_{\text{Predicate}}$ the best candidate]]]

   b. [[*op* the best candidate]$_2$ T($= \lambda$)+is$_1$($= \rho$)   [Brian] t$_1$ t$_2$]

(13) a. a jewel **of** a village

   b. [[F = similar a jewel]$_2$ **of**($= \lambda$)+ρ_1 [a village [t$_1$ t$_2$]]]

The nominal linker *de* in Chinese is another example, illustrated in (14), where *de* is considered a Linker that triggers raising of the empty Aux (see also Simpson 2002, who argues that the linker *de* can be identified as a determiner):

(14) a. hongsede   fangzi
       red   DE   house
       'red house'

   b. D [$_{\text{CP}}$ house [Aux [red]]]

   c. D [[red]$_2$ Aux$_1$-DE $_{= \text{Linker}}$ [house [t$_1$ t$_2$]]]

Den Dikken's analysis provides a novel insight to several cross-linguistic constructions. However, it raises some theoretical concerns. One of the major theoretical concerns is on the restrictiveness of the Relator-Linker analysis. In a way, it is impossible to define (or to falsify) the notion of Relator. Relator is a general term that is designed to cover the functional categories that connects an argument to its predicate. It is sometimes difficult, however, to define precisely what the notion of "predicate" is. In terms of "predicate," for instance, den Dikken (2006) only considers the predication of a subject and its predicate, but he offers no discussion on an object in a transitive predicate:

(15) a. [Subject [**Relator** = v Predicate]]

   b. [Predicate [**Relator** = ? Object]]

There seems little theoretical reason to exclude the configuration in (15b) (involving an object) from being an instance of predication. But what is the Relator here? If it can be identified as a determiner (a functional category between verb and NP object), then it is a puzzle why the determiner of the subject cannot be analyzed in the same fashion (the Relator in (15a) is identified as a light verb in den Dikken). We may also assume instead that the Relator is another light verb in (15b) (an object light verb, in parallel to the subject light verb). A Relator, then, may be identified as some type of "conjunct" that conjoins various levels of parallel projections. In fact, den Dikken may have already pointed to a similar direction since the Relator-Linker analysis is extended to many other configurations, where the connected elements are not simply a typical argument–predicate combination, but units of similar structural statuses (from den Dikken 2006:chapter 2):

(16) a. nice and easy

  b. [$_{AP}$ nice [$_{RP}$ and$_{(= Relator)}$ easy]]

(17) a. Susan danced beautifully.

  b. Susan –ed [dance [$_{RP}$ –ly $_{= Relator}$ beautiful]]

(18) a. Imogen regards the president as a fool.

  b. Imogen regards [the president [$_{RP}$ as $_{= Relator}$ a fool]]

Based on this, it is conjectured in den Dikken (2006:17) that the Relator "might uniformly be the logical operator '∩,' with predication being semantically represented as set intersection." We shall elaborate on this conjecture and present a unified analysis (of Kayne's and den Dikken's approaches) under the Merge-marker analysis introduced in the following sections.

2. ON THE DUAL-CONSTITUENT DP AND CONNECTIVES

One way to generalize the analyses proposed in Kayne (2005) and den Dikken (2006) is to assume a connective pair, represented as {k, k'}, as part of our grammatical devices:[6]

(19) a. Kayne (2005):   (of, OF)

  b. den Dikken (2006): (Linker, Relator)

These elements are generalized connectives that may connect various domains. In effect, the remnant movement analysis and the dual-constituent analysis can be reanalyzed as a conjoined structure of two VP domains (by the connective pair, (of, OF)):

(20) a. have lots of money
  b. [have lots] of [have money] OF

As usually assumed, in the pronounced structure, the lower instance of V undergoes deletion under identity:[7]

(21) [have lots] of [~~have~~ money] OF

Applying the same analysis to the classifier and the noun, then, the classifier-noun structures can be reanalyzed as:

(22) a. Lisi he-le   san   ping   (de)   shui

       Lisi   drink-Asp   three   bottle$_{CL}$ DE   water

       'Lisi drank three bottles of water'.

   b. [he   san   ping]   (de)   [he   shui]   (DE)

       drank   three   bottle$_{CL}$ DE   drink   water   DE

Here, what are conjoined by the connective pair ((*de*, DE) in Chinese) are not simply CL and N, but larger VP constituents (hence the Kaynean analysis is recaptured here).

One advantage of adopting such an analysis is that Riemsdijk's problem can be resolved. Recall the problem in (5) and (6), repeated here as (23) and (24):

(23) a. John ate a tray of **pastries**.   [head = pastries]

   b. John carried a **tray** of pastries.   head = tray]

   c. John turned over a **tray** of **pastries**. [head = tray or pastries]

(24) a. John **he-le**   [san   ping   **shui**].   (head = water)

       John drank   three   bottle   water

       'John drank   three bottles of water'.

   b. John da-po   [san   **ping**   shui].   (head = bottle)

       John break   three   bottle   water

       'John broke three bottles of water'.

Applying our analysis to the preceding examples, the following structures can be derived:

(25) a. [eat a tray = N1] of [eat **pastries** = N2] OF

   b. [carry a **tray** = N1] of [carry pastries = N2] OF

   c. [turn-over a **tray** = N1] of [turn-over **pastries** = N2] OF

The structural analysis directly captures the strict locality of theta-assignment (Williams 1994). It can be assumed verbs should freely assign theta-roles to their associated arguments, and at the interface related to interpretations (e.g., LF), the interpretations that are (semantically or pragmatically) deviant will be filtered out.[8]

The analysis proposed here may also be related to the verb-copying constructions in Chinese in (26). The matrix noun, *water,* can either remain in the canonical position following the classifier, as in (26a), or it can be preposed with an additional copy of the verb, as in (26b):

(26) a. Zhangsan   he-le   [san   ping]   (de)   [shui]
        Zhangsan   drink-Asp   three   bottle$_{CL}$ DE   water

   b. Zhangsan   [he   shui]   [he-le   san   ping]
        Zhangsan   drink   water   drink-Asp   three bottle$_{CL}$
        '(both a and b): Zhangsan drank three bottles of water'.

Under the proposed analysis, one can reduce the verb copying construction to an instance of predicate inversion transformation, where the pronunciations of the connectives, or the {de, DE} pair, may vary according to the positions of the predicates these elements are associated with:

(27) a. [he san bei] de [[he shui] DE
   b. [he shui] DE$_i$ [he san bei] de

Compare the verb-copying constructions in (27) with the predicate inversion structures in (28). Both transformations simply involve rearrangement of the connected domains and different pronunciation rules of the connective pairs:

(28) a. [v the man] be [V Sherlock] BE.   = *The man is Sherlock.*

   b. [V Sherlock] be [v the man] be.   = *Sherlock is the man.*

3.   BEYOND PHRASE STRUCTURES

3.1.   Merge-Markers in the Nominal Domains

Recall that the problem of the dual-constituency analysis lies in the local selection of CL and N (yet, they belong to independent VPs). We believe that this problem suggests that syntactic computation actually involves a more abstract structure, which we shall refer to it as Merge-markers (M-markers). As phrase-markers to the standard theory, we take M-markers as the most fundamental syntactic units in syntactic computation. Due to limited space, we summarize the main ideas as follows.[9] It has been hypothesized in chapter 5 that the standard phrase structures are always derived from an underlying more abstract syntactic representation, subject to the conditions in (29) (from Liao 2011):

(29) The Vergnaud Conjectures

    a. The underlying syntactic representation (or M-marker) is a Cartesian product of the primitive syntactic relations (R_n):

$$\text{M-marker} = R_1 \otimes R_2 \otimes R_3$$

    b. Lexical items (or syntactic formatives) are inserted in the M-marker, and 'merge' is defined upon any two adjacent nodes in the M-marker.

    c. Phrase-markers are constructed from the abstract M-markers.

From (29a), Liao (2011) further proposes that the underlying computation involves three fundamental relations, i.e., {N, V}, {Substantial (Sb), Functional (Fn)}, and {k, k'}. {N, V} describes the *argument-of* and *spec-head* relations, {Sb, Fn} describes the relation between a substantive root and the functional category that defines its grammatical function in the structure, and {k, k'} describes the Kayne-den Dikken connectives that are introduced in the last section. When the primitive syntactic relations are simultaneously satisfied, a Merge-marker is obtained, as illustrated in (30):

(30) A canonical M-marker = {V, N} $\otimes$ {Sb,Fn } $\otimes$ {k,k'}

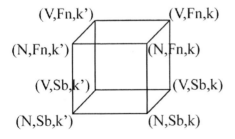

Subject to (29a), each M-marker is a domain where all primitive relations have been combined with one another. One can, though not exclusively, represent such combinations in a graph-theoretical way, the "product" can be mapped to a three-dimensional cube in (30). (29b) states that when a syntactic formative is inserted into a node in the M-marker, a "syntactic role" is assigned by the combination of the primitive syntactic relations. For example, the node (N, Sb, k) and (N, Sb, k') corresponds to a pair of nominal substantial items that are related to each other by the connectives {k, k'} (i.e., the relation of CL and N). On the other hand, (N, Sb, k) and (N, Fn, k) characterize the relation between a nominal substantive root and its paired nominal functional item, which subsequently defines the grammatical function of the substantive root (see the next section). For our purpose here, the CL-N domain is used as illustration (note that M-markers may also constitute other syntactic domains; see Liao 2011 for details):

(31) The CL-N domain

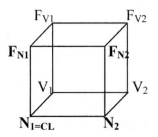

After lexical insertion, each node has a well-defined "syntactic role" that interacts with one another by the primitive syntactic relations. Under this configuration, CL and N are the two substantive nouns that are locally connected by the "extension" relation {k, k'}.

Turning to (29c), when a M-maker is mapped to a phrase structure (triggered by the asymmetric requirement of the interfaces), the dual-VP analysis is directly derived (recall Kayne's analysis). Here, the connective pair that introduces the embedding transformation would be interpreted in PF as the linking elements (of, OF). The transformation from M-marker to phrase markers is shown as follows (see chapter 6 of this volume and chapter 3 in Liao 2011 for details):[10]

(32) a. [have lots] of [~~have~~ money] OF

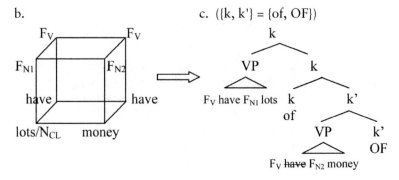

An advantage of the current proposal is that the tension between the single-constituent analysis and the dual-constituent analysis can be neutralized, and in addition, this treatment sharpens the small clause analysis in Kayne (2005). Under the analysis proposed here, the underlying structures are constructed by a set of "small clauses" that are formed by the primitive syntactic relations, while the surface constituent structures are derived from the asymmetric nature of the phrase structure (in alternation to the remnant movement analysis in Kayne 1994).

Going back to (32b), an important question concerns the functional categories that are coupled with the substantive N's (including the noun and the classifier). The next section focuses on the functional items and their interactions in the M-markers. It will be shown that employing M-markers in the syntactic analyses not only sheds some light on the classifier/counting constructions, but also on the cross-linguistic syntax-semantic mappings of mass-count distinction and plural marking.

3.2. Functional Categories in the Nominal Domain

This section deals with the functional items in the nominal dimension of M-markers in (33). Crucially, the functional items need to explain (at least) the following three semantic (LF) properties in (34):

(33) The CL-N domain

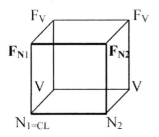

(34) a. Mass-Count Distinction

    b. Semantic/Morphological Plurality

    c. Quantifiers

An observation is crucial in Higginbotham (1994): Every mass quantifier can always find a count counterpart, but not vice versa:

(35)

	COUNT	MASS
a.	many N's	much N
b.	some N's	some N
c.	(a) few N's	(a) little N
d.	one N	n.a.
e.	two N's	n.a.

The pattern suggests that except for numeral count nouns, other plural count nouns and mass nouns in fact share many underlying features. To this end, we propose a compositional analysis of the mass/count and plurality as in (36), in contrast to the standard taxonomy in (37):

(36) The proposed taxonomy

	A*	Ø
[unit]	plural	Singular
Ø	mass	n.a.

(37) The standard taxonomy

$$
\left\{
\begin{array}{l}
\text{count} \left\{
\begin{array}{l}
\text{singular} \\
\text{plural}
\end{array}
\right. \\
\text{mass}
\end{array}
\right.
$$

We propose that the mass-count distinction can be further decomposed to combinations of [unit] and A*: The functional item [unit] reflects a semantic criterion of atomicity, or more precisely, the notion of integrity (Moltmann 2005) while the A* operator (standing for a set formation operator: AND) reflects a grouping function of the atomic units, or cumulativity (to be made specific in the following subsection). Simply speaking, our proposal here is that a plural count noun is understood as a set formed by atoms, so that it is cumulative and atomic. The analysis is further backed up by the fact that plurality shares features with both singular terms and mass nouns (Landman 1995). A plural and a singular term are both countable, in the sense that they can be counted by numerals, and are hence atomic. A plural noun, at the same time, shares with a mass noun the property of being cumulative:

(38) a. [Water and water] ran out.   = [Water] ran out.

   b. [Animals and animals] ran out. = [Animals] ran out.

Link (1983) proposes a semantic formulation for the mass/count distinction in terms of semilattice structures, which are illustrated in the following (Doetjes 1996):

(39) a. singular

   {a,b,c}

   b. plural [11]

   {a,b,c},{a,b},{b,c},{a,c}

   c. mass (x^+ represents an item with vague boundary)

   {$a^+,b^+,c^+, \ldots$},{a^+,b^+},{b^+,c^+},{a^+,c^+} … (*portions of material parts*)

Semantic singular terms are understood as the atoms in the semilattice structure, while plural terms are understood as the nonatomic parts, which consist of two or more atoms per set. Mass terms are identified as inherently plural, but their atoms are vague (represented here as x^+), in the sense that the recursion of the part-of relation is unbounded (i.e., the sizes of atoms are vague; cf. Chierchia 2010). The semilattice framework can be reduced to two elementary features: atomicity and cumulativity. The former defines an atomic level of a semilattice, while the latter gives rise to different groupings ordered by the *part-of* relation.

As discussed earlier, we adopt a functional item [unit] to refer to the semantic notion of atomicity (or integrity). When the functional item [unit] is coupled with a substantive noun, the merger yields a count structure, as in (40a); otherwise, a mass structure in (40b):

(40)

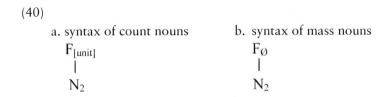

a. syntax of count nouns   b. syntax of mass nouns

$F_{[unit]}$ $F_\emptyset$

| |

N_2 N_2

The coupled structure characterizes the syntactic relation of a substantive root and a (grammatical) functional item, i.e., the {Sb, Fn} relation. The functional items also define the syntactic roles of its paired substantive items, and therefore, the nouns in (40) take the roles of matrix nouns. On the other hand, when a substantive root is coupled with a Numeral, it takes the role of a classifier. The two domains, when connected by the {k, k'} relation, constitute a nominal syntactic structure:

(41) Coupling in the CL-N domains

$$\text{Num}_{-A*} \quad\text{——}\quad F_{[unit]}$$
$$|\qquad\qquad\qquad|$$
$$N_1 \quad\text{——}\quad N_2$$
$$(= CL) \qquad (=main\ N)$$

Let us turn to the structural representation of cumulativity/plurality, in association with the functional item $A*$ operator. Here, a distinction needs to be drawn between semantic plurality and morphological plural markings. It is not an uncommon assumption that semantic plurality includes mass nouns (like *water* and *furniture*), as well as plural nouns, because both categories of nouns give rise to cumulativity (X and X → X; Link 1983). On the other hand, morphological plurality refers to the nouns that carry morphological plural markings, which are subject to surface linguistic variations. Let us focus on semantic plurality first. Chierchia (1998a, 1998b) treats mass nouns as lexicalized plural terms since mass and plural nouns behave alike in many contexts. For example, they are both compatible with collective predicates, and they have the same interpretations when they occur in stage-level and individual-level predicates (Carlson 1977). In fact, Harris (1982) has noted that the connective operator + (his AND) distinguishes plural and mass nouns on the one side, from singular nouns, on the other:

(42) a. (Wherever I looked,) I saw lava *and* lava.   → I saw lava.
      b. I saw cats and cats.   → I saw cats.
      c. I saw a boy *and* a boy.   ≠ I saw a boy

Let us adopt Harris's proposal by assuming an operator $A*$ for the logical connective +, and we shall also follow his idea that quantifiers are defined upon such an operator. Within such a proposal, we may assume that singular terms do not contain an $A*$ operator anywhere in the structures, while both plural and mass nouns contain $A*$, but the sources of the $A*$ are different. For plural nouns, the $A*$ operator comes from the recursive function of the numerals per se (e.g., two = one + one), while for mass nouns, the $A*$ comes from the "mass" classifier, or a silent AMOUNT (Kayne 2005) (to be made explicit later). In this way, the difference between singular, plural and mass terms can be visualized by the following taxonomy:

(43) The proposed taxonomy

	A*	Ø
[unit]	plural	singular
Ø	mass	n.a.

Note that the proposed combinatory analysis may provide a new perspective on the long-standing paradox of the so-called plural mass nouns (McCawley 1979):

(44) Some **plural mass nouns** in English (Ojeda 2005)

clothes, chattel(s), effects, stocks, victuals, vivers, sweetmeats, molasses, oats, hops, weeds, brains, bowels, cinders, curds, embers, grounds, guts, dregs, hards, lees, proceeds, remains, vails, contents, belongings, (paper) hangings, leavings, sharings, sweepings, winnings, ashes, chemicals, vegetables, greens, eatables, drinkables, sweets, sours, bitters, cordials, movables, valuables, necessaries, dues, assets, goods, wages, measles, mumps, hysterics, shingles, shivers, rickets, chills, throes, vives, blues, creeps, dumps, jumps, sulks, sullens.

Plural mass nouns are not typologically rare, and have been noted in many other languages. To name a few, see Ojeda (2005) for plural mass nouns in Bantu, Alexiadou (2010) and Tsoulas (2006) in Greek, and Wiltschko (2008) in Halkomelem (a Salish language):

(45) Bantu (Ojeda 2005) (PL = Noun Class 6)

a. PLURAL	ma-kolo 6-leg 'legs'	ma-tama 6-cheek 'cheeks'	ma-ndoki 6-rifle 'rifles'
b. MASS	ma-i 6-water 'water'	ma-kila 6-blood 'blood'	ma-bele 6-soil 'soil'

(46) Greek (Alexiadou 2010; Tsoulas 2006)

epesan	nera	sto	kefali	mu
fell-3Pl	water-Pl	on	head	my

'Water fell on my head'.

(47) Halkomelem Salish (Wiltschko 2008)

    a. tsel   kw'e´ts-l-exw   te/ye   th'exth' e´xet

       1Sing.Subj   see-Trans-3Obj Det/Det-Pl   gravel.Pl

       'I saw a lot of gravel'.

    b. tsel   kw'e´ts-l-exw   te/ye   shwela´thetel

       1Sing.Subj   see-Trans-3Obj Det/Det-Pl   fog.Pl

       'I've seen a lot of fog'.

Under the standard mass/count taxonomy, where plural and mass nouns fall into separate natural classes, the existence of plural mass nouns should be ruled out in principle. Under the proposed analysis, however, the compositionality of plurality provides a direct solution to this problem. If we assume that morphological plural marking is subject to (surface) parametric variation across languages, then in languages that allow plural mass nouns, the plural marking can be regarded as a morphological realization of the A* operator, which can also be found in the mass structure:[12]

(48)

$$\varnothing_{\text{Num}} \quad \text{——} \quad \varnothing_{[\text{unit}]}$$

$$\text{AMOUNT}_{\text{-A}*} \text{——} \text{money} \quad \rightarrow \text{PL(-s)}$$

On the other hand, count plural marking (*–s* and its allomorphs) in English can be formulated as a morphological realization of the combination of A* and [unit], as in (49):

(49)

$$\text{two}_{\text{-A}*} \text{——} [\text{unit}] \rightarrow \text{PL(-s)}$$

$$\text{NUMBER} \text{——} \text{cat}$$

The analysis presented here may also sharpen the proposals in Wiltschko (2008) and Alexiadou (2010) on mass plural nouns. In particular, Wiltschko (2008) suggests that plural markers can be heads in some languages, or they can be adjoined to different nominal categories (N, n, #, and D) in other languages, as a modifier. However, her analysis overlooks the close semantic associations between mass and plural nouns, and entirely separates semantic plurality from morphological plurality. Alternatively, our analysis assumes that plurality universally comes from the inherent logical A* operator, and it is the surface morphological parameters of the A* operator that yield different surface patterns.

4. SYNTAX OF CLASSIFIERS

In this section, the classifier constructions in Chinese are studied at length, in comparison with the nominal constructions in English. Three types of classifier/nominal constructions will be examined, including number/shape classifiers, vague classifiers, and measure classifiers. We shall adopt as a guiding principle the assumption of silent structures in Kayne (2005). The goal of our analysis is to develop a unified analysis of classifier/nominal structures under the proposed framework.

4.1. Count Classifiers: Number versus Shape Classifiers

In (Mandarin) Chinese, count classifiers function as the counting units in a general sense, and according to the criteria for counting, they can be further classified into two subclasses: shape classifiers and number classifiers. Shape classifiers agree with the "shapes" of nouns they attach to, while number classifiers agree with other properties of the nouns that may provide some concept of counting units, such as the default classifier (literally means "single"), honorific forms, or other abstract/metaphoric features. The following list illustrates some common examples of number and shape classifiers:

(50) Two types of count classifiers

a. shape CL	b. number CL
zhang (for sheets, papers, etc.), *ben* (for books), *zhi/gen* (for sticks, pens, etc.), *tiao* (for snakes, necklace, etc.), *zhi* (for dogs, cats, cows, etc.), *kuai* (for a load or a chunk of objects), etc.	*ge* 'single' (default), *wei* 'chair' (for honorific professions), *men* 'door' (for academic subjects), etc.

(i)   yi   da zhang   zhi
      one big CL   paper
      'a big sheet of paper'
(ii) yi   xiao ben shu
      one small CL book
      'a small book'
(iii) yi   xiao zhi bi
      one small CL pen
      'a small pen'
	(i) yi (*da) ge xiaoyuan
	      one big CL campus
	      'a (big) campus'
	(ii) yi (*xiao) wei/ge laoshi
	      one small CL teacher
	      'a (small/young) teacher'
	(iii) yi (*da) men/ge xuewen
	      one big CL knowledge
	      'a (big) branch of knowledge'

It has been claimed that the two subtypes of counting classifiers can be distinguished through adjective modification.[13] Shape classifiers allow a modifier like *big* and *small,* as in (50a), while number classifiers do not. Close scrutiny, however, suggests that adjectival modification of the classifiers is in fact sensitive to the lexical semantics of the classifiers. Number classifiers generally come from default/honorific/metaphoric forms without any reference to shapes. Therefore, attributing the availability of adjectival modifications to the syntax proper does not seem adequate (cf. Cheng and Sybesma 1998). Furthermore, it is not the case that number classifiers resist any modifications, an intensifier like *zheng* 'whole' can modify both number and shape classifiers (Tang 2005):

(51) a. Yi   zheng   bei/wan   shui/tang.   [shape CL]
          one   whole   cup   /bowl   water/soup
          'A whole cup/bowl of water/soup'

      b. Yi   zheng   ge   hanbao/nian-tou.   [number CL]
          one   whole   CL   burger/year-Dim.
          'a whole burger/year'

We suggest that the relation between shape and number classifiers be formulated as an implication rule encoded in grammar from "shape" to "number." If correct, this rule amounts to saying that the shape CL may simply be a subset of the number CL. We believe the implication rule is a domain-general rule that derives from the fact that reference to visual shapes may serve as a natural criterion for counting (Grinevald 2000; Moltmann 1998; Svenonius 2008). The implication rule from shape to number also gains empirical supports in language. Two pieces of evidence will be discussed here. Schwarzschild (2009) observes that several predicates in English always (preferably) apply to singular participant events (to the atomic parts), which are referred to as Stubborn Distributive Predicates:[14]

(52) a. The boxes are large. → Each box is large.

      b. The boxes are round. → Each box is round.

(53) a. ?The wine is big.

      b. ?The snow is round.

      c. ?The cocaine is long.

Schwarzschild (2009), however, does not offer a clear explanation why these predicates show such a behavior. Given the implication rule from shape to number, on the other hand, the "stubbornness" of these predicates can be accounted for. The shape adjectives directly imply counting units (e.g., individual boxes), which bring about distributivity of the predicate:

(54) The boxes are large$_{[shape]\rightarrow[number]}$.

The second piece of evidence comes from the Southern Min (or Hokkien), where shape adjective predicates require the presence of shape classifiers, as in (55):

(55) a. Hit gi enbit gai dua *(gi)

   that-one CL pencil Aux. big CL

   'That pencil is long'.

  b. Hit jia gao gai dua *(jia).

   that-one CL dog Aux big CL

   'That dog is big'.

We may therefore conclude that, although hidden in different surface patterns, languages seem to encode this universal implication rule (from shape to number) in one way or another.

 To recapitulate, the parallel syntax of number classifiers is illustrated in (56). Shape classifiers share the same structure with number classifiers, the only difference being restricted to the feature of CL (with the implication rule from shape to number):

(56) a. liang ge xuesheng.

   two CL students

   'two students'

  b. liang$_{-A*}$ —— [unit]

   | |

  ge$_{(=CL)}$ —— xuesheng

From the perspective of a parallel structure, the functional item numeral has two major functions. It defines the syntactic "role" of the coupled substantive item as a classifier, and at the same time, it specifies the quantity of [unit] (with the recursion function A*). As a pivot, it associates a count classifier to the count structure. We therefore capture the fact that a counting numeral (or quantifiers with similar functions), selected by a count classifier, must occur in a count structure (i.e., with [unit]).[15] We also predict that some classifiers, which do not select a counting numeral (such as the numeral *yi* 'one/a' in *yi xie / yi dian* 'some' in Chinese) would show different selectional properties with respect to the numeral/quantifier. We shall come back to the latter by examining the vague counting classifiers in section 4.3.

The functional item [unit] examined so far is assumed to be phonologically null. On the other hand, it can be overtly realized in several linguistic contexts. Chao (1968) notes that the a group of 'strict count' nouns in Mandarin form a compound with the classifier. Notably, these N-CL compounds are strictly count, and they resist mass interpretations:

(57) a. hua-duo   b. ma-pi   c. chuan-zhi   d. che-liang
        flower-CL   horse-CL   ship-CL   car-CL
        'flowers'   'horses'   'ships'   'cars'
     e. shui-di   f. bu-pi
        water-drop   cloth-CL
        'drops of water' 'pieces of cloth'

The morphological compounding rule of N+CL is not productive in modern Mandarin, however. One cannot freely form a strictly count noun by compounding a noun with its classifier:

(58) a. *gou-zhi   b. *ren-wei   c. *jiu-di   d. *guo-li
        dog-CL   person-CL   wine-drop   fruit-CL
        'dogs'   'people'   'drops of wine' 'fruits'

In addition, these strictly count nouns can still be counted with a classifier phrase. This indicates that the N-CL compounds are not formed through N-to-CL head-incorporation. Also, numerals/quantifiers in these constructions prefer to be plural and/or vague (judgments vary with respect to the numeral *yi* 'one'):

(59) a. xuduo   duo   hua-duo   b. ji   tai/liang che-liang
        many   CL   flower-CL   some   CL   car-CL
        'many flowers'   'a good many cars'
     c. wu/%yi   di   shui-di
        five/one   drop   water-drop
        'five/one drop(s) of water'

Under our theory, one can take the CL suffix in the N-CL compounds as a morphological realization of the functional item [unit], as shown by *ji duo hua-duo* in (60). Since the numeral and the $-CL_{[unit]}$ suffix are local, the analysis may also account for the selectional restriction between the vague quantifiers and the suffix -CL:

(60)

$$ji_{-A^*} \text{——} -duo_{[unit]}$$
$$duo_{(=CL)} \text{——} hua$$

A similar example can be found in Dutch, where a class of strictly count nouns is accompanied by diminutive suffixes. Wiltschko (2006) and De Belder (2008) notice that in Dutch and German, diminutive suffixes (in addition to plural markers) always give rise to plural interpretations (hence strictly count):

(61) a. veel   zout   b. veel   zout-je-s
       much   salt   many   salt-Dim-PL
       'much salt'   'many salt crakers'

(62) a. veel   brood   b. veel   brood-je-s
       much   bread   many   bread-Dim-PL
       'much bread'   'many rolls'

The paradigm suggests that the diminutive suffixes may also occupy the position of the functional item [unit], on a par with the suffix –CL in Mandarin Chinese.

4.2. NUMBER and AMOUNT: Unpronounced Nouns in English

Let us turn to the corresponding expressions in English. Against the standard theory, where the numerals and quantifiers take noun phrases as their immediate complements, Kayne (2005, 2007) argues that a covert unpronounced noun is located between the numeral/quantifier and the head noun. Therefore, (63a) should be analyzed as involving a covert NUMBER, as in (63b):

(63) a. two cat-s

      b. two NUMBER cat-s

Kayne's (2005, 2007) analysis gains empirical support from expressions like *a few students,* and *a little money:*

(64) a. **a few** NUMBER student-s

b. **a little** AMOUNT money

Under standard analyses, these syntactic phrases are anomalous. The plural modifier *few* appears to be a modifier of *students,* but the indefinite article *a,* nevertheless, requires a singular noun. Kayne's solution is to assume hidden unpronounced nouns. For count structure, a covert noun NUMBER situates between *a few* and *students* in (64a), and for mass structure, a covert AMOUNT appears between *a little* and *money* in (64b). Kayne shows that such a proposal provides a straightforward solution to another inconsistent pattern in (65), where *few* and *famous* are both adjectives, but only *few* can function as a subject:

(65) a. Few are very intelligent.

b. *Famous are very intelligent.

The pattern is accounted for if a covert noun NUMBER is hidden in the structure. The covert noun NUMBER, however, does not appear for an adjective like *famous:*

(66) a. Few **NUMBER** are very intelligent.

b. Famous *****NUMBER** are very intelligent.

In a footnote, Kayne (2005:147n17) suggests that the unpronounced NUMBER be treated in a classifier-like fashion. Elaborating on his account, we propose (67) for English numeral constructions. A covert NUMBER (NUM) occupies the "classifier" position, in comparison to the classifier constructions in Chinese (cf. (56)):

(67)

a. two student-s
b. two$_{-A*}$ ——— [unit]   (morphological spell-out: A*+[unit] = PL-*s*)
    | |
  NUM$_{(=CL)}$ ——— student

On the other hand, in a mass structure, where the functional item [unit] is unavailable (represented here by [Øunit]), a counting numeral is not licensed, and only mass quantifiers, such as *much,* can appear in the structure, coupled with the silent noun AMOUNT:

(68)

    a. much money

    b. much   —— $F_{[\varnothing unit]}$

       | |

    AMOUNT$_{-A*}$—— money

4.3. Vague Classifiers: *A few* and *a little* versus *xie* and *dian*

Turning back to Kayne's original examples *a few* and *a little* in English, let us refer to the expressions that do not express exact quantities as Vague Quantity Constructions (including things like *many/much, some, several,* among others). Assume that *a few students* and *a little water* have the structures in (69) and (70), respectively:

(69)

    a. a few students

    b. ONE/a —— [unit]   (A*+[unit] = PL -*s*)

        | |

      NUM —— student

        |

      few$_{-A*}$

(70)

    a. a little water

    b ONE/a   —— $F_{[\varnothing unit]}$

       | |

    AMOUNT$_{-A*}$ —— money

       |

    little

We take *few* and *little* as modifiers of NUMBER and AMOUNT, respectively. We also assume that the numeral is occupied by a default numeral ONE, pronounced as *one* or *a* (the reduced form) in English.

    It is crucial, when we compare (67), (69) and (70), to identify the sources of A* in these constructions. The A* operator comes from the plural counting numeral in (67), from the plural modifier *few* in (69), and from the mass classifier AMOUNT in (70). The complimentary distributions of A* operators suggest an important property of the A* operator. It is a quantificational property extended from the lexical node to the whole classifier domain (reminiscent of Quantifier Raising). The complimentary distributions of A* also explain why the following expressions are illicit:

(71) a. *two few students   (intended: two groups of few students)

   b. *two little water   (intended: two amounts of waters)

Under the current analysis, the ungrammaticality of (71) is due to the conflict/redundancy of two A* operators in a single CL-N domain:

(72) a. two$_{-A]^*}$ few$_{-A^*}$ NUMBER students

   b. two$_{-A^*}$ little AMOUNT$_{-A^*}$ water

Chinese also has vague classifier constructions similar to the English *a few* and *a little*. They are the *yi-xie* and *yi-dian* constructions. In their lexical semantics, *yi* means the numeral 'one' in Chinese, *xie* means 'fewness', and *dian* means 'little amount' or 'spot'. However, unlike English, where *a few/a little* selects count/mass nouns, *yi xie* may lead to ambiguous count or mass readings, while for most native speakers, *yi dian* may only bring about mass readings. Consider the following examples:

(73) a. Ta   du-guo   yi   xie   shu
       he   read-Asp   one   XIE   book
       i. 'He read some books'.   [count]
       ii. 'He received some education'. [mass]

   b. Ta   du-guo   yi   **dian**   shu
       he   read-Asp   one   DIAN   book
       i. *'He read some books'.   [count]
       ii. 'He received some education'. [mass]

(74) a. Zhangsan   chi-le   **yi**   xie   pingguo.
       Zhangsan   eat-Asp   one   XIE   apple
       i. 'Zhangsan ate some apples'.   [count]
       ii. 'Zhangsan had some apple (parts)'. [mass]

   b. Zhangsan   chi-le   **yi**   **dian**   pingguo.
       Zhangsan   eat-Asp   one   DIAN   apple
       i. *'Zhangsan ate some apples'.   [count]
       ii. 'Zhangsan had some apple (parts)'. [mass]

In the literature, *yi xie* and *yi dian* are usually analyzed as single morphological units, and *yi xie* and *yi dian* are treated syntactically on a par with other bimorphemic quantifiers, such as *yi-qie* 'all' and *yi-ban* 'half'. However, such analyses cannot be maintained in view of the following contrasts in (75) to (77). In classifier reduplication constructions, only *xie* and *dian* can be reduplicated, but not *–qie* and *–ban*:

(75) a. Zhangsan shuo-chu yi jian-jian shiqing
      Zhangsan say-out one CL-Red thing
      'Zhangsan discloses many things (one after another)'.

   b. Zhangsan chi-le yi ke-ke pingguo.
      Zhagnsan eat-Asp one CL-Red apple
      'Zhangsan ate many apples (one after another)'.

(76) a. Zhangsan xiang zhidao yi-qie(*-qie) shiqing
      Zhangsan want know one-cut-cut thing
      'Zhangsan wants to know everything'.

   b. Lisi zhi shuo-chu yi-ban(*-ban) shishi.
      Lisi only say-out one-half-half fact
      'Lisi only reported half of the fact'.

(77) a. Zhangsan xiang zhidao yi xie(-xie) shiqing
      Zhangsan want know one XIE-Red thing
      'Zhangsan wants to know some things'.

   b. Lisi zhi shuo-chu yi dian(-dian) shishi.
      Lisi only say-out one DIAN-Red fact
      'Lisi only reported a partial fact'.

Classifier reduplication is productive in typical Num-CL structures, as evidenced in (75), and the rule is sensitive to their syntactic components. For bimorphemic quantifiers that happen to use *one* in the numeral position, classifier reduplication is prohibited, as in (76). Therefore, *xie* and *dian* should be treated as syntactic classifiers. We further suggest that *yi* in *yi xie* and *yi dian* should be treated as the numeral one. In Mandarin Chinese, only the numeral *yi* 'one' may undergo *one*-omission in postverbal positions:

(78) a. Zhangsan zuo-le (yi) fen zaocan.
      Zhangsan make-Asp one CL breakfast
      'Zhangsan fixed a breakfast'.

   b. Lisi zhu-le (yi) bei kafei.

Lisi   cook-Asp   one   cup   coffee

'Lisi made a cup of coffee'.

As evidenced in (79), the numeral *yi* in *yi xie* and *yi* dian may also undergo *one*-omission, indicating that they are real numeral. In contrast, the lexical compounds *yi-qie* and *yi-ban* are not subject to the *one*-omission rule, as in (80):

(79) a. Zhangsan   chi-le   (yi)   xie   shuijiao.   [*yi* omission okay]

   Zhangsan   eat-Asp   one   XIE   dumpling

   'Zhangsan had some dumplings'.

b. Lisi   he-le   (yi)   dian   kafei.   [*yi* omission okay]

   Lisi   drink-Asp   one   DIAN   coffee

   'Lisi drank some coffee'.

(80) a. Zhang sanzhidao   *(yi-)qie   shiqing.   [no *yi* omission]

   Zhangsan   know   one-cut   things

   'Zhangsan knows everything'.

b. Zhangsan   zhi   he-le   *(yi-)ban   kafei.   [no *yi* omission]

   Zhangsan   only   drink-Asp   one-half   coffee

   'Zhangsan only drank half a cup of coffee'.

The preceding paradigms then argue for a syntactic analysis that treats *yi xie* and *yi dian* as an instance of numeral classifier constructions. However, while *xie* and *dian* are classifiers, they differ from the typical count classifiers in not allowing sequential counting. Instead, they simply describe a vague quantity, and display sensitivity to mass/count distinctions.[16] These properties of vague classifiers are then reminiscent of *a few* and *a little* in English. A universal representation of vague classifiers (or vague quantifiers) is therefore possible by analyzing Chinese *xie* and *dian* as overt realizations of the morphological fusions of *few-NUMBER* and *little-AMOUNT* in English. To illustrate, syntax of *yi xie* and *yi dian* can be analyzed in the following fashions:

(81)

   a. yi   xie   xuesheng
      one XIE   student
      'a few students'
   b.   ONE/yi —— [unit]
             | |
          xie-$_{A*}$ —— student
   (= few-NUMBER)

(82)

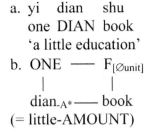

   a. yi dian shu
     one DIAN book
     'a little education'

The differences of vague classifiers/quantifiers in Chinese and English, then, are reduced to simple selectional properties of lexical features. Specifically, while *(few) NUMBER* and *(little) AMOUNT* in English select a count and mass structure, respectively, in Chinese, *XIE* optionally, while *DIAN* strictly, selects for the mass structure. The nominal constructions in English and Chinese are identical in their underlying syntax. The parameters between the two languages are reduced to lexical/morphological properties (or pronunciation patterns).

One particular note here is that the default numeral ONE (or a reduced *a*) does not seem to have a strict selection for [unit], or for the count structure. Instead, it may also occur in mass contexts (such as *a little* in English and *yi dian* in Chinese), where AMOUNT is coupled with a default numeral ONE. The loose selectional properties of the numeral ONE can be evidenced by the fact that singular count nouns, but not plural ones, are rather flexible in having a mass interpretation. Consider the following examples with the distributive quantifier *dou* 'all' in Chinese:

(83) a. Shui dou shi   hong-se   de
         water all   Aux   red-color DE
         'The whole water is red'.

      b. Zhe liang tai che dou shi hong-se   de.
         this two   CL   car all   Aux red-color DE
         'These two cars are both red (but not necessarily every part)'.

      c. **Zhe yi (zheng)   tai   che** dou shi   hong-se   de.
         this one whole   CL   car all   Aux   red-color DE
         (i)   'The whole car is red (in every visible parts)'.
         (ii) #'This is a red car (but not necessarily every part)'.

The distributive quantifier *dou* requires a mass or a plural argument, and resists a singular argument. Nevertheless, when *dou* takes a singular argument, such as *zhe yi tai che* 'this car' in (83c), the singular argument is in fact interpreted as a mass term, which looks into subparts of the singular term, and therefore cancels the atomicity. This is indicated by the interpretation (*the whole N → every part of N*) in (83c). That is, the singular noun no longer denotes an atomic singular object by itself, but rather a collection of its subparts (see Moltmann 1998). The semantic interpretation of the singular object is then close to a noncountable mass noun, like *furniture* in English. Under our analysis, the property of *whole* in English and *zheng* in Chinese can be directly accounted for if we assume that they are in fact modifiers of the unpronounced noun AMOUNT in mass structures.

4.4.   Measure Classifiers

Measure words are used in the so-called pseudo-partitive constructions, where the *of*-complement NP of the measure word can only be mass or plural terms, as shown in (84a, b). Additionally, plural agreement with the numeral shows on the measure word, but not on the main noun, as in (84c, d), which indicates that numerals and measure words form a single constituent, i.e., (84c)

(84)   a. a cup [of **chocolate**]   *[mass]/*[singular]*

b. a cup [of **chocolates**]   *[plural]*

c. [**two** [cup-s]] of chocolate

d. *[**two** [cup of chocolate-s]]

Although Chinese does not display overt plural agreement morphology, the following phrase is also ambiguous:[17]

(85)   yi   bei   qiaokeli

one   cup$_{CL}$ chocolate

a. 'a cup of chocolate (drink)'   [mass]

b. 'a cup of chocolates'   [plural]

The ambiguity shows that the same mass/plural distinction is observed in the measure classifier constructions, in spite of lack of overt morphological cues. The plurality of (85b) can be revealed by predicates that are sensitive to count structures, such as the verb *compare,* as shown in (86). Since mass readings are not compatible with count-sensitive predicates, as in (86a), only plural readings are available with such predicates, as in (86b):

(86)   Zhangsan   zixi-de   bijiao-le   zhe   yi   bei   qiaokeli,

Zhangsan   carefully   compare-Asp this   one   cup$_{CL}$ chocolate

(faxian   mei   ke   dou   bu   yiyang   da)

discover   every   CL   all   not   same   big

a. #'Zhangsan carefully compared this cup of chocolate'.

b. 'Zhangsan carefully compared this cup of chocolates, (and he found that they are all different in sizes'.

If one assumes the rather standard analysis that [*this one cup*$_{CL}$ *chocolate*] straightforwardly corresponds to the structure [D Num CL N], the contrast in (86) will not be easily accounted for without further stipulations. Moreover, in canonical pseudo-partitive constructions in English: [N$_1$ of N$_2$], one can even modify N$_2$ with another quantifier. The same holds in Chinese, and N$_2$ can be modified by an overt quantifier in the measure classifier constructions (Chao 1968). Compare (87) and (88):

(87) a. a box of many chocolates

   b. a bowl of many eggs

(88) a. yi   he   henduo   de   qiaokeli
      one   box   many   DE   chocolate
      'a box of many chocolates'

   b. yi   wan   shu   ke   de   dan
      one   bowl   several CL   DE   egg
      'a bowl of several eggs'

Reflecting the independent status of N$_2$, let us assume that the pseudo-partitive constructions actually consist of two nominal domains of equal size, which are connected by a higher-ordered connective pair {K, K'} (where in English, they are also realized as {of, OF'}), and the connective carries a predication function (recall the Relator-Linker analysis in den Dikken 2006), and may display selectional relation. The structure of the two connected nominal domains can be visualized as in (89), where the boldfaced lines represent a higher-ordered connective pair that connects the two parallel nominal domains:

(89) a. two cups of (many) chocolates

   b. liang   bei   qiaokeli
      two   cup   chocolate
      'two cups of chocolates'

   c. two$_{-A*}$ ——   [unit]   #$_{-A*}$ ——   [unit]
       | | —— | |
       NUMBER —— cup   NUMBER —— chocolate

Due to this predicative connective, a selection of the A* operator holds between the two connected nominal domains. This explains why only mass or plural readings may appear in the pseudo-partitive constructions (recall that mass and plural both carry A* operators). The preceding structure illustrates how the plural reading of the second NP comes from the structure (the A* operator of the covert numeral #), whereas the structures in (90) illustrate the source of the mass reading, in which the A* operator comes from the unpronounced AMOUNT in the second NP:

(90) a.   two cups of chocolate

     b.   liang   bei   qiaokeli

         two   cup   chocolate

         'two cups of chocolate'

     c.

$$\begin{array}{ccccccc}
\text{two}_{-A*} & \text{---} & [\text{unit}] & & \varnothing & \text{---} & [\varnothing\text{unit}] \\
| & & | & \text{---} & | & & | \\
\text{NUMBER} & \text{---} & \text{cup} & & \text{AMOUNT}_{-A*} & \text{---} & \text{chocolate}
\end{array}$$

Other verbal syntactic predicates may also display selection of the A* operator. One illustrative example is the selection of a collective verb and its argument. For example, (89) and (90) both consist of two A* operators. This accounts for the source of ambiguity in the following example (modified from Link 1983):

(91) John reshuffled [two decks of (MANY) cards].

     a.   'John separately reshuffled two decks of cards'.

     b.   'John reshuffled the cards that consist of two decks in total'.

The example in (91) has two A* operators from *two* and an unpronounced *MANY* before *cards*. *Reshuffle* being a verb (like *compare*) that selects the A* operator as its argument, the reading in (91a) is available when the first A* operator (of *two*) is selected as its main argument, while the reading in (91b) is obtained when the A* of the unpronounced MANY is selected as the main argument.

Notice that the "dual status" of the measure classifier is reminiscent of the adjunction analysis of mass classifiers (Cheng and Sybesma 1998):

(92)

a.

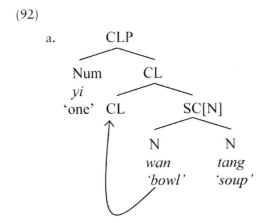

The proposed structure in Cheng and Sybesma attempts to capture the dual syntactic status of classifiers by employing an analysis with small clauses and head adjunctions. We reinterpret the mixed analysis as a chain relation between the unpronounced AMOUNT and *wan* 'bowl' (the former may undergo morphological fusion with the latter on the surface representation), and the substantive role of the classifier comes from the fact that the surface "classifier" is analyzed in our framework as a substantive noun root coupled with the functional item Numeral.

5. CONCLUSION

This chapter presents a novel theory of nominal constructions in English and Chinese. It is shown that the (symmetric) parallel syntax that results in Merge-markers can capture several important properties of cross-linguistic nominal constructions, some of which are problematic for the standard analyses. For example, Riemsdijk's problem (i.e., both classifier and noun are able to be assigned a theta role) can be resolved by the assumption that both the classifier and the noun are substantive roots, and it is their associated functional categories that eventually define the syntactic roles of the classifier and noun. We have also shown that the functional categories that are coupled with CL and N are Numeral and [unit], respectively. In semantics, the combination of Numeral (or the A* operator) and [unit] provides us with new insight of looking at the mass-count distinction. Such a proposal may also shed light on the plural mass noun problem. We have also argued that the theory of unpronounced nouns in Kayne (2005, 2007) can be nicely incorporated into our theory, and thus allows us to achieve a universal account of the nominal syntax.

NOTES

1. I owe much to Jean-Roger Vergnaud for his constant insights and inspiring ideas. During our collaboration, it is remarkable that Jean-Roger was always able to point out so many crucial aspects in the Chinese grammar that I have overlooked (given the fact that he knows little Chinese). I would also like to thank Tommi Leung, Audrey Li, Katy McKinney-Bock, Andrew Simpson, and Iris Wang for their comments and suggestions. All errors remain mine alone.
2. Some have proposed a parametric view of DP structure, and argue that a determiner is lacking in languages like Chinese and Japanese languages, where bare nouns and bare numeral NPs are productive (Cheng and Sybesma 1998, 1999; Chierchia 1998a, 1998b). However, in line with the **language uniformity principle** (Chomsky 1995), there is also abundant evidence against such a parametric view (Borer 2005; Li 1999; Liao and Wang 2011; Simpson 2005; Tang 1990; Watanabe 2006; Zamparelli 2000). Here, we will assume the latter.
3. Note that Watanabe's (2006) analysis differs from Borer's and Li's analyses in assuming that a classifier is the head of Number Phrase (#P) (equivalent to the CLP above), whose specifier is occupied by a numeral. That is, a numeral does not belong to an impendent nominal projection.
4. One might argue that only measure/mass classifiers may receive a theta role, but a count classifier cannot. This is not empirically attested. Consider the singular agreement of the plural subject, acceptable by many native speakers in English (NUMBER being an unpronounced noun):

   (i)   Three NUMBER people is/are enough to carry the sofa.

   The quirky agreement pattern is explained if we assume that semantic plurality may have been involved in syntactic agreement, and the real subject of (i) is actually the unpronounced NUMBER (Kayne 2005), which carries a theta role of Amount/Quantity. As will be argued below, count classifiers in Chinese can be identified as over realizations of the unpronounced NUMBER in English.
5. The *de* marker in many cases looks like the linker element *of* in English (though they are not alike in every aspect). We limit our discussion to the use of *de* in numeral-classifier constructions. See note 11 for more discussion on *de*.
6. A similar effect is observed in Larson (2009), who refers the pair to ezafe and reversed-ezafe, based on the data of the linking elements in the Iranian languages (e.g., Farsi and Kurdish).
7. The analysis presented here assumes a copy-and-deletion approach to remnant movement, which is more compatible with the current minimalist assumption (Chomsky 1995). For a pioneer work suggesting such an analysis, see Fanselow and Cavar 2002.
8. For example, the head can be ambiguous between tray and pastry in (25)in a scenario where the pastry is put on a tray made of bread.
9. We refer readers to Liao 2011 for details.
10. The mapping from a (symmetric) graph-theoretical representation to an asymmetric phrase structure can be achieved by imposing asymmetric linear orders upon the vertices. Different linear orders would then create a 'family' of trees, each of which are different surface arrangements of the same underlying syntactic relations.
11. From the entailment of negative sentences (*John saw no students → John didn't see a student*), Chierchia (2010) concludes that the extensions of a plural noun should include singular objects. We shall ignore this difference since it bears no direct relation to our analysis.

12. Following Kayne (2005), I assume that covert AMOUNT and NUMBER occupy the classifier position in non-classifier languages. We shall return to this point later.

13. Cheng and Sybesma (1998, 1999) propose that classifiers can be distinguished into count and mass classifiers through the tests of *de*-insertion and adjective modifications. The first test, however, is not without judgmental variations among native speakers. The second test is often challenged as well (Kobuchi-Philip 2007). We shall not adopt the first criterion. The second criterion, as we argue here, has to do with whether a given classifier provides shape information or not (most mass classifiers are only a subset of such classifiers).

14. For the same observation as in Schwarzschild 2009, see Moltmann 1998, who explicitly attributes the distributivity to the part-structure sensitive nature of some predicates.

15. In some dialects of Chinese and many Southeast Asian languages, bare CL-N sequences can be found. This phenomenon is not a counterexample to our analysis, however. Simpson et al. (2010) argue convincingly that cross-linguistically CL-N constructions (whether interpreted as definite or indefinite) necessarily involve an unpronounced ONE (being a default numeral).

16. The fact that *xie* and *dian* are classifiers should pose problems to the popular view that the semantics of classifiers is simply to facilitate counting in grammar.

17. The ambiguity also recalls the language uniformity principle (Chomsky 2001:2), and a reasonable analysis is that Chinese employs a covert plural morphology that is not PF-interpreted (at least for non-human objects; see Li 1999 for the discussion of the plural marking *–men* in Chinese).

REFERENCES

Abney, S. 1987. The English noun phrase in its sentential aspect. Doctoral dissertation, MIT.

Alexiadou, A. 2010. Plural mass nouns and the morpho-syntax of number. Paper presented at WCCFL 28. USC.

Belder, M. de 2008. Size matters: Towards a syntactic decomposition of countability. *WCCFL* 27:116–122.

Borer, H. 2005. *In Name Only: Structuring Sense.* Vol. I. Oxford: Oxford University Press.

Carlson, G. 1977. Reference to kinds in English. Doctoral dissertation, MIT.

Chao, Y. R. 1968. *A Grammar of Spoken Chinese.* Berkeley: University of California Press.

Cheng, L. L.-S., and R. Sybesma. 1998. *Yi-wan tang, yi-ge tang*: Classifier and massifier. *Tsing Hua Journal of Chinese Studies* 28:385–412.

———. 1999. Bare and not-so-bare nouns and the structure of NP. *Linguistic Inquiry* 30:509–542.

Chierchia, G. 1998a. Reference to kinds across languages. *Natural Language Semantics* 6:339–405.

———. 1998b. Plurality of mass nouns and the notion of "semantic parameter." In *Events and Grammar*, ed. by S. Rothstein. Dordrecht, Netherlands: Kluwer.

———. 2010. Mass nouns, vagueness and semantic variation. *Synthese* 174:99–149.

Chomsky, N. 1977. On *wh*-movement. In *Formal Syntax*, ed. by P. Culicover et al. New York: Academic Press.

————. *The Minimalist Program*. Cambridge, MA: MIT Press.

————. 2001. Derivation by phase. In *Ken Hale: A life in language*, ed. by M. Kenstowicz, 1–52. Cambridge, MA: MIT Press.

Dikken, M. den 2006. *Relators and Linkers: The Syntax of Predication, Predicate Inversion, and Copulas*. Cambridge, MA: MIT Press.

Doetjes, J. 1996. Mass and count: Syntax or semantics? *HIL Occasional Papers in Linguistics: Proceedings of Meaning on the HIL* 1:34–52.

Fanselow, G., and D. Cavar. 2002. Distributed deletion. In *Theoretical Approach to Universals*, ed. by A. Alexiadou. Amsterdam: Benjamins.

Fukui, N., and Y. Takano. 2000. Nominal structure: An extension of the symmetry principle. In *The Derivation of VO and OV*, ed. by P. Svenonius. Dordrecht, Netherlands: Kluwer.

Grinevald, C. 2000. A morphosyntactic typology of classifiers. In *Nominal Classification*, ed. by G. Senft. Cambridge: Cambridge University Press.

Harris, Z. 1982. *A Grammar of English on Mathematical Principles*. New York: John Wiley.

Higginbotham, J. 1994. Mass and count quantifiers. *Linguistics and Philosophy* 17:447–480.

Huang, C.-T. James. 1982. Logical relations in Chinese and the theory of grammar. Doctoral dissertation, MIT.

Kayne, R. 1994. *The Antisymmetry of Syntax*. Cambridge, MA: MIT Press.

————. 2005. *Movement and Silence*. Oxford: Oxford University Press.

————. 2007. *Several, few* and *many*. *Lingua* 117:832–858.

Kobuchi-Philip, M. 2007. Floating numerals and floating quantifiers. *Lingua* 117:814–831.

Landman, F. 1995. Plurality. In *Handbook of Contemporary Semantics*, ed. by S. Lappin. London: Blackwell.

Larson, R. K. 2009. Chinese as a reversed ezafe languages. *Yuyanxue Luncong* [Journal of Linguistics] 39:30–85.

Lebeaux, D. 1988. Language acquisition and the form of the grammar. Doctoral dissertation, University of Massachusetts.

Li, Y.-h. A. 1999. Plurality in a classifier language. *Journal of East Asian Linguistics* 8:75–99.

Liao, W.-w. R. 2011. The symmetry of syntactic relations. Doctoral dissertation, University of Southern California.

————, and Y.-y. Wang. 2011. Multiple-classifier constructions and nominal expressions in Chinese. *Journal of East Asian Linguistics* 20:145–168.

Link, G. 1983. The logical analysis of plurals and mass terms: A lattice-theoretical approach. In *Meaning, Use, and Interpretation of Language*, ed. by R. Bauerle et al. Berlin: de Gruyter.

McCawley, J. 1979. *Adverbs, Vowels, and Other Objects of Wonder*. Chicago: University of Chicago Press.

Moltmann, F. 1998. Part structures, integrity, and the mass-count distinction. *Synthese* 116:75–111.

————. 2005. Part structures in situations: The semantics of individual and whole. *Linguistics and Philosophy* 28:599–641.

Moro, A. 2000. *Dynamic Antisymmetry*. Cambridge, MA: MIT Press.

Ojeda, A. E. 2005. The paradox of mass plurals. In *Polymorphous Linguistics*, ed. by S. Mufwene et al. Cambridge, MA: MIT Press.

Park, S.-Y. 2008. Functional categories: The syntax of DP and degp. Doctoral dissertation, University of Southern California.

Riemsdijk, H. van 1998. Categorial feature magnetism: The endocentricity and distribution of projections. *Journal of Comparative Germanic Linguistics* 2:1–48.

Ritter, E. 1991. Two functional categories in noun phrases: Evidence from modern Hebrew. In *Syntax and Semantics 25: Perspectives on Phrase Structure*, ed. by S. Rothstein. New York: Academic Press.

Schwarzschild, R. 2009. Stubborn distributivity, multipaticipant nouns and the count/mass distinction. Paper presented at NELS 39, Cornell University.

Simpson, A. 2002. On the status of modifying de and the structure of the Chinese DP. In *On the Formal Way to Chinese Languages*, ed. by S.-W. Tang and C.-s. Liu. Stanford, CA: CSLI.

———. 2005. Classifiers and DP structure in Southeast Asian languages. In *The Oxford Handbook of Comparative Syntax*, ed. by G. Cinque and R. Kayne. Oxford: Oxford University Press.

———, H. L. Soh, G. Le, and H. van Nomoto. 2010. Bare classifiers and definiteness: Cantonese and beyond. Paper presented at IACL-18 and NACCL-22, Harvard University.

Svenonius, P. 2008. The position of adjectives and other phrasal modifiers in the decomposition of DP. In *Adjectives and Adverbs: Syntax, Semantics, and Discourse*, ed. by L. McNally and C. Kennedy. Oxford: Oxford University Press.

Tang, C.-C. J. 1990. A note on the DP analysis of the Chinese noun phrase. *Linguistics* 28:337–354.

———. 2005. Nouns or classifiers: A non-movement analysis of classifiers in Chinese. *Language and Linguistics* 6:431–472.

Tsoulas, G. 2006. Plurality of mass nouns and the grammar of number. Paper presented at the 29th GLOW colloquium, UAB-Casa Convalescencia, Barcelona.

Watanabe, A. 2006. Functional projections of nominals in Japanese: Syntax of classifiers. *Natural Languages and Linguistic Theory* 24:241–306.

Williams, E. 1994. *Thematic Structure in Syntax*. Cambridge, MA: MIT Press.

Wiltschko, M. 2006. Why should diminutives count? In *Organizing Grammar: Linguistic Studies in Honor of Henk van Riemsdijk*, ed. by H. N. Covert et al. Berlin: Mouton de Gruyter.

———. 2008. The syntax of non-inflectional plural marking. *Natural Language and Linguistic Theory* 26:639–694.

Zamparelli, R. 2000. *Layers in the Determiner Phrase*. New York: Garland.

Contributors

EDITORS

Katherine McKinney-Bock completed her PhD in the Department of Linguistics at the University of Southern California and is joining Reed College for the academic year 2013–14 as a visiting assistant professor of linguistics. Her dissertation revisits foundational issues within the Minimalist Program in syntax. Working from Vergnaud's Items and Contexts Architecture, she takes narrow syntax to be a more abstract representation from which constituent structure is derived, using graph theoretic principles. Her research also includes theoretical work on the semantics and syntax of adjectives and experimental work, using eye-tracking methods, on the real-time processing of adjectives.

Maria Luisa Zubizarreta completed her PhD in the Department of Linguistics at MIT in 1982 and joined the University of Southern California in 1988 as professor of linguistics. Her primary research is in theoretical linguistics, with a particular focus on the relationship between lexicon and syntax and on the interface between syntax, prosody, and information structure. Her publications include *Focus, Prosody, and Word Order* (1998), *On the Syntactic Composition of Manner and Motion* (2008), *Foundational Issues in Linguistic Theory* (2008) with co-editors Robert Freidin and Carlos Otero.

CONTRIBUTORS

Jean-Roger Vergnaud graduated from the Ecole Polytechnique (Ingenieur Diplomé) in 1967, from MIT (PhD in philosophy and linguistics) in 1974, and from Université Paris 7 (Doctorat d'Etat es-Sciences, computer science track) in 1982. He joined the University of Southern California in 1988, where he was the Andrew W. Mellon Professor of Humanities until his death on January 31, 2011. Vergnaud's formal works on vowel harmony and stress theory (in collaboration with Morris Halle) and Case Theory in generative syntax were foundational contributions to the field of linguistics. His publications include *Dépendances et niveaux de représentation en syntaxe* (1985) and "An Essay on Stress" (with M. Halle; 1987).

Robert Freidin is professor of linguistics in the Council of the Humanities at Princeton University. His research concerns syntax and semantics, focusing on the foundations of syntactic theory (the central concepts of syntactic analysis and their evolution) and its role in the study of language and mind. Some of this work is collected in *Generative Grammar: Theory and Its History* (Taylor and Francis, 2007). His most recent publications include "The Roots of Minimalism" (with Howard Lasnik) in *Oxford Handbook of Linguistic Minimalism* (2011, "A Brief History of Generative Grammar" in *Routledge Companion to the Philosophy of Language* (2012, "Noam Chomsky's Contribution to Linguistics: A Sketch" in *Oxford Handbook to the History of Linguistics* (2013, and *Syntax: Basic Concepts and Applications* (2012).

Tommi Leung is assistant professor of linguistics at United Arab Emirates University. He graduated from the University of Southern California (2007) under the supervision of Jean-Roger Vergnaud and Roumyana Pancheva. His research interest focuses on the theoretical issues of syntax, phonology, and biolinguistics. Of late, he is also interested in the mathematical foundations of linguistic theories.

Wei-wen Roger Liao is assistant research fellow in Academia Sinica. Liao completed his PhD at the University of Southern California in 2011 and his MA at National Tsing Hua University in 2004. His primary research interests are generative syntax, semantics, and Chinese linguistics. His dissertation is titled "The Symmetry of Syntactic Relations." Pursuing Jean-Roger Vergnaud's idea, Liao applies the mathematic principles of symmetry and symmetry breaking to generative syntax and develops a theory of symmetric syntax. His recent publications include "Multiple-Classifier Constructions and Nominal Expressions in Chinese," *Journal of East Asian Linguistics*, Volume 20, Issue 2 (2011).

Index